CRIMINAL BEHAVIOR SYSTEMS

A Typology

Third Edition

Marshall B. Clinard

University of Wisconsin — Madison

Richard Quinney

Northern Illinois University

John Wildeman

Hofstra University

 anderson publishing co.
p.o. box 1576
cincinnati, oh 45201-1576
513-421-4142

Midwood

On the cover: *No Flowers* by Jack B. Yeats
Courtesy of the National Gallery of Ireland

CRIMINAL BEHAVIOR SYSTEMS: A Typology
Third Edition

ISBN 0-87084-180-7
Library of Congress Catalog Number 93-71747

 Printed on recycled paper.

Ellen S. Boyne *Project Editor*   *Managing Editor* Kelly Humble

3/24/99

In remembrance of John Wildeman
Our friend, colleague and coauthor

Preface

Criminal behavior covers a wide variety of violations of criminal laws. For purposes of explanation, this behavior must be broken down into types. In this book, after first discussing the construction of the types of crime, we go on to formulate and use a typology of criminal behavior systems. We are convinced that continued progress in criminology depends greatly on the study of the types of criminal behavior. Typology construction is the beginning of theory. It is the beginning of making sense of our experience of crime.

This is the third edition of *Criminal Behavior Systems: A Typology*, which was first published in 1967. The first edition was enthusiastically received both as a textbook and as a substantial contribution to criminology. The original typology has been reprinted and referred to frequently in numerous other books and articles.

The second edition, published in 1973, reflected considerable revision and extensive substantive changes. In the original edition a discussion and commentary followed the research articles on each type of criminal behavior. The second edition dropped this format. Instead, the authors integrated the research findings into the presentation and discussion. The second edition was reprinted in 1986, and in the 20 years, from 1973 to 1993, *Criminal Behavior Systems: A Typology, Second Edition* has frequently been cited, parts of it have been reprinted in other books and articles, and a number of colleges and universities continue to adopt it for classroom use.

The third edition is the result of the continued interest in the typological approach of this book. The original authors, Marshall B. Clinard and Richard Quinney, invited John Wildeman to join them as a coauthor. Wildeman assumed the major responsibility for the revising, research updating and references. Unfortunately, however, he was not able to see the book in print, as he died before the galleys were produced. Major theoretical advances in criminology and many of the research findings published since the second edition have been incorporated. The category of corporate crime has been clarified further and clearly distinguished from the category of occupational crime, and the category labeled *political criminal behavior* has been extensively expanded. Finally, some proposed solutions to various types of criminal behavior have been incorporated into the text—solutions that depart from violent responses to criminals on the part of the state.

We hope that this book continues to be of use to students in the field of criminology and to criminologists formulating their own theories and research on criminal behavior.

We are deeply indebted to those who in the past and present have devoted much time and effort to criminological research on various forms of criminal behavior. Our typology has grown out of such work. Finally, we wish to express our appreciation of Ellen S. Boyne's interest and her competent editing of the manuscript.

Contents

9. Organized Criminal Behavior   219

10. Professional Criminal Behavior   247

Subject Index   267

Name Index   275

Chapter 1

Types of Criminal Behavior

We all try to give meaning to our existence. Our common goal is to make the world understandable and familiar, thus rendering it amenable to reason and control. The most important way we achieve understanding is by generalizing beyond the singular, the unique and the particular. Whether we are participants or observers of the social scene, we understand largely by searching for the recurrent and uniform. Thus, through *abstraction* we are able to comprehend and grasp the world of concrete experience.

All phenomena are unique in time and space. "There is rarely if ever a one-to-one correspondence between any typology and the complexity of reality" (Wrong 1992, 385). But in order to make our experiences intelligible, we often reduce the infinite variety of life to categories. We construct images or concepts in our attempt to "know" the world around us. These constructs are a reduction of our experiences, a reduction that treats occurrences *as if* they were similar, recurrent and general. Phenomena thus become comparable, and comparison is the beginning of scientific and philosophical reflection.

Thus, as with all human endeavors, the systematic study of behavior is based on an ordering of the diversified world of discrete phenomena. This is accomplished in the sciences by the development of classifications or typologies, where concrete occurrences are ordered and compared by categorizing single observations into groups called classes or types. As abstractions, these types deviate from the concrete in that they accentuate attributes relevant to a particular analysis. A type consists of characteristics that have empirical referents, even though these characteristics may not be experienced directly in the form of a given type. When they do, sociology calls this an "ideal type."

Typologies have been used for centuries in the study of physical and human phenomena. For example, an important typology was created by the Swedish botanist Linnaeus two centuries ago when he developed the modern scientific classification of plants and animals. The use of typologies is common today, not only in botany, but in zoology, geography, geology and other physical sciences.

1

Similarly, in the area of human behavior, the social scientist attempts to derive types, whether they be types of social organizations, types of occupations or types of deviants. The use of types in ordering the diversities of observed phenomena has been instrumental in the development of the social sciences, from Comte through Marx, Durkheim and Weber, to our more contemporary theorists.

Types not only reduce phenomena to more systematic observation, they also assist in the formulation of hypotheses and serve as guides for research. The construction of types may lead to theoretical formulation. The constructed type, in fact, as Hempel noted over 40 years ago, can serve as a theoretical system in itself by "(1) specifying a list of characteristics with which the theory is to deal, (2) formulating a set of hypotheses in terms of those characteristics, (3) giving those characteristics an empirical interpretation, and (4) as a long-range objective, incorporating the theoretical system as a 'special case' into a more comprehensive theory" (Hempel 1952, 84).

Thus, the construction of types from a broad range of phenomena is a necessary stage in the development of specific theories; it also offers the possibility of formulating a comprehensive theory for the explanation of all the phenomena under observation. Conversely, a typology can be derived from a general theory of a specified phenomenon. There is, indeed, an interaction between theory construction and typology. While types may emerge from theory, they also are instrumental in the reformulation and expansion of theory. Typology and its relation to theory construction are essential to the further development of general theory.

Typologies in Criminology

A diverse and wide range of behaviors is included in the category of crime. In fact, law-violating behavior is every bit as varied as is law-abiding behavior. Just as law-abiding (or lawful) behavior follows categorizable patterns and falls into types, so too does law-violating (or criminal) behavior. The one characteristic that all criminal behaviors have in common is that they have been defined as criminal by some recognized political authority.

Much of the work of criminology has been concerned with crime in general. However, because of the increasing realization that crime refers to a limitless variety of behaviors, criminologists have turned their attention to the study of particular types of crime. Thus, criminologists now give greater attention to the identification, classification and description of types of criminal behavior as defined by the government.

Figure 1.1

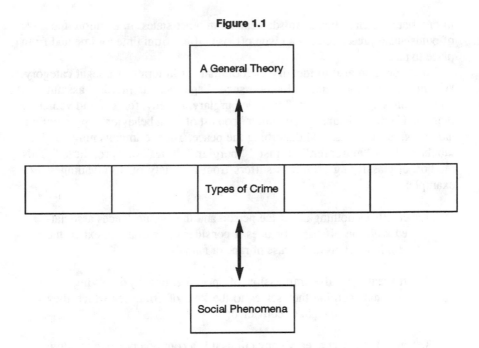

Figure 1.1 diagrams a method of theory construction in criminology. The interdependence of typology and theory construction is clear. Theoretical assumptions are necessary for the formulation of types, whether those assumptions are stated or implicit; and a typology forces the reformulation of general theory.

Criminologists in the past have constructed and used many different typologies of crime and criminals. The most common typologies have been (1) the legalistic, (2) the individualistic, and (3) the social.

Legalistic Typologies

The oldest and most frequently used forms of classification are based on the legal definition of the offense. Perhaps the most commonly used legalistic classification is in terms of the seriousness of the offense, as indicated by the kind of punishment provided for the behavior. The most serious offenses are called felonies and are usually punishable by confinement in a state prison for more than one year (or by death in those states that still permit it). Less serious offenses are called misdemeanors and are normally punishable by fines or by confinement in a county jail for up to one year. As a classification of crime this is not very useful because it is difficult to make clear-cut distinctions between the two major types of offenses. For example, many criminal acts classified as felonies in one state are classified as misdemeanors in other states. In addition, the form of punishment prescribed for a given offense differs from time to time and from place to place.

It is common also to identify the criminal act in terms of a legal category. "Crimes against the person" include such illegal acts as murder, assault and rape; "crimes against property" include burglary, larceny, forgery and vehicular theft; and "crimes against public order" consist of such behavior as prostitution, gambling, drunkenness and disturbing the peace. Thus, criminals may be given labels such as "murderer," "rapist," "burglar," "thief" or "prostitute." This method of classifying criminals suffers from a variety of disadvantages. For example:

1.   It tells us nothing about the person and the circumstances associated with the offense, nor does it consider the social context of the criminal act, as in the case of rape or auto theft;

2.   It creates a false impression of specialization by implying that criminals confine themselves to the kind of crime for which they happen to be caught or convicted;

3.   In order to secure easy convictions it is a common practice to allow offenders to receive a reduced sentence by a number of different plea bargaining strategies—for example, by pleading guilty to a lesser charge or by pleading guilty in order to receive a reduced sentence. In these cases the final legal status of the original criminal action will bear little resemblance to the actual behavior;

4.   Because the legal definition of a criminal act varies according to time and place, the legal classification of crime presents problems for comparative analysis; and

5.   The use of legal categories in a classification assumes that offenders with a certain legal label, such as burglars, robbers, auto thieves and rapists, are all of the same type or are products of a similar process.

There have been a number of attempts to overcome some of the problems of legalistic classifications of crime, while still using the legal categories themselves. Although the categories of crime defined in the criminal law may not be appropriate for sociological purposes, they may nevertheless be used in forming types of crime. One possibility is that types may be defined *within* specific legal categories. For example, burglars, depending upon their mode of operation, could be divided into housebreakers, bank robbers, professional burglars and amateur burglars. Another possibility is that related legal categories may be *combined.* Criminologists who favor the strategy of defining types according to legal categories claim that doing so is desirable because official data concerning criminal histories appear in terms of legal nomenclature, and because the criminal code contains specific operational definitions of criminal behavior.

One legalistic typology, formulated in the 1960s, was based on arrest patterns: the *single arrest pattern* (many arrests for one type of crime), the *multiple arrest pattern* (many arrests for two or more types of crime), the *mixed pattern* (many arrests for all sorts of crime) and *no pattern* (arrested only once or twice) (Roebuck 1967). While this typology is useful in pointing out the error of using a single arrest to type an offender, and is suggestive of career patterns instead, a serious limitation is that such inductively derived typologies could mount up indefinitely by this method of using arrests.

An important problem with the construction of legal typologies of crime concerns the controversy over what behaviors and what persons should be regarded as criminal (Quinney and Wildeman 1991, Chapter 1). At what stage of the criminal defining process should persons and behaviors be regarded as criminal? Is it at the stage of official detection, at the stage of arrest, at the stage of official adjudication or at the stage of official disposition? Or, to state the extreme, should a typology of crime include persons and behaviors irrespective of official legal action? This is not a light question, for many progressive criminologists have long argued that the discipline should go beyond the state definition of crime to include those actions that bring social harm and social injury to masses of citizens. If we extend the definition of crime to these actions and their perpetrators, clearly many actions or nonactions of the state itself fall under our definition. The progressives argue that to fail to go beyond the state's definition of crime is to render criminology a "handmaiden of the state" (Platt 1974; Schwendinger and Schwendinger 1970). Even if the criterion of official legal action is dropped in the construction of a typology, there is still the problem of how long a person remains a criminal after he or she violates the criminal law. Ultimately the selection of the stage of legal action to be used in defining the persons and behavior to be included in a typology of crime depends upon the purpose of the typology and the kinds of research problems that are anticipated. In other words, the needs of the research sometime dictate the kind of typology employed.

The use of legal categories of crime is valid when the purpose is to understand the process by which behavior becomes defined as criminal (Beirne and Messerschmidt 1991; Quinney 1970; Turk 1969). Since criminality is not inherent in behavior but is a quality conferred upon individuals and acts by others, the study of the formulation and administration of the law is important to the criminologist. The legal definition of crime is the best indication of how the category of crime is created as a form of public policy. Any typology could incorporate the legal aspects of criminal offenses. The legal category itself is a social construction.

Individualistic Typologies

Several Italian criminologists who rejected the legal definitions of crime more than 100 years ago were instrumental in turning the attention of criminologists to classification and to the use of criteria other than those found in the criminal law (Beirne 1988; Lombroso 1876; Mannheim 1960). The early criminologists of the Italian, or "positivist," school delimited types of offenders in terms of a heterogeneous collection of personal attributes. Lombroso (1835-1909), for example, identified, to his own satisfaction at least, a "born criminal" with a unique, inferior physique. Later, he recognized other types of criminals, including (1) the insane criminal, (2) the criminal by passion, and (3) the occasional criminal, a type that emphasized the social aspects of the offender as well as individualistic characteristics.

Another member of the positivist school, Garofalo, a jurist, maintained that criminals are characterized by psychological anomalies. He divided these "defectives" into four categories: (1) typical criminals, or murderers who kill for enjoyment, (2) violent criminals, (3) criminals deficient in pity and probity, and (4) lascivious criminals. In a not too different fashion, Ferri (1856-1929), of the same school, distinguished between five types of criminals: (1) the insane, (2) the born, (3) the habitual, (4) the occasional, and (5) the passionate.

Clinical psychologists and psychiatrists have subsequently attempted to classify criminal offenders by utilizing either a single personality trait or a syndrome or grouping of traits. Accordingly, criminal offenders have been grouped according to whether they are immature, emotionally insecure, dependent, hostile, antisocial, nonconformist or aggressive. Sometimes a single trait has been used to apply to a variety of criminal careers differing in both the nature and seriousness of activity. Consequently, personality trait syndromes by themselves have little meaning for distinguishing types of criminal careers or the behavior of criminals from noncriminals who may also have these traits.

Recently a limited individualistic typology of offenders has been developed on the basis of the psychodynamics of criminal motivation and rationalization: (1) novice shoplifters, (2) youthful "badasses," (3) gangbanging "street elites," (4) "hardman" robbers, (5) "righteous" killers, and (6) cold-blooded murderers (Katz 1988). Critics have pointed out that this typology fails to incorporate social-structural variables and is overly phenomenological in its emphasis on popularly disapproved individual behaviors (Turk 1991).

In terms of individualistic factors, offenders also have been divided according to their gender, age, race, ethnic background, rural-urban background, educational level and other personal attributes. Gender is not a very meaningful criterion for classification because, with the exception of prostitution, women in the Western world commit almost as wide a variety of offenses as men, although not as frequently. It is increasingly difficult to distinguish clearly among offenders merely upon the basis of gender. Likewise, age is a somewhat meaningless classification because all types of crime are committed by persons of varying ages, although at far different rates (for example, rapists are seldom over the age of 60). Offenders committing the most overt serious crimes against the person, however, are more frequently under 25 years of age, while white-collar and corporate crimes are generally committed by middle-aged persons with access to the means of breaking the law. Classification of offenders by age has little merit, for the criminal development of an offender may have little relation to age. An offender may be considered "developed criminally" if he or she has unfavorable attitudes toward laws, property and the police; professional knowledge of techniques to commit crimes and avoid prosecution; and a framework of rationalizations to support his or her conduct. These qualities can be present in a teenage offender and be comparatively absent in a middle-aged one, or vice-versa.

The individualistic approach to criminal classification employs the questionable assumption that individuals with particular personal characteristics commit certain types of crime. In addition, the individualistic approach implies that persons with these characteristics specialize in particular offenses. Finally, while individualistic classifications may offer some diagnostic possibilities for treatment, they have little utility for the construction of sociological theories of criminal behavior.

Social Typologies

Crime does not evolve in a social vacuum. If it is to be studied as a social phenomenon, it is necessary to delineate types of criminal behavior according to the *social* context of the criminal offender and the criminal act. A number of such types have been developed. Two European criminologists of the nineteenth century, Mayhew and Moureau, proposed criminal types based on the way in which crime is related to the various activities of the criminal. Mayhew distinguished between *professional criminals,* who earn their living through criminal activity, and *accidental criminals,* who commit criminal acts as a result of unanticipated circumstances. Moureau added one other type of criminal to Mayhew's types. Recognizing that many of the criminals who commit crimes against the person cannot be included in either of Mayhew's types, Moureau designated the *habitual criminal* as one who continues to commit criminal acts for such diverse reasons as a deficiency in intelligence or lack of self-control.

Building on the Mayhew-Moureau criminal types, in the twentieth century Lindesmith and Dunham devised a continuum of criminal behavior ranging from the *individualized criminal* to the *social criminal* (Lindesmith and Dunham 1941). The criminal acts of the individualized criminal are committed for diverse and personal reasons, with the behavior finding little cultural support.

The criminal behaviors of the social criminal, on the other hand, are supported and prescribed by group norms. The social criminal through criminal behavior achieves status and recognition within a tight and limited group, such as an organized crime group or gang. In addition, although the social criminal uses illegitimate means, the goals he or she seeks, such as economic gain and personal security, are valued by the broader culture. The types of criminals found between the extremes share in varying degrees the characteristics of one or the other polar types. Research subsequent to the developmnent of this typology has indicated considerable group and social factors in such offenses as murder, aggravated assault and forcible rape, which Lindesmith and Dunham regarded as of the individual type.

Zeroing in on the relationship between age and criminality, or crime and the life cycle in general, some criminologists have highlighted the vocational aspects of certain forms of crime. They have seen that some crimes are committed by persons who pursue criminal behavior as a *career* (Blumstein et al. 1986; Gottfredson and Hirschi 1990; Hirschi and Gottfredson 1983; Inciardi 1975; Nagin and Paternoster 1991; Sampson and Laub 1990).

In a pioneering study, Reckless (1967) suggested two types of criminal careers: *ordinary* and *professional*. As career crimes, these two types of crime are similar in that they usually involve property offenses for the purpose of gain; the criminals tend to specialize in particular violations; the commission of the offenses requires various degrees of skill and experience; crime is pursued as a way of life; and career criminals continue in crime for a long period of time, possibly for a lifetime. In terms of differences among the career types, ordinary criminals represent the lowest rank of career crime, engaging in conventional crimes requiring limited skills. Professional criminals, on the other hand, are highly skilled and able to obtain considerable amounts of money without being detected. Whereas Reckless's distinction is important and valid, it is limited to those who make an occupation or career out of crime.

Farr and Gibbons (1990) offer a classificatory system based upon five dimensions: (1) organizational level at which crime occurs, (2) legitimacy of organizational context, (3) organizational alignment of offender, (4) range of crime forms, and (5) primary victims. This typology is useful in that it brings clearly to the fore the complexities of crime with which criminologists must deal. However, the scheme has not been widely adopted and it requires further refinement.

A more comprehensive typology has been developed by Gibbons (1992). It is based primarily on what he calls "role-careers," in which identifiable changes occur in different offender types.

Some delinquent patterns lead to adult criminal careers, whereas others do not. In turn, some criminal careers begin with delinquent behavior, whereas others develop in adulthood. Some role-careers involve more changes in episode than others. For example, many adult predatory offenders begin their lawbreaking with minor offenses in early adolescence. As the offenders age these frequently lead to more serious forms of delinquency, which in turn result in repeated police contacts, commitment to juvenile institutions, "graduation" into adult forms of crime, and more contacts with law-enforcement agencies and correctional institutions. Over this lengthy developmental sequence, the social-psychological characteristics of the offenders also change.

This role-career perspective provide(s) the foundation for a typology of lawbreakers based on the illegal role behavior they exhibit and on their self-image patterns and role-related attitudes. (Gibbons 1992, 206)

Using his role-career model, Gibbons developed a uniform frame of reference employing the criteria of "definitional dimensions" and "background dimensions." The definitional dimensions consist of: (1) the nature of the offense behavior, (2) the interactional setting with others in which the offense takes place, (3) self-concept of the offender, (4) attitudes toward society and agencies of social control such as the police, and (5) the steps in role-career of the offender. The background dimensions are: (1) social class (by which, presumably, he means socioeconomic status group), (2) family background, (3) peer group associations, and (4) contact with defining agencies such as the police, courts and corrections. Originally his system identified 15 adult offender types and 9 juvenile offender types, but he subsequently refined this to 20 types, including both adults and juveniles.

1.	professional thieves	11.	"psychopathic" assaultists
2.	professional "heavy" criminals	12.	statutory rapists
3.	semiprofessional property criminals	13.	aggressive rapists
4.	naive check forgers	14.	violent sex offenders
5.	automobile thieves—"joyriders"	15.	nonviolent sex offenders
6.	property offenders, "one-time losers"	16.	incest offenders
7.	embezzlers	17.	male homosexuals
8.	white-collar criminals	18.	opiate addicts
9.	professional "fringe violators"	19.	skid row alcoholics
10.	personal offenders, "one-time losers"	20.	amateur shoplifters

All typologies of crime and criminals are bound to be problematic on some level or other, because classifying any form or kind of human behavior is an elusive task. The weakness in this case is that some of Gibbons' types are not sharply delineated and tend to overlap or be unclear as to their specific characteristics. Other types depart from an essentially general group and cultural frame of reference and present a largely individualistic psychological orientation that is somewhat contradictory to the overall frame of reference. On the other hand, the strengths of the typology lie in the various definitional and background dimensions.

A somewhat different typology was developed by Cavan, which gives principal consideration to the public reaction to crime and the criminal's reaction to the public (Cavan 1962). In an analysis of the interaction between the public and the criminal, seven types of criminal behavior are constructed: (1) *criminal contraculture* (professional crime, robbery, burglary), (2) *extreme underconformity* (for example, occasional drunkenness), (3) *minor underconformity* (for example, embezzlement), (4) *"average" conformity* (minor pilfering), (5) *minor overconformity* (exactness in obeying laws and moral codes), (6) *extreme overconformity* (attempts to reform society by persuasion and legal means), and (7) *ideological contraculture* (strenuous efforts to remodel society, possibly through the use of illegal means). Because societal reaction is crucial to the criminal's self-concept and subsequent behavior, it is an important variable to be included in a typology of crime. However, the flaw here is that the variable "societal reaction" is only one dimension of criminal behavior.

An indication of the importance of the typological approach in modern criminology can be seen in the attention devoted to the subject in virtually all contemporary criminology textbooks. Typology construction is far from "perfect" (all such systems are based on unstated assumptions about what the world is "really like"); nonetheless, without typologies of crime and criminals, theory itself becomes impossible.

Principles of Criminal Typology

There are a number of methodological problems in the construction of typologies of crime. These problems themselves serve as the basic principles of such typological systems. We now reflect on these problems.

Classification and Typology

While not always followed in practice, a distinction can be made between a *classification* (composed of classes) and a *typology* (composed of types). A strict classification consists of a set of variables or attributes that are linked to form a number of logically possible classes. A typology, in contrast, attempts to specify the ways in which the attributes of observable phenomena are empirically connected in the formation of particular types. Thus, for example, we make classifications of insects and typologies of behavior patterns. Moreover, in a classification there is the assumption that all cases within a class share the properties of that class to the same extent. A type, however, "acts as a point of reference that determines the extent to which any empirical case conforms to it, the principle consideration therefore being degree of approximation" (Rhoads 1967, 348). It is the construction of types rather than classes that interests the criminologist.

Ideal and Empirical Typologies

Another distinction that is sometimes drawn is between two kinds of typologies: the *ideal* and the *empirical*. Following the lead of Weber, an ideal type is an abstraction that does not necessarily describe concrete cases, but represents possible or even extreme cases. An ideal type may be conceived of as a distortion of the concrete. All empirical occurrences can then be viewed in terms of the ideal type. Theoretically, the ideal type never can be found in reality, just as Michelangelo's statue of David represents a level of perfection of the male body that is never seen in real life.

The empirical typology, on the other hand, is composed of types that describe patterns that exist in the real world. The ideal type is the observer's abstraction; the empirical type is supposed to represent what actually exists.

The distinction between ideal and empirical types is, however, arbitrary. Moreover, the distinction suffers from a faulty epistemology. The problem is related to the age-old controversy between realism and nominalism. "There is no reason to believe in the objective reality of anything. Our concern, rather, is with the formulation of constructs that are meaningful for the purposes at hand." (Quinney 1970, 138). Certainly we construct types on the basis of our perceptions and our experiences. Nothing is either totally *a priori* or completely the result of induction. To conceive of types as developing from either source is to ignore the metaphysical problem of the nature of reality and our grasp of it. We construct that which gives meaning to our lives and to the problems of living that are posed by our need to survive.

Theoretical Assumptions and Underlying Dimensions

No matter how hidden and implicit they may be, there are always some assumptions about the nature of crime and society present when we construct criminal typologies. These implicit assumptions are what Gouldner called *"domain assumptions"* (Gouldner 1970). In addition, the particular selection of dimensions is guided by the interests of the criminologist. In other words, the purpose at hand determines how the typology is constructed. Also, the level of explanation desired by the criminologist will play a part in the selection of dimensions in the typology. We create typologies that meet our particular needs, just as we create social structures that meet our needs.

General characteristics for the construction of typologies can be developed in the course of criminological research. With the use of such techniques as factor analysis and regression analysis, and through time studies, for example, common characteristics of offenders can be found. These dimensions in turn can be used in the construction of a typological system. Typologies also can be constructed through the use of findings from other research studies on crime and delinquency. Related to the selection of characteristics underlying typologies is the determination of the phenomena to be included in the typology. The phenomena associated with crime include (1) the formulation and administration of criminal law, (2) the development of persons and behaviors that become defined as criminal, and (3) the social reactions to crime.

The distinction between these three subject areas is crucial in the construction of typologies in criminology. For example, if a typology is based on *criminal law,* attention is focused on the process by which criminal definitions are imposed on human behavior by authorized agents of the state. On the other hand, if the objective is a typology based solely on the criminal and his or her behavior, the emphasis is on the process by which persons who are subject to criminal definition acquire their self-conceptions and values, and how they associate with others in social and cultural contexts. Alternatively, a typology could be constructed on the basis of the nature and extent of social reaction to crime.

Yet another typology, a *criminal behavior system,* could be constructed that would consider all three areas of phenomena associated with crime. Such a typology would suggest how persons with certain characteristics and behaviors develop patterns that have a certain probability of becoming defined as criminal and that elicit particular reactions from various segments of society. The development of a multidimensional and integrative typology is this book's primary concern.

Comprehensiveness and Homogeneity of Types

There is also the question of whether a typology should include the entire range of crime or be limited in scope. A typology that attempts to be comprehensive must formulate types at a fairly high level of abstraction. When this is done it is unlikely that many cases will remain outside of the typology. Also, we must remember that the higher the level of abstraction and the more behavioral phenomena included, the less specificity is realized.

Should a typology incorporate both adults and juveniles? Many of the offenses of juveniles are the same as those of adults, as far as the behavior itself is concerned. Therefore, in constructing types, there may be little reason to create separate types for minors and adults. Instead, various forms of juvenile delinquency can be included in a single typology (as we have done). When an offense committed by a juvenile would be a crime if committed by an adult, it is included within our typology. It is possible to construct a typology based on uniquely juvenile offenses, such as truancy, but this is not our intent here.

No typology, unless it is on a very low level of abstraction, can contain purely homogeneous types. For every type, several subtypes could be delineated. The level of abstraction of the typology in general, and each type in particular, determines the extent to which subtyping may be appropriate. It is always the *purpose* of the analysis, combined with the desired level of abstraction, that influences the construction of types. Understandably, many of our types could eventually be broken down into subtypes, but this will have to await further work.

The Future of Criminal Typology

Whatever the nature of typology construction, the trend in criminology is clearly toward further study of types of crime. In the development of typologies we cannot expect to achieve a system that all criminologists will agree is the most desirable. Although some classifications will at various times be more popular than others, there are a number of reasons why we cannot look forward to one unifying typology in criminology.

First, as already mentioned, typologies differ according to the purposes they are to serve. Since there will continue to be a multitude of purposes and goals, including levels of analysis and degrees of generality, there will always be a number of typologies. Second, there is the fact that crime is relative. The definitions of crime change from time to time and from place to place, depending on the political structure and culture of a community. Therefore, the behaviors and persons to be included in a typology will vary according to time and place. Future typologies may be developed that will include the crimes of other historical periods. Third, theory within criminology will continue to develop. As this happens, typologies will be adjusted. Finally, theories, theoretical frameworks and the related typologies will change as the orientations of criminologists change. Inevitably, as with all intellectual and political developments, the interests of criminologists will be attuned to the developments in the larger society. Typologies, like theories, are historical, time-bound mental constructions. For example, a typology of criminal behavior in the former Soviet Union under Communist rule is likely to be extensively altered now that Communism has collapsed. We can expect to see a different political spin put on the work of criminologists in the former "Iron Curtain" nations. After all, criminology, like the other social sciences, is developed to meet human needs.

Theoretical Dimensions of a Typology of Criminal Behavior

All human social behavior is patterned. As such, it can be conceptualized as a patterned *system* of behavior. Crime as well is best seen as a system of behavior that follows patterns. As a result, in the typology we present here, types of crime are viewed as *systems* of behavior (Clinard and Meier 1992).

The theoretical assumptions of our typology are contained in five dimensions:

1.   Legal Aspects of Selected Offenses
2.   Criminal Career of the Offender
3.   Group Support of Criminal Behavior
4.   Correspondence between Criminal and Legitimate Behavior
5.   Social Reaction and Legal Processing

Included in these five dimensions are diverse phenomena associated with crime, that is, the formulation and administration of criminal law, which takes place within specific social structures dictating the distribution of power and wealth; the development of persons and behaviors that may be defined as criminal, which unfolds in another structure of wealth distrubution; and the social reactions to the behaviors, which are largely dictated by media-influenced perceptions. Together these five dimensions with their specific assumptions form the theoretical basis for our typology of criminal behavior systems.

Legal Aspects of Selected Offenses. Crime, according to most criminologists, is a definition of human conduct that is created by authorized agents in a politically organized society (Quinney 1970; Siegel 1992, 17). Criminal laws are formulated by those segments of society that have the power to translate their values, ideologies and interests into public policy. Criminal laws thus consist of definitions of behaviors that are regarded as threatening to the dominant class as well as behaviors that are a threat to other classes (as is the case with violent personal crime). The social history of criminal laws is a reflection of changes in the power structure of societies (Reiman 1984).

Criminal Career of the Offender. The criminal career of the offender includes the social roles he or she plays, his or her conception of self, his or her progression in criminal activity and his or her identification with crime. Offenders vary in the degree to which criminally defined behavior has become a part of the organization of their life (more often than not in the absence of other, legitimate job possibilities). The behavior of the offender is shaped by the extent to which criminally defined norms and activities have become a part of the individual's career (Blumstein et al. 1988).

Group Support of Criminal Behavior. The behavior of offenders is supported to varying degrees by the norms of the groups to which they belong

(Hagan 1991; Hagan and Palloni 1988). To some offenders, group support—or in many cases gang support—is a viable substitute for family support. Persons defined as criminals act according to the normative patterns learned in relative social and cultural settings. Group support of criminal behavior varies according to offender associations with differential norms and the offender integration into social groups.

Correspondence between Criminal and Legitimate Behavior. Criminal behavior patterns are structured in society in relation to legitimate and legal behavior patterns. Within this context persons develop and engage in actions that have relative probabilities of being defined as criminal. Criminally defined behaviors thus vary in terms of the extent to which they correspond to legitimate patterns of behavior in society. The behavior of the offender is viewed in relation to the norms of the segments of society that have the power to formulate and administer criminal law and with regard to what *they* perceive to be the norms of the general public.

Societal Reaction and Legal Processing. Criminally defined behaviors vary in the intensity and amount of reactions they provoke from different sectors of society. Social reactions range from degree of approval or disapproval to the official sanctioning procedures of the criminal justice system. Different policies of punishment and treatment are established and administered for each type of crime. Social reactions are also affected by the visibility of the offense and the degree to which the criminal behavior corresponds to the interests of the power structures of society. Finally, types of criminal behavior vary in the ways that they are processed through the legal system. Patterns of detection, arrest, prosecution, conviction, sentencing and punishment or treatment exist for each type of crime.

A Typology of Criminal Behavior Systems

Nine types of criminal behavior systems are constructed in relation to the five theoretical dimensions. The types are:

1. Violent Personal Criminal Behavior
2. Occasional Property Criminal Behavior
3. Public Order Criminal Behavior
4. Conventional Criminal Behavior
5. Political Criminal Behavior
6. Occupational Criminal Behavior
7. Corporate Criminal Behavior
8. Organized Criminal Behavior
9. Professional Criminal Behavior

The nine criminal behavior systems are summarized and diagrammed in table form in Figure 1.2.

Violent Personal Criminal Behavior. The criminal laws of homicide, assault and rape are found in most societies, yet the legal categories are qualified and interpreted in their respective social and historical contexts. Most offenders do not usually conceive of themselves as criminals. They are often persons without previous criminal records who commit a personal offense because of certain circumstances. The offenses are not directly supported by any group, although there may be cultural and subcultural definitions favorable to the general use of violence. There generally is strong reaction to these offenses.

Occasional Property Criminal Behavior. Criminal laws protect the material interests of the propertied classes, specifically prohibiting forgery, shoplifting, vandalism and automobile theft. The offenders do not usually conceive of themselves as criminals and are able to rationalize their criminal behavior. They are usually committed to the general goals of society and find little support for their behavior in group norms. The behaviors violate the value placed on private property in American culture. Societal reaction is not severe in those cases where the offender has no previous record and there is leniency in legal processing.

Public Order Criminal Behavior. Specific criminal laws embody the mores of particular segments of the community. Such offenses as prostitution, homosexuality, drunkenness and drug use may be "victimless," but they are disturbing to some community members. The violators may conceive of themselves as criminals when they are repeatedly defined as criminals by others. There is considerable association with other offenders, and some of the behaviors are supported by rather clearly defined subcultures. There is some correspondence between the illegal behaviors of public order offenders and legitimate patterns of behavior. Some of the behaviors defined as illegal are desired by many in legitimate society. There are strong social reactions by some segments of the community and weak reactions by others. Only a small portion of the offenses result in arrest, and many are tolerated as long as they do not become too visible.

Conventional Criminal Behavior. The laws that protect private property include such crimes as larceny, burglary and robbery. Offenders begin their careers early in life, often in gang associations. Offenders vacillate between the values of the larger society and those of a criminal subculture. Some offenders continue primary association with other offenders well into adulthood, while others pursue different careers later in life. The behaviors are consistent with the goal of economic success; thus they are "rational" but inconsistent with the sanctity of private property. There may be a series of arrests and convictions. Rehabilitation programs generally preserve the status quo without changing the social conditions that produced the behavior.

Political Criminal Behavior. Criminal laws are created by governments to protect their own existence, among other things. Specific criminal laws, such as "conspiracy" laws or laws prohibiting political demonstrations, are made to control and punish those who threaten the state. However, government structures, agencies and officials also violate criminal laws. Political offenders, acting out of conscience, do not usually think of themselves as criminals. They receive support for their behavior by particular segments of society. Often the behaviors of citizens against the government are consistent with the ideal of political freedom and basic human rights. Governmental crimes correspond to the belief in political sovereignty. Public acceptance of political crime depends on the extent to which the policies of the government are regarded as being legitimate at the time.

Occupational Criminal Behavior. Legal regulation of occupations serves to protect the public and consumer from the vested interests of occupational and professional groups and associations. These offenders violate the law in the course of their occupational activities. The behavior corresponds to the pursual of business activities. Occupational offenders are easily able to rationalize their conduct. Some occupations (or groups within occupations) tolerate or even support these offenses. Official penalties have been lenient, often restricted to the sanctions administered by the professional associations themselves. Because such offenses are committed by "respectable" persons, social reaction traditionally has been mild or tolerant.

Corporate Criminal Behavior. Criminal and civil laws and administrative regulations of corporations have been established to control such behavior as the restraint of trade, false advertising, misuse of trademarks, insider trading, the manufacture of unsafe foods and drugs, hazardous working conditions and environmental pollution. Such laws serve to protect honest and socially conscious corporations and a capitalist economy. In addition, they exist to protect the consuming public (though this appears to be a less vigorously pursued goal). The criminal behaviors may be an integral part of corporate business operations. Violations are rationalized as being basic to business enterprise. Corporate crime involves a great amount of organization and cooperation among the participants. The offenses are consistent with the prevailing ideology that encourages maximum profits in advanced capitalist societies. Strong legal actions have not traditionally been taken against corporations and their officials. However, negative public reactions and legal actions are increasing as corporate crime becomes more widespread and more costly to the taxpayer.

Organized Criminal Behavior. Many traditional laws have been used in the attempt to control organized crime. Special laws also have been enacted in recent years to deal with organized criminal activity in legitimate business and racketeering. These offenders pursue crime as a livelihood. In the lower echelons they conceive of themselves as criminals, associate primarily with other criminals and are isolated from the larger community and society. In the top levels offenders associate with people of legitimate society and often reside in the more desirable residential areas. There is considerable correspondence between the criminal

Figure 1.2 Typology of Criminal Behavior Systems

	Violent Personal Criminal Behavior	Occasional Property Criminal Behavior	Public Order Criminal Behavior
Legal Aspects of Selected Offenses	The criminal laws of homicide, assault and forcible rape are of ancient origin. Yet the legal categories are qualified and interpreted in their respective social and historical contexts. Likewise, the ruling class is able to exclude the forms of violence that enhance its own position.	Criminal laws protect the material interests of the propertied classes. Specific laws prohibit forgery, shoplifting, vandalism and auto theft.	Specific criminal laws embody the moral sense of particular segments of the community. Such offenses as prostitution, homosexuality, drunkenness and drug use are disturbing to some community members. Many of the crimes are "victimless" in that only willing participants are involved. Yet it is easier for the power elite to outlaw these behaviors than to either accept them or to change the social arrangements that produced the behaviors.
Criminal Career of the Offender	Crime is not part of the offender's career. He or she usually does not conceive of self as criminal.	Little or no criminal self-conception. The offender does not identify with crime. He or she is able to rationalize his or her behavior.	Most offenders do not regard their behavior as criminal. They do not have a clearly defined criminal career. Ambiguity in self-concept produced in continued contact with legal agents.
Group Support of Criminal Behavior	Little or no group support. Offenses committed for personal reasons. Some support in subcultural norms.	Little group support. Generally individual offenses. Associations tend to be recreational.	Offenses such as prostitution, homosexual behavior and drug use grow out of, and are supported by, rather clearly defined subcultures. Considerable association with other offenders.
Correspondence between Criminal and Legitimate Behavior	Violations of values on life and personal safety.	Violation of value on private property. Offenders tend to be committed to the general goals of the society.	Some of the offenses are required by legitimate society. Much of the behavior is consistent with legitimate behavior patterns.
Societal Reaction and Legal Processing	Strong social reaction. Harsh punishments. Long imprisonment.	Social reaction is not severe when the offender does not have a previous record. Leniency in legal processing. Probation.	Strong reaction by some segments of society, weak reaction by others. Only a small portion of the offenses result in arrest. Sentences are strong for some offenses, such as the possession of narcotic drugs.

Figure 1.2 *continued*

Conventional Criminal Behavior	Political Criminal Behavior	Occupational Criminal Behavior
The laws that protect private property include such crimes as larceny, burglary and robbery. Since the primary interest is in protecting property, general laws regarding property do not need to distinguish the career nature of many property offenders.	Criminal laws are created by governments to protect their own existence. Specific criminal laws, such as conspiracy laws, as well as traditional laws, are made to control and punish those who threaten the state. Yet the government and its officials often violate criminal laws. Political criminal behavior thus includes crimes *against* government and crimes *by* government.	Legal regulation of occupations has served to protect the interests of occupational groups, and in some cases to regulate harmful occupational activities. The legal codes that control occupations and professions tend to be made by the occupations and the professions themselves, representing their material interests.
Offenders begin their careers early in life, often in gang associations. Crimes committed for economic gain. Vacillation in self-conception. Partial commitment to a criminal subculture.	Political offenders do not usually conceive of themselves as criminals and do not identify with crime. They are defined as criminal because they are perceived as threatening to the status quo (as in crime against government) or they are criminal when they violate the laws that regulate the government itself (crime by government).	Little or no self-conception. Occasional violation of the law, accompanied by appropriate rationalizations. Violation tends to be a part of one's work. Offenders accept the conventional values in the society.
Behavior supported by group norms. Early association with other offenders in slum areas. Status achieved in groups. Some persons continue primary association with other offenders, while others pursue different careers.	Support is received by particular groups or by segments of society. They identify or associate with persons who share similar values. Behavior is reinforced by specific norms.	Some occupations (or groups within occupations), tolerate or even support offenses. The offender is integrated into social groups and societal norms.
Consistent with goals of economic success, but inconsistent with sanctity of private property. Gang delinquency violates norms of proper adolescent behavior.	Crimes against government usually correspond to basic human rights. The actions and beliefs, however, are opposed by those who are threatened by these freedoms. Crimes by government correspond to contrary behavior patterns that promote the sovereignty of government rulers.	Behavior corresponds to the pursual of business activity. "Sharp" practices and "buyer beware" philosophy have guided work and consumption patterns.
A series of arrests and convictions. Institutionalization and rehabilitation of the offender. Agency programs that preserve the status quo without changing social conditions.	Official reactions tend to be severe in the case of crimes against government. Considerable harassment may be experienced and heavy sentences may be imposed. Public acceptance of political offenses depends on the extent to which the policies and actions of the government are accepted. Reactions to governmental crime depend on the consciousness of the public regarding the activities of the government.	Reactions have traditionally been mild and indifferent. Official penalties have been lenient, often restricted to the sanctions administered by professional associations. Public reaction is becoming less tolerant.

Figure 1.2 *continued*

	Corporate Criminal Behavior	Organized Criminal Behavior	Professional Criminal Behavior
Legal Aspects of Selected Offenses	With the growth of corporations, criminal laws have been created to regulate such activities as restraint of trade, false advertising, fraudulent sales, misuse of trademarks and manufacture of unsafe foods and drugs. Criminal laws—especially administrative regulations—have been established by the corporations themselves to secure a capitalist economy.	Many traditional laws have been used in the attempt to control organized crime, especially those regarding gambling, prostitution and drug trafficking. The government has more recently enacted special criminal laws in order to infiltrate organized criminal activity in legitimate business and racketeering. But since organized crime is closely tied to the general business economy, these laws tend to invade the privacy of all citizens rather than control organized crime.	Professional crimes are distinguished by the nature of the criminal behavior rather than by specific criminal laws. Such professional activities as confidence games, pickpocketing, shoplifting, forgery and counterfeiting are regulated by the traditional laws that protect private property.
Criminal Career of the Offender	The violating corporate official and the corporation have high social status in society. Offenses are an integral part of corporate business operations. Violations are rationalized as being basic to business enterprise.	Crime is pursued as a livelihood. There is a progression in crime and an increasing isolation from the larger society. A criminal self-conception develops.	A highly developed criminal career. Professional offenders engage in specialized offenses, all of which are directed toward economic gain. They enjoy high status in the world of crime. They are committed to other professional criminals.
Group Support of Criminal Behavior	Crime by corporations and corporate officials receives support from similar (even competing) businesses and officials. Lawbreaking is a normative pattern within many corporations. Corporate crime involves a great amount of organization among the participants.	Support for organized criminal behavior is achieved through an organizational structure, a code of conduct, prescribed methods of operation and a system of protection. The offender is integrated into organized crime.	Professional offenders associate primarily with other offenders. Behavior is prescribed by the norms of professional criminals. The extent of organization among professional criminals varies with the kind of offense.
Correspondence between Criminal and Legitimate Behavior	Corporate crime is consistent with the prevailing ideology that encourages unlimited production and consumption. Only recently has an alternative ethic developed that questions practices that support corporate crime.	While organized crime may be generally condemned, characteristics of American society give support to organized crime. The values underlying organized crime are consistent with those valued in the free enterprise system.	Professional criminal activity corresponds to societal values that stress skill and employment. Some of the offenses depend upon the cooperation of accomplices. The operations of professional crime change with alterations in the larger society.
Societal Reaction and Legal Processing	Strong legal actions have not usually been taken against corporations or their officials. Legal actions often have been in the form of warnings and injunctions, rather than in terms of criminal penalties. Public reactions and legal actions, however, are increasing in respect to corporate crime.	Considerable public toleration of organized crime. Offenses are not usually visible to the public. Immunity of offenders, as provided by effective organization, prevents detection and arrest. Convictions are usually for minor offenses.	Considerable public toleration because of the low visibility of professional crime. Offenders are able to escape conviction by "fixing" cases.

activities of organized crime and legitimate business activities. Illegal services desired by legitimate society are provided by organized crime. The public tolerates organized crime and its activities, partly because of the services it provides and partly because of the problems in dealing with its operation. Conviction is usually for minor offenses. However, as a result of recent federal legislation, more major organized crime figures have been successfully prosecuted.

Professional Criminal Behavior. Professional crimes are distinguished by the nature of the criminal behavior rather than by specific criminal laws. The laws that protect private property are used to control confidence games, pickpocketing, forgery and counterfeiting. Professional criminals pursue crime as a livelihood. They see themselves as criminals, associate with other criminals involved in the same activities and have high status in the "world" of crime. The extent of organization among professional offenders varies with the kind of offense. There is some correspondence between professional crime and dominant behavior patterns, in that professional offenses involve hard work and often a high degree of skill. The public tolerates many of the offenses because of the low visibility of the behaviors. Many cases of professional criminal behavior are "fixed" in the course of legal processing.

The organization of this book is based on the typology constructed above. A separate chapter is devoted to each of the nine criminal behavior systems. Each chapter contains a detailed description of a particular type, an analysis of that type according to each of the five theoretical dimensions (i.e., legal aspects of selected offenses, criminal careers of the offender, group support of criminal behavior, correspondence between criminal and legitimate behavior, and societal reaction and legal processing) and a discussion of related research and writings. A selected bibliography is provided at the conclusion of every chapter.

References

(Note: An asterisk is placed before those works we consider of greater importance to students. We have adopted this format for the reference section at the end of all the chapters.)

Akers, Ronald (1985). *Deviant Behavior: A Social Learning Approach.* Belmont, CA: Wadsworth.

Beirne, Piers (1988). "Heredity versus Environment: A Reconsideration of Charles Goring's *The English Convict* (1913)." *British Journal of Criminology* 28 (3): 315-339.

Beirne, Piers, and James Messerschmidt (1991). *Criminology.* New York: Harcourt Brace Jovanovich.

*Blumstein, Alfred, Jacqueline Cohen, Jeffrey A. Roth, and Christy A. Visher (1986). *Criminal Careers and Career Criminals.* Washington, DC: National Academy Press.

*Blumstein, Alfred, Jacqueline Cohen, and David P. Farrington (1988). "Criminal Career Research: Its Value for Criminology." *Criminology* 26 (1): 1-36.

Cavan, Ruth Shonle (1962). *Criminology.* 3rd ed. New York: Thomas Y. Crowell.

*Clinard, Marshall B., and Robert F. Meier (1992). *Sociology of Deviant Behavior.* 8th ed. New York: Harcourt Brace Jovanovich.

*Farr, Kathryn Ann, and Don C. Gibbons (1990). "Observations on the Development of Crime Categories." *International Journal of Offender Therapy and Comparative Criminology* 34:223-237.

Ferri, Enrico (1917). *Criminal Sociology,* trans. J. Kelly and J. Lisle. Boston: Little, Brown. (First published in Rome in 1881.)

Gibbons, Don C. (1992). *Society, Crime, and Criminal Behavior.* Englewood Cliffs, NJ: Prentice-Hall.

Gottfredson, Michael and Travis Hirschi (1990). *A General Theory of Crime.* Palo Alto, CA: Stanford University Press.

Gouldner, Alvin Ward (1970). *The Coming Crisis in Western Sociology.* New York: Basic Books.

*Greenberg, David F. (1991). "Modeling Criminal Careers." *Criminology* 29 (1): 17-46.

Hagan, John (1991). "Destiny and Drift: Subcultural Preferences, Status Attainments, and the Risks and Rewards of Youth." *American Sociological Review* 56 (5) 567-582.

*Hagan, John, and Alberto Palloni (1988). "Crimes as Social Events in the Life Course: Reconceiving a Criminological Controversy." *Criminology* 26:87-100.

Hempel, Carl G. (1952). "Typological Methods in the Natural and Social Sciences." Proceedings, American Philosophical Association, Eastern Division. Philadelphia: University of Pennsylvania Press.

*Hirschi, Travis and Michael Gottfredson (1983). "Age and the Explanation of Crime." *American Journal of Sociology* 89:552-584.

Inciardi, James (1975). *Careers in Crime.* Chicago: Rand McNally.

*Katz, Jack (1988). *Seductions of Crime.* New York: Basic Books.

Lindesmith, Alfred, and H. Warren Dunham (1941). "Some Principles of Criminal Typology." *Social Forces* 19:307-314.

*Lombroso, Cesare (1876). *L'Uomo Delinquente.* Milan: Hoepli.

Mannheim, Hermann, ed. (1960). *Pioneers in Criminology.* London: Stevens & Sons.

McKinney, John C. (1969). "Typification, Typologies, and Sociological Theory." *Social Forces* 48:1-11.

*Nagin, Daniel, and Raymond Paternoster (1991). "On the Relationship of Past to Future Delinquency." *Criminology* 29:163-189.

Nagin, Daniel, and David Farrington (1992). "The Stability of Criminal Potential from Childhood to Adulthood." *Criminology* 30 (2): 235-260.

Petersilia, Joan, Peter W. Greenwood, and Marvin Lavin (1978). *Criminal Careers of Habitual Felons.* Washington, DC: National Institute of Law Enforcement and Criminal Justice.

Platt, Tony (1974). "Prospects for a Radical Criminology in the United States." *Crime and Social Justice: A Journal of Radical Criminology* 1:1-12.

*Quinney, Richard (1970). *The Social Reality of Crime.* Boston: Little, Brown.

Quinney, Richard and John Wildeman (1991). *The Problem of Crime.* Mountain View, CA: Mayfield.

Reckless, Walter (1967). *The Crime Problem.* New York: Appleton-Century-Crofts.

*Reiman, Jeffrey (1984). *The Rich Get Richer and the Poor Get Prison.* New York: John Wiley.

Rhoads, John K. (1967). "The Type as a Logical Form." *Sociology and Social Research* 51:346-359.

Roebuck (1967). *Criminal Typology: The Legalistic, Physical-Constitutional-Hereditary, Psychological-Psychiatric and Sociological Approaches.* Springfield, IL: Charles C Thomas.

Rowe, David C., D. Wayne Osgood, and Alan W. Nicewander (1990). "A Latent Triad Approach to Unifying Criminal Careers." *Criminology* 28:237-270.

Sampson, Robert, and John Laub (1990). "Stability and Change in Crime and Deviance over the Life Course: The Salience of Adult Social Bonds." *American Sociological Review* 55:609-627.

Schrag, Clarence (1961). "A Preliminary Criminal Typology." *Pacific Sociological Review* 4:11-16.

Schutz, Alfred (1963). "Concept and Theory Formation in the Social Sciences." Maurice Nathanson, ed. *Philosophy of the Social Sciences.* New York: Random House.

Schwendinger, Herman, and Julia Schwendinger (1970). "Defenders of Order or Guardians of Human Rights?" *Issues in Criminology* 5:123-157.

Siegel, Larry J. (1992). *Criminology.* Saint Paul, MN: West.

Turk, Austin T. (1969). *Criminality and Legal Order.* Chicago: Rand McNally.

Turk, Austin T. (1991). "Seductions of Criminology: Katz on Magical Meanness and Other Distractions." *Law and Social Inquiry* 16 (1): 181-194.

*Walker, Samuel (1989). *Sense and Nonsense about Crime: A Policy Guide.* Monterey, CA: Brooks/Cole.

Wrong, Dennis (1992). "The Lonely Crowd Revisited: A Review Essay." *Sociological Forum* 7 (2): 381-389.

Chapter 2

Violent Personal Criminal Behavior

Felonious violent crimes against the person include acts in which physical injury is inflicted against one or more others, including criminal homicide, aggravated assault, forcible rape or attempts to inflict such injuries. What has been referred to as "suicide by proxy," where a despondent and depressed person kills his or her loved ones and himself/herself in order to spare them humiliation, falls into the same category (Livingston 1992, 165). So-called "assisted deaths" (in the style of Dr. Jack Kevorkian), wherein one person aids and abets the death of another, have been defined legally as homicides. Kidnapping involves the element of physical force, and child abuse sometimes also involves the use of force and violence against the person. Armed robbery involves an element of force, such as the use of a gun, knife or threat of violence in obtaining money, jewelry or other items of value.

The use of violence and the reaction of society to it can be viewed in an even wider perspective. The use of personal and institutional violence has played a critical role in human history from riots to wars. The history of the United States is a case in point.

Apart from its role in the formation and preservation of the nation, violence has been a determinant of both the form and the substance of American life. The threat to the structure of society mounted by the criminal and the disorderly has been met energetically by the official and unofficial violence of the forces of law and order. Often perceiving a grave menace to social stability in the unsettled conditions of frontier life and racial, ethnic, urban, and industrial unrest, solid citizens rallied to the cause of community order. They did this indirectly by granting to the police and other duly constituted agents of the community the power to commit violence to preserve order. Not confining themselves to passive approval of police action, these upright citizens revealed their deep commitment to community order by their own violent participation in lynch mobs and vigilante movements and related extralegal bodies. . . . Established groups have been quick to resort to violence in defense of the status quo they dominate. (Brown 1969, 4-5)

Wars, civil riots and violent demonstrations may involve thousands of individual acts of assault, murder, arson, vandalism and theft (Garofalo and Hindelang 1977; Mulvihill, Tumin and Curtis 1969; Short and Wolfgang 1972; U.S. Dept. of Justice 1982; Weiner and Wolfgang 1990). The worst riot in United States history since the so-called "Irish Riots" in New York City in 1864 occurred in Los Angeles in May of 1992 in reaction to a police violence case and the subsequent acquittal of the defendants. Wars offer testimony to the involvement of hundreds of thousands in mass violence. As these are forms of collective violence, however, on the whole, their origin and nature are quite different from individual violent personal acts like homicide, assault and rape. Collective acts of violence will be discussed in the chapter on political criminal behavior (Chapter 6).

This chapter deals only with criminal homicide, aggravated assault and forcible rape, inasmuch as there is significant research and empirical data on these offenses. Robbery is not included as a violent personal crime, though it typically involves the threat of force, because the behavior is generally associated with a career of theft and will thus be discussed as a type of conventional crime. By the same token, although arson can be the occasion of violent death, it is not discussed here because it is chiefly directed toward the destruction of personal property (usually residential or commercial buildings). Child molestation is not included here, because only a relatively small percentage of child molestation involves force in order to gain the compliance of the child (Gelles and Straus 1988; McCaghy 1967; U.S. Dept. of Health and Human Services 1984).

Legal Aspects of Selected Offenses

For most of the history of the human race, generally the murder of or assault on a person was considered be to a private wrong for which the relatives of the deceased or assaulted person either took vengeance or demanded compensation. Such individual acts of violence were, on the whole, of minor concern to the tribal or political state and in fact, required law enforcement beyond the capacity of existing law enforcement institutions. But in modern industrial societies, minimizing crimes of violence is the stated goal of the legal order. However, the United States, described by many on the basis of solid empirical data as the most violent advanced industrial society on the face of the earth, has experienced an alarming increase in crimes of a violent nature since World War II.

The distinction between criminal and noncriminal homicides required many centuries of development under English law (upon which American law has largely been modeled). Excusable homicides include killings by misadventure and, under certain circumstances, self-defense. Whereas excusable homicides were never considered felonies in common law, they required the king's pardon and generally resulted in the confiscation of the offender's property (although this practice was later eliminated).

Further, the distinction between murder and manslaughter (womanslaughter also?) can be traced to the Norman Conquest. Originally, murder (*murdrum* in medieval Latin) applied both to the killing of a Norman and the fine levied by the king on a district if the offender was not brought to justice. This distinction between the killing of Normans and English people was not eliminated until the fourteenth century, when murder acquired the meaning of willful homicide. At this point, pardonable homicides were distinguished from those that had "malice aforethought." Early English law did not distinguish between degrees of homicide; all were considered murder. Distinctions in modern law have their roots in statutes enacted in the late fifteenth and sixteenth centuries that excluded "murder upon malice aforethought" from benefit of clergy. Thus, a second category was created: all criminal homicides that were not murder, namely, *manslaughter*. Before that, in the old common law of England, one who inadvertently killed another while committing some other felony was guilty of murder.

The type of *criminal homicide* that will be referred to here as "murder" consists of *murder,* first- or second-degree; *nonnegligent manslaughter,* excluding justifiable homicide or attempts or assaults to kill; and *negligent manslaughter* other than manslaughter connected with the operation of motor vehicles. Murder is the unlawful killing of a human being with "malice aforethought." Malice aforethought represents a "guilty mind," or *mens rea,* but not necessarily premeditation and planning. In many jurisdictions of the United States there are degrees of murder, first-degree and second-degree, often dependent on the situation or the means used. This constitutes a legal situation that affects the length and type of sentence. This distinction is of great importance, for it can mean the difference between life in prison (for second-degree murder in states that do not have the death penalty) or capital punishment, the ultimate punishment of which the state is capable (Bedau 1982).

The concept of malice aforethought eventually took on a meaning under criminal law quite different from its original usage. Today a killing may be said to have malice aforethought when the accused (1) intended to kill either the victim or another, (2) intended to inflict serious bodily injury on the victim, (3) did not intend to kill but engaged in conduct of extreme recklessness, (4) killed another in the course of committing some other felony, or (5) killed a police officer while resisting arrest. Some of these acts are treated as first-degree murder and others as second-degree murder, depending on the jurisdiction's legal code. Under present-day law one may legally kill an assailant when there is a reasonable belief of imminent danger of loss of life or of suffering serious bodily injury. The "reasonableness" of this belief was the central issue in the much publicized case of Bernhard Goetz, the so-called "subway shooter" in New York in 1984 (Siegel 1992). Goetz was a subway passenger who felt physically threatened by the behavior of four youths, all of whom he shot. He was eventually found guilty only on the charge of unlicensed possession of a handgun. Reasonableness must be proven to the satisfaction of law enforcement authorities and the court. Generally a person may also use deadly force to save a third party who is a member of the actor's household or to whom the actor has special commitments.

Manslaughter is unlawful or criminal homicide without malice aforethought, that is, without *mens rea*. It covers a wide range of acts, including those that result in accidental death. A person might attack another without the intention of causing death or severe bodily harm but death may be the outcome. The unlawful killing may be in a sudden heat of rage or anger and without premeditation. The element of provocation by the victim is often considered an element in manslaughter. In many cases of a mate slaying his or her physical abuser over many years of abuse, the element of provocation is taken into account (Livingston 1992, 214-216; Yllo and Straus 1981). All such manslaughter is termed voluntary or nonnegligent manslaughter. Involuntary manslaughter is death arising from unintentional killing, primarily from negligence, such as death resulting from the collapse of an improperly constructed building. This is death attributable to the negligence of some person other than the victim.

In general, murder and aggravated assault are similar, for both involve the use of physical force to settle a dispute. In aggravated assault there is an attempt to cause a person injury or kill him or her. *Nearly all murders thus represent some form of aggravated assault, the chief difference being whether the victim in fact died.* Serious assaults are invariably considered felonies by the courts, as they cover such behavior as an attempt to inflict severe injury or to kill. These include assault with a deadly weapon, assault to commit murder or assault by shooting, cutting, sticking, stabbing, maiming, etc. Whether the behavior results in injury or is only an attempt to cause injury, it remains a case of aggravated assault. In most cases it is probably the element of chance that prevents the offense from slipping over into criminal homicide by the death of one of the participants.

Compared to other crimes, homicide is fairly accurately reported and recorded so that it is possible to make useful and valid international comparisons. The United States homicide rate is considerably higher than that of most of the countries in the European Economic Community and Japan. The homicide rates in South Africa, Angola, Sudan and Kenya are extremely high as a result of rapid social change, intertribal strife and civil wars. It is a generally accepted conclusion, based on solid empirical evidence from cross-national studies, that there is a strong positive relation between the degree of social inequality in a country and the levels of homicide. This suggests that higher levels of political and military organization of societies are positively correlated with homicide rates.

If we look at homicide and aggravated assault that result in serious personal injury, we see that the United States has the highest rate of violent crime among all the industrialized nations of the world. In the decade of the 1980s the rate per 100,000 of homicide and assault resulting in serious bodily injury was 10.5. This was followed by Canada (2.4), Australia and Italy (1.9), Austria (1.7) and France and Japan (1.0) (United Nations 1986). These figures are striking, in view of the fact that this country has the highest ratio of citizens behind bars or under some sort of correctional supervision. The United States also is alone among the advanced industrial nations still to execute offenders. Penal policies in the United States have, by and large, failed to control violent crime. Peace-making, nonviolent alternatives are currently being sought by many (Pepinsky and Quinney 1991). The driving idea behind this search is that state violence against offenders only provokes more violence on the part of citizens and fails to have any positive effect on the offender. Another factor to be considered is that homicide and other forms of violence have a wide variety of purposes and meanings in different cultural settings (Riches 1986).

If we look at homicide rates in large cities, a complex picture takes shape. Studies have shown that, contrary to popular belief, city size is not directly correlated with homicide rates. The important variable seems to be the population size of the city in relation to the size of the country in which it is located, that is, population density. Further, it is suspected that social forces operative in large cities of the advanced industrial nations—social forces often created by the mass media—are diminished or absent in large cities of the developing and underdeveloped world (Archer and Gartner 1984). Another key factor in homicide rates is the degree of income inequality that characterizes the city. In other words, high levels of income inequality correlate with high rates of homicide (Messner 1980).

Forcible rape, the act of having unlawful sexual intercourse with a woman against her will, is distinguished from statutory rape, sexual intercourse with a female under a specific age (16 in most jurisdictions) with or without her consent. Although the actual percentage is not known because of problems in reporting this felony, it appears that forcible rape constitutes only a small proportion of all arrests and prosecutions for rape. By United States law, rape involves sexual intercourse accompanied by force and against the woman's consent. The precise definition of "force" is often difficult to determine in cases of rape. For example, a woman's consent to having sexual intercourse may have been given with great reluctance and/or because there has been a threat of force used to obtain her consent. If she consents to intercourse, although the consent may be reluctantly given and although there may be some force used to obtain it, the offense may or may not be considered by the court to constitute rape. Problems of underreporting rape have diminished somewhat as a result of three factors: (1) an increased willingness of girls and women to step forward and complain to the police of victimization, (2) an increasing tendency among district attorneys across the country to accept and vigorously pursue rape charges instead of, as in the past, discouraging the victim from pressing charges, and (3) the establishment in many cities of special rape investigation units made up of female police officers. The pressures of organized advocacy groups for the advancement of women's rights have secured these progressive steps within the past quarter of a century.

Criminal Career of the Offender

As a rule, murderers, assaulters and rapists are not career criminals in these violent behaviors. In the case of homicides it is rare to find a person arrested for this crime who has previously committed such an offense, although the individual may have arrests for other offenses, violent as well as nonviolent. Few people make "careers" out of assaulting others. Of all those arrested in the United States between 1964 and 1967 for serious crimes, only 35 percent of those arrested for aggravated assault had been arrested previously for this same offense (Mulvihill, Tumin and Curtis 1969). These statistics tend to remain remarkably stable over time. With regard to using actual or threatened violence in the form of assault and even homicide as part of their careers in crime, the exceptions are organized criminal offenders (so-called "hit men") who will be discussed in a later chapter.

Most murderers and assaulters do not think of themselves as being real "criminals"; rather, they look upon themselves as being unable to control their impulses. Generally, they do not identify with crime, and criminal behavior is not a significant part of their life organization. The situation is somewhat different with rapists; they are reported by some to have a fairly extensive criminal record for other offenses, particularly against property. On the psychological level, according to clinical findings, rape—a crime of aggression as opposed to one of sexual lust—is likely to be the crime of men who were themselves the victims of sexual abuse as children. As a result, they are prone to feel the impulse to rape throughout much of their lives unless treated (Groth 1979).

In a 1989 study of 28,884 men in Denmark, researchers found that specialization in violence exists for offenders with three or more arrests. Violent offenders often have a pattern of violence, and hence, past violence is a predictor of future violence.

> Our results suggest that groups at high risk of committing future violence can be identified by examining their records of arrest. We found that individuals who had committed one violent offense were more than twice as likely as other individuals in the criminal population to commit a future violent offense. More-

over, individuals with four or more arrests whose second or third offense was their first violent offense were much more likely than similarly classified non-violent individuals to commit future violent crimes. . . . Thus, we suggest that the utility of a past record of violence in predicting future violent offending would be increased if predictive indicators of higher levels of recidivism were also apparent (Brennan, Mednick and John 1989).

An earlier study of persons in St. Louis convicted of assault concluded that violent persons are not likely to be involved in other types of crime. The majority of offenders did not have prior arrest records, and of those who did, relatively few were for crimes against the person. Two-thirds of the cases in the 20-34 age bracket, however, had no prior arrest record (Peterson, Pittman and O'Neal 1962). On the other hand, Wolfgang's classic study of homicide in Philadelphia found that 66 percent of the offenders had been previously arrested for offenses against the person (48 percent for aggravated assault) and only 34 percent had any record for property or other offenses. Of those offenders with an arrest record, a larger proportion had a record of aggravated assault involving woman abuse and fighting than of all types of property offenses combined (Wolfgang 1958). Studies of this nature, however, have come under fire recently as lacking in attention to and analysis of disaggregated rates, that is, their "failure to disaggregate the overall homicide rate into more refined and conceptually meaningful categories of homicide" (Williams and Flewelling 1988, 421). Some studies have focused on the need for greater attention in homicide research to variables such as population structure, resource deprivation/affluence, unemployment rates and geographical location (Land, McCall and Cohen 1990).

Another study based on cluster analysis methodology concluded that (1) the number of an individual's prior violent crimes is strongly associated with that person's number of nonviolent crimes; (2) offenders with psychiatric histories display a greater tendency than other offenders toward violent crime; (3) addicted offenders (to alcohol and controlled substances) are more likely to be convicted of burglary than of violent personal crime; (4) individuals with no psychiatric history who are convicted of homicide are more likely to do so with a gun, away from their own residence, and to choose a friend or acquaintance as their victim, whereas offenders with psychiatric histories tend to slay spouses or relatives, within their own homes, and not use a gun as their weapon (Toch and Adams 1989).

Many rape offenders appear to have had a record of arrests for criminal offenses. One study of 1,292 rape offenders in Philadelphia showed that 50 percent of them had a past arrest record, and there was little difference in the extent of this past record between black offenders and white offenders (Amir 1971). Only 20 percent of those with a past arrest record, however, had previously committed a crime against the person, with blacks far outnumbering whites in this respect. Approximately one in 10 had committed rape in the past. Another study has shown that by the age of 26, 87 percent of rapists had been convicted of some crime; two-thirds had been convicted of a felony, one-half of them "non-sex" offenses. For slightly more than half, the forcible rape was their first sex offense, and for about one-fourth, it was their second. A substantial number (22 percent) had a record of juvenile offenses, but only 5 percent had prior sex offenses (Gebhard et al. 1965).

A great deal of violent behavior is linked to social situations and differences in power that people have over one another. Nevertheless, there are some people who react with violence in a variety of situations and circumstances. It is highly probable that such people have extensive criminal records and a long history of antisocial conduct in other areas of their lives, such as school maladjustment and family problems. A study of 50 such offenders found that they experience an increasing sense of violence as a solution to some present problem (for example, a feeling of being "dissed" or "pushed around") and in so doing come to see themselves as violent individuals (Athens 1989).

Dangerous violent offenders generally go through a series of four stages.

1. *Brutalization:* These offenders were typically coerced by physical force to submit to authority as children and adolescents. They are accustomed to seeing the brutalization of others and they have been taught by others in their primary groups to resort to violence in order to accomplish their objectives.

2. *Belligerency:* This is a consequence of the first stage. At this stage offenders have become deeply convinced that they must use violence in their future relations with others.

3. *Violent Performances:* These offenders set out performing a series of violent acts in which they intentionally and gravely injure other people.

4. *Violent Personality:* As a result of their violent performances, others come to define them as violent people instead of simply people who are capable of violence. As a result, others in their peer group come to confer a sense of empowerment on them, and this in turn reinforces their use of violence. The way they experience violence is graphically illustrated by a person in his late teens convicted of aggravated assault:

> After the stabbing, my friends told me, "Hey man, we heard about what you did to Joe. It's all over school. Everybody's talking about it. You must really be one crazy ass motherfucker." My girlfriend said, "Wow, you stabbbed that dude." Finally, things came together and hit right for me. My girlfriend and all my other friends were impressed with what I

had done. I didn't really care what my parents thought. Everybody acted like nobody better piss me off any more unless they wanted to risk getting fucked up bad. People were plain scared to fuck with me. My reputation was now made.

I was on cloud nine. I felt like I climbed the mountain and reached the top. I had proven to my friends and myself that I could really fuck somebody up. If something came up again, I knew I could hurt somebody bad. If I did it once, I could do it again. . . . I knew I could fuck somebody's world around, send them sideways, upside down and then six feet under. There was no doubt at all in my mind now that I was a bad son of a bitch, a crazy motherfucker. I could do anything, kill or murder somebody.

Now that I had reached the top of the mountain, I was not coming down for anybody or anything. The real bad dudes who wouldn't associate with me before because they thought I was a nobody, now thought I was a somebody and accepted me as another crazy bad ass. (Athens 1989, 76-77)

Some continue perpetrating such acts of violence, meanwhile learning from the way others react in the wake of such actions. These individuals are perceived by themselves and others as dangerous, powerful people not to be fooled with. The unpredictability of their violence is also a potent factor. In short, others bestow the mantle of power on the person, and that reinforces the use of violence.

Group Support of Criminal Behavior

The general cultural and subcultural pattern seems to determine the frequency of crimes of violence. Accceptance of the use of violence varies from country to country, region to region and state to state. It also varies by neighborhood (within a city), social class, occupation, race, sex and age (Langan and Innes 1990). The existence of *subcultures of violence,* normative systems of a group or groups smaller than the total society, has been advanced as a concept (primarily by Wolfgang and Ferracuti) to explain these variations (Ferracuti, Lazzari and Wolfgang 1970). According to this view, specific populations, such as social classes, ethnic groups and so forth, have different attitudes toward the use of violence. Favorable attitudes toward violence are organized into a set of norms that are culturally transmitted. Subcultural groups exhibit norms about the importance or lack of importance of human life in the scale of values, and the kinds of reactions to certain types of social stimuli, in the evaluation of such stimuli and in the socialization process in general. For example, during the 1980s in America's inner-city areas it became normal, even necessary in the minds of many adolescents, to carry guns for self-protection and status among peers. Some popular films were woven around this subcultural pattern of extreme violence, mainly presenting it in a positive but destructive light. The assumption that violence is a normal, expected part of one's life grew widespread—with deadly results.

A subculture of violence represents values that stand apart from the dominant, central or "parent" culture of society. It should be pointed out, however, that the proponents of a "subculture" of violence actually base the existence of the theory of differences on rates of violence between various groups, for example, warring gangs or drug dealers. This does not, of course, mean that *all* persons in any group share the values supposedly reflected in a subculture of violence or, conversely, in a subculture of nonviolence.

Different segments of society define different social situations as violence-appropriate. Some males "must" defend their mothers' honor, often to the point of violence. For some, a sneer, a "dis" or simply being stared at is considered enough to call for a violent response, while for others, being taken advantage of monetarily is what merits a violent response. Many American adolescents (males, in the vast majority of cases) consider violence an appropriate response to being denied a request for money or even use of the family car from parents or relatives.

It has been argued persuasively by a number of criminologists, philosophers and other social scientists that state-mandated executions constitute a powerful support and reinforcement for violence in the minds of many citizens. The reasoning is, "if it is legitimate for the state to punish a wrong by killing the wrongdoer, why is it not legitimate for me to do the same when I am wronged?" The reasoning, of course, is flawed, but the conclusion is suggested and not entirely unreasonable (Pepinsky and Quinney 1991; Reiman 1992).

In general, American popular culture encourages and nurtures violence. From the athletic entertainment industry, there is ice hockey, stock car racing, boxing and football. There is also rap and heavy metal music with lines such as "I've got something to say. I killed your baby today" (Metallica). Even television nature programs have become more realistic: "I think the average audience would watch violence more easily than mating (in nature shows), because Americans are conditioned to violence ever since they watched cartoons as kids" claimed the president of ABC/Kane Productions International (*New York Times* 1992). Taken as a whole, one would be challenged to find much that encourages peacemaking and nonagression in American culture.

The parent (or carrier) culture itself condones violence; and the greater the degree of integration of an individual into a subculture of violence—in terms of appropriate reactions to certain types of stimuli and the importance of human life—the more likely it is that a particular individual will resort to violence in a dispute to gain an objective. Child rearing practices and peer group associations that employ violence are part of this subculture. There are many cultural and subcultural socialization patterns that lead to social interaction patterns and personal decisions that produce people who are ready to inflict serious physical harm with only minor provocation (Athens 1989). Violence is defined as an appropriate response to provocation among poor, disenfranchised male adolescents and young adults in urban ghettos. This has been the case at least since the Irish Riots in New York in 1864. Wolfgang noted it again back in 1961 (Wolfgang 1961). Violent crimes are more closely linked to males, particularly young males, partly because of the felt need to display "machismo," as the display of male pride is called in Latin America. Typically, this feeling of maleness is equated with physical aggression. Often these young males have no other way to assert themselves or to prove their worth.

Regional Differences

As a general proposition, it is safe to say that homicide rates in various countries and regions of the world are related to cultural differences regarding the use of violence rather than to penal laws or individual personality characteristics. In Europe, for example, Switzerland and Sweden have low rates, especially in comparison to the newly united Germany and the disintegrated former state of Yugoslavia. Rape and sexual assault are virtually nonexistent in Japan. The United States has far and away the highest rate in the world of homicide by handguns. (In this book we will deal with violent political crime, such as terrorism, in a later chapter.)

Aside from those regions and countries suffering from civil war and severe ethnic strife, Colombia, along with the United States, has one of the highest rates of violence in the world, with what is probably the most striking example of large-scale cultural violence—called *violencia Colombiana*. There are two reasons for this: one, the violence caused by drug production and trafficking, and two, the tremendous range in the distribution of wealth. A handful of families own and control the vast majority of that country's wealth. While other Latin American countries always have had high homicide rates, Colombia has experienced a fantastic increase in the use of violence since World War II, when the rate was 11.2 per 100,000, increasing to a high of 51.4 by 1958, and a rate of 33.8 in 1960 (Guzman 1964). In the 1990s, the rate of violence is considerably higher in Colombia, with murders of high court judges, newspaper editors and journalists. In northern India the fierce and bitter struggle between the Sikhs and the Kashmiris and the Indian government has brought about increasing violence. In addition, the bitter struggles between the minority Muslims and the Hindus have been characterized by much violence. Great Britain, traditionally a country of control and tranquility, is experiencing an increase in violence because of immigration and unemployment in its industrial centers. Israel is a special case: the *intifada,* the Palestinian uprising of recent years, wreaked havoc on domestic tranquility. The fall of the Soviet Union sparked ethnic violence in that region of the world. These situations of rapid social change, and in some cases civil war (for example, in what was formerly Yugoslavia) are unique and are thought of separately from rates of violence in relatively stable societies.

The importance of cultural definitions in criminal homicide was revealed several decades ago when wide regional differences in the United States were found (Brearley 1932). Even today, homicide rates in the former "Dixie states" of the South are considerably higher than those of other regions. Some cultural definitions demand personal violence in certain situations, and weapons are more frequently carried in some areas than in others. Moreover, the pattern of Southern violence cannot be explained by the rural nature of the population, relative poverty or backwardness or underdevelopment. After examining these explanations, one researcher suggested the problem may possibly lie in historical factors such as the influence of slavery as a repressive system on the culture, the type of immigration (Scotch-Irish and fundamentalist) and, above all, "the development of a Southern world view that defines the social, political and physical environment as hostile" (Hackney 1969). Moreover, another study showed that, contrary to the general pattern of other offenses, murder and aggravated assault are negatively correlated with most socioeconomic variables, whether they occur in rural, urban or standard metropolitan statistical areas (Quinney 1966). "Offenses against the person regardless of the population area may become institutionalized and perceived by people in these structures as the most appropriate solutions to interpersonal problems" (Quinney 1966, 49).

The Use of Weapons

Based on current data, it is becoming increasingly apparent that violent crime in the United States is largely the problem of city dwellers. Certainly, this is true of young, black, male city dwellers in particular. But it should be noted that the size of the city is not directly correlated with violent crime rates in this population. For example, a study of firearm homicides among young black males that was conducted by the National Center for Health Statistics found that the cities of Washington, DC, Los Angeles, Detroit, Jacksonville and New Orleans, in that order, were the top five in firearm homicides of black males from age 15 to 19 (*Journal of the American Medical Association* 1992). "The most common weapon used to commit murder in the United States is a firearm. In 1987 approximately 59 percent of all murders were committed with a firearm, 44 percent with a handgun . . . the handgun [is] the weapon of choice in all three major types of murder—family, acquaintance and stranger (Beirne and Messerschmidt 1991, 67). According to the *Santa Barbara News Press,* in 1990, 37,155 Americans died of gunshot wounds; almost 5,000 of the victims were below the age of 20. In California alone, 2,692 persons were murdered by handguns. Japan, whose population is four times greater, had only 69 murders involving handguns.

Both the possession of firearms and familiarity with the norms governing their use are part of the subculture of violence. The weapon of choice among men who were armed during their conviction crime was the handgun, as opposed to a shotgun, rifle or knife (Wright, Rossi and Daly 1983). There are five categories of citizens who are prohibited by federal law from purchasing firearms in the United States (persons referred to in "disability categories" in the legislation): (1) unlawful users of controlled substances, (2) "mental defectives," (3) illegal aliens, (4) dishonorably discharged persons, and (5) those who have renounced their United States citizenship (Tien and Rich 1990). Nonetheless, as of 1994, handguns are widely available.

Unfortunately, the United States does not have a strictly enforced and uniform firearm registration program. Consequently no one knows for certain how many Americans or American households own what kind of weapons. We do have estimates, however, based on inferences from known data. One estimate is that there are 50 million unregistered handguns in the country, and that two-thirds of law enforcement officers slain in the line of duty are killed by these weapons (Siegel 1992). In 1994 there were an estimated 200 million firearms of all types in private possession in the United States. One problem is that, although the domestic production and sale of firearms can be known with a fair degree of accuracy, it is impossible to know the number imported and sold, either legally or illegally. A number of innovative people make their own firearms, usually for self-protection. A steel pipe, a trigger mechanism and a cartridge chamber are all that is needed. One study reported that two out of three homicides, one out of five aggravated assaults and one out of three robberies involved firearms (handguns in the vast majority of cases) (Newton and Zimring 1969). Guns unquestionably contribute to violence, but in complex ways (Kleck 1991).

Use of a handgun in the commission of crimes is a frequent occurrence in American cities. Every day, children, families at home, individuals in cars and pedestrians in public places are victims of drug-related "drive-by" shootings, gang warfare and simple shootouts between people who have a conflict of interest with one another. According to a report released by the Centers for Disease Control and Prevention in June of 1992, the nationwide homicide rate for young people in the 15 to 19 year old age group is 11.15 per 100,000 from handguns alone. Firearm homicides in the United States actually declined from 1979 to 1984, but have risen sharply since that year. The greatest increases in death from gunshot have been among white men and women in both large and small cities, and among black young men in small cities (*Journal of the American Medical Association* 1992).

Nearly all industrialized nations either forbid civilian possession or ownership of handguns, or rigidly regulate it. As a result, there are pronounced differences in the weapons of choice in aggravated assault and murder in these countries. In the United States it has been estimated that about one in five serious assaults are committed with the use of a firearm, as opposed to about two-thirds of homicide cases. About one-fourth of assault cases are committed with hands, fists and feet, as compared with 10 percent of homicides. In assault cases, the heaviest thing at hand is normally used. A candlestick, a poker, an iron pipe or—lacking these—one's fists.

Demographics

Rates for murder and assault that are similar in type vary a great deal by local area, geographical area, race, social class and age. This fact illustrates the role of group factors in criminal violence. An interesting study made in Houston found the characteristics of nearly all homicide and aggravated assault offenders to be similar, indicating that they represent basically similar behavior.

> Criminal homicide and aggravated assault seem to be similar in all of the analyses. They tend to occur in the same census tracts of the city. The distributions for the hour of the day and the day of the week are remarkably similar. They have a very similar age distribution, with regard to victims and offenders. The race and ethnic proportions in the two categories of offenses are quite similar. So is the representation of the sexes, in both victims and offenders. (Pokorny 1965)

Community. Violence occurs primarily in large cities. Approximately one-quarter of all violent crimes of assault and homicide are committed in the cities of (in rank order): New York, Los Angeles, Chicago, Detroit, Houston, Philadelphia and Washington, DC (Federal Bureau of Investigation 1991). As far as area of the city is concerned, violent crime is more frequent in communities that have exceptionally high rates of unemployment, overcrowding and housing decay, and that are characterized by considerably substandard schools, drug dealing and poverty. Frequently referred to as the inner city, these areas are typical of cities with extremely high levels of income inequality. In other words, income inequality is an indicator of level of violence. The use of interpersonal violence as a means of settling disputes has become common in the inner-city subculture.

Today a great deal of this violence is the result of drug traffic. Often, members of gangs and organizations that deal in drugs kill each other in the competition for customers and marketing territory, even when they are not personally acquainted. Furthermore, "drive-by shootings" or drug shootouts involve innocent victims ("mushrooms") who happen to be in the wrong place at the wrong time. In these incidents, which are occurring with alarming frequency, the victims are totally unknown to the killers.

It does, however, remain true that in crimes of violence it is more common that the offender and the victim were on some level of intimacy or acquaintance at the time of the offense. In his classic study of criminal homicide, Wolfgang found that in 87 percent of the cases the murderer and the victim had known each other before the murder and that two-thirds of all the homicides in Philadelphia occurred during weekends, particularly Saturday night (Wolfgang 1958). In this connection, Riedel and Zahn identify three separate categories of criminal homicide: (1) *family homicide,* wherein the offender and victim are members of the same family, blood- or marriage-related; (2) *acquaintance homicide,* wherein they knew each other to some degree of interpersonal intimacy; and (3) *stranger homicide,* wherein victim and offender do not know one another at all. They found that approximately two-thirds, or 66 percent, of all homicides are either family or acquaintance homicides, and less than one-fifth were between strangers (Riedel and Zahn 1985).

Finally, it is a telling commentary on the American family that many crimes involving interpersonal violence occur during holidays when families assemble to celebrate the occasion. At such times, alcohol use tends to be a component of the occasion, and intense emotions and interaction are part of the mix. Being under the influence of a controlled substance is a factor in violent crime. According to the Bureau of Justice Statistics, victims of violent crime—excluding homicide, of course—report that they believed their assailants were under the influence of drugs or alcohol in about 36 percent of these crimes. Approximately 54 percent of the inmates of state prisons reported that they were under the influence of drugs and/or alcohol at the time they committed the violent offense for which they were currently incarcerated (Dillingham 1991).

Race. One explanation for racial differences in homicide rates must be sought in the pressures of subcultural factors, such as the norms of ghetto life in America's cities. These subcultural factors, in turn, are the direct results of the conditions of the inner city. Racial disparity is greatest in arrest rates for crimes of violence. African-Americans account for approximately 12 percent of the population, and yet they account for 55.7 percent of the arrest rate for homicide and nonnegligent manslaughter. For aggravated assault they account for 40.1 percent of arrests, and for burglary they account for 36.5 percent of arrests. For all offenses classified as violent crime (murder, rape, robbery and aggravated assult), African-Americans account for 46.6 percent of arrests (*Sourcebook of Criminal Justice Statistics* 1990, 426). These official data must be approached with great care, for other variables are surely at work here. For example, discrimination in the criminal justice system's institutions and the inadequacy or lack of legal self-defense mechanisms available to disenfranchised citizens may play a role. In a Chicago study in the 1960s, the black criminal homicide rate was approximately 10 times that of whites; in fact, the rate for black females was about twice that of white males (Voss and Hepburn 1968).

Currie summed up the relationship between violence and race in this way:

> Homicide is the leading cause of death for blacks of both sexes between the ages of fifteen and twenty-four: 39 percent of black men and 25 percent of black women who die at these early ages are murdered. At this age, homicide death rates are five times higher for blacks than whites among men and four times higher for women. (Currie 1985)

Social Class. Violent crime is found to be concentrated among citizens of the lower socioeconomic status groups. It has been thus since the colonial period in our history. Wolfgang found that nine out of 10 criminal homicides in Philadelphia were among the lowest echelons of the secondary labor force. Laborers, for example, committed far more criminal homicides than did those in clerical positions (Wolfgang 1958). One study of assault in London found that the majority of the offenders were unskilled or casually employed workers (McClintock 1963). The higher clerical and professional workers accounted for no more than 5 percent of the total. Of those involved in a sample group of assaulters, four-fifths of the offenders, as well as a like percentage of the victims, were from the working class. The same relationship between violence and socioeconomic status has been found in several other studies (Currie 1985; Elliott and Huizinga 1983; Rao 1968; Sismondi 1970; Thornberry and Farnworth 1982). It is important, however, to place these findings in context. As Beirne cautions:

> . . . when we consider this class/crime link, it is clear the vast bulk of avoidable (physical) harm and economic loss originates from the professional-managerial class. Consequently, the *type and seriousness* of crime are associated with social class position: conventional crimes tend to be committed more often by the poor and the working classes; white-collar and political crimes tend to be committed more often by the professional-managerial class. (Beirne and Messerschmidt 1991, 535)

Criminal homicides do occur among middle- and upper-class socioeconomic segments of society, but they are relatively rare, even in countries and areas with high homicide rates such as southern United States and many countries in Latin America. When homicide is committed among such socioeconomic groups, it is likely to be more rational and planned. Deterrence most likely operates with this group more than with the lower groups, for the consequences can be potent and meaningful to their lives. In general, however, the cultural phenomenon of interpersonal violence does not pervade middle- and upper-class strata of bourgeois societies.

A study of 646 cases of forcible rape in Philadelphia showed that the offense is generally committed by young unmarried males, aged 15 to 25, who come from the lower classes. Ninety percent of the offenders from both races belonged to the lower part of the occupational scale. Approximately four in 10 were from the lower class; if the lower middle class is added, the figure is six in 10. A disproportionate amount of the violence involved in these cases was in the offender group from the lower class. It was also found that there was a significantly higher number of black offenders than white offenders. The proportion of black offenders was four times that of the general population, as was the proportion of black victims. The inner-city areas had the highest rates of forcible rape (Amir 1971).

Amir's study also shows the role of group factors in that areas with high rates of forcible rape have been found to correspond to areas having a high rate of crimes against the person generally. According to the Bureau of Justice Statistics, 37 percent of the defendents in rape charges in the largest 75 counties in the United States had one or more prior felony charges (U.S. Dept. of Justice, Bureau of Justice Statistics, *Felony Defendants in Large Urban Counties* 1990). Of the 646 cases, 43 percent involved multiple offenders. A total of 912 (71 percent) offenders, were involved in multiple-rape cases. Group factors were also indicated by the fact that black offenders were more likely to be involved in a group rape. Inner cities are extremely dense population areas involving constant and intense social interaction and exposure. Those who hold a structural view see rape as a product of unequal social relations such as poverty and inequality. Thus, inequality in economic and social conditions produces increased violence and aggression among the population condemned to the lower end of the distribution (Blau and Blau 1982).

Age and Gender. Most violent crime is perpetrated by males. In this country one-tenth of 1 percent of persons arrested for murder and nonnegligent manslaughter are women. Only 2.4 percent of arrests for assault, simple or aggravated, are of women. The overall arrest rate for females for all violent offenses is 3.2 percent. In most cases of arrests for females on the charge of homicide and assault, the victim is a spouse or male companion who has abused the perpetrator. Recent findings strongly suggest that the availability of legal and extralegal resources to these abused women can give them nonviolent alternatives (Browne and Williams 1989; Quinney and Wildeman 1991). For abused mates and spouses, further research along these lines is necessary, especially in light of the fact that the vast majority of these women have dependent children.

Interpersonal violence, such as homicide and assault, is higher in urban areas (inner-city neighborhoods in particular) and among young age groups. Specifically, homicide rates are considerably higher among males aged 18 to 24 than for any other group (Luckenbill 1984; Wolfgang and Zahn 1983). Many studies of criminal violence have shown that the vast majority of assaultive behavior, including murder, occurs during later adolescence and early adult years (Weiner 1989). Further, most young people tend to murder and assault those similar to them in age, race, sex and socioeconomic status.

Studies have shown that criminal justice policies with respect to violent crimes committed by juveniles largely reflect similar policies adopted for adult violent offenders. (Armstrong and Altschuler 1982; Fagan, Forst and Vivona 1987). One finding is that the perception that juvenile homicides are on the increase is largely erroneous. Further, the idea that homicide by juveniles is simply a younger version of adult homicide appears somewhat erroneous: "Juvenile homicides are more likely to involve multiple offenders. If the homicide does entail multiple offenders, juvenile homicides are more likely to involve a concurrent felony, firearms, male offenders, and male victims, and are more likely to be cross-race homicides" (Cheatwood and Block 1990). Juvenile violent crime of all categories is much more likely among inner-city youth. These youths are literally immersed in a subculture of violence

Rape arrest rates for both white and black juveniles in both urban and rural areas are disproportionately high. In 1988, 44 percent of arrests for rape in urban areas were arrests of white youths, while 55 percent were of black youths. This is reversed in rural areas: 69 percent of young people arrested on the charge of rape in rural areas are white and 31 percent are black. In this case, "youth" and "young people" includes individuals under 18 years of age. It is important also to take into account the absolute numbers: urban youth arrests for rape total 3,732; rural youth arrests total 1,389. These figures are not surprising in view of the distribution of population in this country (U.S. Dept. of Justice, Bureau of Justice Statistics 1990, 294, 433).

Intraracial Nature of Violence

The relation of group factors to crimes of violence can be seen in the fact that in nearly all crimes of violence in the United States both offender and victim are of the same race. This is true of homicide, aggravated assault and rape. Crimes of violence tend to be *intraracial* rather than interracial. This may be because social relations in this country are largely between members of one's own race and living patterns are extremely segregated in most areas of the country.

The finding of a large-scale study of 17 large United States cities supports the intraracial nature of violence. "Racial fears underlie much of the public concern over violence, so one of our most striking and relevant general conclusions is that serious 'assaultive' violence—criminal homicide, aggravated assault and forcible rape—is predominantly *intra* racial in nature" (McClintock 1963). The majority of these crimes involve blacks assaulting blacks; most of the remainder involve whites victimizing other whites. Where race was known, 24 percent of the homicides were between whites and 66 percent between blacks. Six percent involved blacks killing whites and 4 percent involved whites killing blacks. In a Houston study 97 percent of the black victims were killed by blacks, 91 percent of the white victims were killed by whites, and 86 percent of the Latin-Americans were killed by other Latin-Americans (Pokorny 1965). In Chicago only 6.6 percent of the criminal homicides were interracial, and of this small number 80 percent involved the killing of whites by nonwhites (Voss and Hepburn 1968). A larger government survey of 1,493 aggravated assault cases in 17 large cities found that 66 percent took place between blacks, 8 percent involved blacks attacking whites, 25 percent took place between whites and 2 percent involved whites attacking blacks. Also, McClintock reports that a study of 17 large United States cities in 1967 found that 90 percent of all forcible rapes were intraracial; of these, 30 percent took place between whites, 60 percent took place between blacks, 10 percent were whites raping blacks and less than 1 percent were blacks raping whites.

Although the studies reported above are from the 1960s, the statistics and the intraracial nature of violence they reflect have remained remarkably constant over the years. A 1984 study showed that, like homicide, forcible rape is predominantly an intraracial crime involving offenders and victims of the same race (Randall and Rose 1984).

Situational Interaction and the Use of Violence

Most murder and aggravated assault represents a response growing out of social interaction between one or more parties in which a situation comes to be defined as requiring the use of violence. Generally in order for such an act to take place, all parties must come to perceive the situation as one requiring violence. If only one responds in a dispute, it is unlikely to become violent; likewise, if only one of the disputants is accustomed to the use of violence, the dispute is likely to end only in a verbal argument, often with a lot of "wuffing" (i.e., posturing). On the other hand, when a cultural norm is defined as calling for violence by a person in interaction with another who harbors the same response, serious altercations—fist fights, physical assaults with weapons and violent domestic quarrels, all of which may end in death—may well be the result. In the process of an argument, person A and person B both define the initial situation as a serious threat, B then threatens A physically, A threatens B, and B then threatens A. By circular reaction, the situation can rapidly build to a climax in which one takes serious overt action, partly because of fear. Consequently, the victim, by being a contributor to the circular reaction of an argument increasing in its physical intensity, may precipitate his or her own injury or death.

Violence may result from a single argument or dispute. Other cases may result from a series of arguments, extending sometimes over a period of years, between spouses, lovers, neighbors or fellow employees. Increasingly, verbalization in these arguments decline, while emotional reactions increase, until in a final argument a climax is reached. With the use of a weapon one of the parties may be injured or killed.

Many cases of violence grow out of what some might regard as trivial disputes. What is considered "trivial" is related to judgments derived from age, social class and other background factors. To an outside observer of a different social class (psychiatrist, prosecutor, judge, middle-class jury member, researcher), such incidents leading to homicide among the lower classes may seem to be no reason for such acts of violence. Homicides may seem to involve the nonpayment of "very small" debts, "minor" disputes or "petty" jealousies, but these may be very important to the person involved. From this point of view, "crime and delinquency are sociocultural phenomena—forms of behavior that result from the routine functioning of the normal sociocultural processes. They must therefore be studied in sociocultural terms and methodologically conceived as existing in their own right" (Hartung 1965). This emphasizes the critical importance of "a jury of one's peers" in the administration of criminal justice.

As are most human behavior patterns, homicide is a situational transaction. Because of this, in many homicide incidents the victim is a partial contributor to his or her own death. This has been called "victim precipitated homicide" (Wolfgang 1958). Goffman referred to what he called a "character contest" in which the homicide is the peak of the escalation of a confrontation (Goffman 1967). He also made a distinction between a "situated transaction," which is a chain of interactions between two individuals during the time they are in one another's immediate physical presence, and a "social occasion," which consists of many situated transactions over a period of time. Social transactions ending in a situated transaction that ends with homicide occur mainly in nonwork situations, during leisure hours and in leisure settings such as the home, the tavern or the car.

In a sample of criminal homicides over a 10-year period in one medium-sized California town, one study found that 75 percent of the homicides took place while the offender and victim were engaged in leisurely activities (Luckenbill 1990). Wolfgang's study in Philadelphia showed that more than one in four homicides were precipitated by the victim, in that the victim first showed or used a deadly weapon or struck a blow in an altercation. Victim-precipitated homicides were found to be significantly associated with blacks, victim-offender relationships involving male victims of female offenders, mate-slaying, alcohol in the homicide situation or in the victim, and victims with a previous record of assault or arrest. Other homicides, not included in this figure, involve the infidelity of a mate or lover, failure of the victim to pay a debt or use of epithets by the victim, such that the victim contributes to the homicide. In a Chicago study

38 percent of the homicides were victim-precipitated; of them 80.5 percent of the victims were black men (Voss and Hepburn 1968). Slightly more than half of the African-American men precipitated their deaths as compared with one-fifth of the white male victims. Even in robbery it is not uncommon for the behavior of the victim to incite the robber to kill.

Luckenbill distinguished five stages of situated interactions that ended in homicide. In approximately half of the cases studied there occurred what he called "rehearsals" between the eventual victim and the offender. *Stage one:* Forty-one percent of the time the victim made the first direct offensive verbal attack. In 34 percent of the cases the victim refused to comply with the request of the offender. *Stage two:* In every case under scrutiny the offender interpreted the victim's previous words and deeds as offensive to him or her. In 60 percent of the cases "the offender learned the meaning of the victim's move from inquiries made of victim or audience" (Luckenbill 1990, 62). *Stage three:* The offender makes an opening move to "pay back" the victim in some manner for the perceived insult or offense. *Stage four:* The eventual victim "stands up" to the offender's opening move, responding with increased hostility. It was found that in 41 percent of the cases, the victim did not comply with the offender's challenge or command. Seventy percent of the cases at this stage took place in the presence of an audience of one sort or another. That is, they were not strictly private events. The audience at this stage intervened or attempted to intervene in 57 percent of the episodes. *Stage five:* "Commitment to battle." In about 35 percent of the homicides the offender carried a handgun or knife to the encounter, and in the remaining 65 percent the offender either left the scene to obtain a gun or knife or used a convenient weapon on the scene, such as a baseball bat, a poker or other object. After the homicide took place, the offender fled the scene 58 percent of the time, remained voluntarily at the scene 32 percent of the time, and was detained by the audience in the remaining cases.

The social interaction leading to rape is varied and complex. The act may be spontaneous and unplanned, or it may be well-planned in advance. It may focus on one particular victim or it may have nothing whatsoever to do with the victim. Finally, it may be a sort of afterthought following the commission of an entirely different crime, such as a burglary (Warr 1988). Formerly it was common to hear the argument that the victim precipitated the rape in a great many cases by dressing or behaving in a seductive manner. This approach—"she asked for it, she wanted it"—has been discredited due in large measure to the work of feminist criminologists, pioneered in part by Susan Brownmiller in the 1970s.

Personal Relationships in Violent Crime

Many studies have revealed that there are close relationships between offenders and victims in crimes involving violence. In fact, a United States government study has concluded that homicide and assault should be examined within the same frame of reference. They are often between relatives, friends, or acquaintances, and most occur indoors (National Commission on the Causes and Prevention of Violence 1969). According to the Bureau of Justice Statistics, of *all* violent offenses—homicide, rape, robbery and assault—41.2 percent are between close (intimate or relative) or known (well known or acquaintance) victims and offenders. The remainder are between strangers. These statistics shift dramatically when we look at homicide and rape alone. In the case of homicide, 57.2 percent are between close or known victims and offenders, and in the case of rape and sexual assault, 64.4 percent are between close or known victims and offenders (U.S. Dept. of Justice, Bureau of Justice Statistics, *Violent State Prisoners and Their Victims* 1990).

A vivid description of deadly assaults between relatives and close acquaintances is conveyed in the following condensed journalistic account, taken from the pages of the *New York Times* the day after a typical Fourth of July holiday, 1992:

A Fourth of July family gathering in a Queens park turned deadly early yesterday morning when a dispute ended with knives drawn, one man dead and six people wounded. The victims, all related by blood or marriage, were among 10 people slain and 22 people wounded in New York City during an eight-hour period over Saturday night and Sunday morning. In addition to the death in Queens, the police reported two other stabbing deaths, also the result of disputes among relatives or acquaintances. The overnight toll also included three children who were wounded by random gunfire. One of the children was a 5-year old who was watching fireworks with his mother in Brooklyn. In the incident in the Queens park, one man was stabbed to death and six other wounded during what police called "a family get-together for the Fourth of July that went bad." In the Bronx another man was stabbed once in the back with a screwdriver when he intervened in a dispute between his sister and her husband. On the Upper East Side of Manhattan a man was fatally stabbed in the chest and abdomen during dispute in his apartment building. His roommate was arrested. Two children were the victims of stray gunshots in the Bronx late Saturday evening. (*New York Times* 1992)

According to the now classic 1967 landmark survey, *The Challenge of Crime in a Free Society,* although people in American cities are often concerned about physical assaults from strangers on city streets, personal violence is far less likely to be perpetrated by a stranger. That same survey found that about 70 percent of all willful killings, nearly two-thirds of all aggravated assaults as well as a high percentage of rapes are committed by family members and others previously known to their victims. Criminal homicides and aggravated assaults result from domestic quarrels, altercations, jealousies and arguments over money and/or property (Millman 1991). Many of the victim-offender relationships have been intimate, primarily involving family members and close friends. The major exception is the small proportion of such homicides occurring in connection with other crimes, such as robbery.

The vast majority of crimes of violence involve male offenders and female victims who are involved in an intimate relationship. In fact, violence against women by men is now beginning to be recognized as a social problem on an international scale. This recognition has prompted a new social movement that seeks to influence state agencies with regard to the processes by which these agencies become aware of violence against women. Specific solutions to violent crimes directed against women can be formulated only on the basis of accurate and efficient processes of reporting and responding to them. Furthermore, male-offender, female-victim violent crimes between intimates are increasingly being viewed as the result of social processes that develop over time rather than of static events taking place outside of any time framework. New terminology is being adopted in research into these crimes between intimates: instead of "domestic violence," "spouse abuse" or "family violence," terms such as "abused women," "battered women," "violence against women" and "woman abuse" are increasingly being used (Hoff 1990; Walker 1990).

Wolfgang's Philadelphia study found that approximately one-third of 588 male and female criminal homicides resulted from general altercations. Quarrels within family structures accounted for 14 percent; jealousy, 12 percent; altercations over money, 11 percent; and robbery—contrary to popular impression—only 7 percent (Wolfgang 1958, 191). Close friends and relatives accounted for over one-half (59 percent) of all homicides and four-fifths of the victimized women. In 28 percent of the cases the victim was a close friend of the murderer, in 25 percent a family relative and in 14 percent an acquaintance. In only one out of eight murders was the victim a stranger. In contrast to men, a much larger proportion of women kill someone in their own families. It was concluded that when a woman committed a homicide, the victim was more likely to be her mate; and when a man was killed by a woman, he was most likely to be killed by his mate (Wolfgang 1958, 325). In those homicide cases in which the offender is a woman and her victim is her mate (be it husband, lover or live-in companion), it is most likely that the female-offender has herself been the victim of violent physical abuse over a long period of time (Browne 1987; Browne and Williams 1989; Jones 1980; Wildeman and Treen 1986).

Correspondence between Criminal and Legitimate Behavior

"Every society is held together by a myth-system, a complex of dominating thought-forms that determines and sustains all its activities. . . . (E)very nation has its characteristic myth-complex. . . . Wherever he goes, whatever he encounters, man spins about him his web of myth, as the caterpillar spins its cocoon. . . .

Inside his myth he is at home in his world (MacIver 1965, 4). One of these myths treasured by all civilized societies is that interpersonal and intergroup violence is to be abhorred and studiously avoided at all costs and must be severely and swiftly punished when it does occur. Both the criminal law and the religious teachings of Judaism, Christianity, Islamism and Buddhism expressly forbid violence as though all violence is antithetical to organized society. In fact, however, the use of violence on other human beings is often sanctioned both by religion and organized society. The killing and other acts of violence directed at enemy soldiers and even enemy civilians is sanctioned, even sanctified, by the political state in wartime. For example, recall the frequent supporting visits to United States troops in the Vietnam War by New York's late Cardinal Francis Spellman. Those persons killed or injured under wartime conditions must certainly exceed by tens of millions all those persons ever killed by civilian murder and assault. For a civilian willfully to kill 10 persons may warrant the death penalty in some states, or life imprisonment without parole in other states; for a soldier to do the same to the enemy warrants a medal or other form of reward for heroism.

The total cost to the principle belligerents during World War I was an estimated 17 million military personnel killed or missing in battle, to which must be added some 20 million civilian deaths. During World War II 10 million military personnel were killed or missing and 43 million civilians were killed. In the Vietnam War approximately 56,000 United States soldiers were slaughtered along with hundreds of thousands of Vietnamese, both civilian and military, from both North and South. When the Soviet army left Afghanistan following eight years of bloodshed, they left behind 1.5 million dead Afghanis and over 50,000 dead Soviet soldiers. No one knows, except perhaps the Pentagon, how many Iraqui soldiers and civilians were killed during the Persian Gulf War. Estimates range between 100,000 and 150,000 Iraqui soldiers.

Thus, it is clear that in the name of the political state large numbers of civilians have been killed for reasons regarding state, religion, class and ethnic characteristics. More examples include the thousands killed during the collapse of the nation state of Yugoslavia in the early 1990s and (probably the most brutal extermination of this type) the planned, deliberate killing and torture deaths of 6.5 million Jews during the Nazi control of Germany and its occupied territories. Yet Richard Speck's notorious killing of eight Chicago nurses in 1965, Charles Whitman's shooting murders at the University of Texas in 1966 and the grizzly murders by Jeffrey L. Dahmer of 17 young men in Milwaukee in 1991 have provoked more horror than the great number of deaths in wartime or the many politically incited civilian deaths. Although society says that human life should not be willfully taken, if a state, which represents certain power interests, does it, the situation may be regarded as of quite a different nature.

State-mandated execution is the ultimate violence against citizens of which the state is capable. Although the majority of Americans approve of it and nearly all states have the death penalty, it has been abolished in all Western European countries and in Canada (Hood 1989). However, there are isolated, but not all that infrequent, instances of "flawed executions" that seriously threaten and erode the public's general support of capital punishment (Haines 1991). Today 36 states allow the death penalty, many of them in the South. From the end of 1930 to the end of 1989 there were 3,979 people executed in the United States. Between 1976, when state-mandated executions were declared constitutional by the Supreme Court, and the end of 1989 120 citizens were executed (U.S. Dept. of Justice, Bureau of Justice Statistics, *Capital Punishment* 1990). At the outset of 1990 there were 2,250 individuals on death row in those states in which capital punishment is legal (U.S. Dept. of Justice, Bureau of Justice Statistics, *Capital Punishment* 1990).

All violence is by no means harmful or dysfunctional to a society. As Coser and others have pointed out, violence in a society may perform a useful function (Coser 1966; Minow, Ryan and Sarat 1992). It may help groups of individuals in a society achieve certain goals that otherwise are difficult or impossible for them to achieve; it may serve as a danger signal of political and economic dislocation in a society; and it may serve as a catalyst for change. Witness the urban riots of the late 1960s and the social changes that followed. Witness the positive responses in the form of financial aid and social improvements to the 1992 Los Angeles riots.

Violence frequently has been resorted to, even on a large scale, in order to achieve certain idealistic moral goals or to reverse the social and political power of interest groups or entire classes. For example, the achievement of the right of labor to organize for collective action was a long and violent struggle in most countries. In the United States, "beginning in the 1870s, workingmen attempting to organize for collective action engaged in more than a half century of violent warfare with industrialists, their private armies, and workers employed to break strikes, as well as with police and troops" (Skolnick 1969). In addition, American women used militant, violent action to secure their right to vote. One historian has referred to all of this as "positive violence" (Brown 1969).

Historically, the United States has been characterized by violence. In general, historical evidence seems to suggest that during the 1960s—with riots and other forms of violence prompted by protests against the Vietnam War, racial discrimination, the assassinations of Malcolm X and Dr. Martin Luther King, Jr., and other issues—Americans were more violent toward one another than in the past years of the twentieth century. However, the Civil War in the nineteenth century, and the enslavement of people before that, attests that the tendency to violence is not unique to the twentieth century. Throughout its history, the diversely populated United States has witnessed fierce competition between ethnic and religious groups. Jews, Catholics and persons of African, Irish, German, Chinese and Italian descent have all been target groups at which riots have been directed. In addition, America's long history of violence and vigilantism on the western frontier was easily adapted to a form of urban or "neo" vigilantism in which various persons (representing religious groups, ethnic minorities, unions, political factions, civil liberties advocates and nonconformists in general) have become victims of violent attacks. More recently, there have been vicious assaults on homosexuals and abortion providers.

Some forms of violence are legally sanctioned within a society while others are not (Haskell and Yablonsky 1970). For a soldier, killing and wounding another person is an approved behavior; in fact, a soldier may be severely punished if he or she does *not* use violence when it is expected or commanded. Similarly, the use of force by law enforcement officers (providing it is not excessive) meets with public approval, while the public condemns police beating or killing of suspects and the violence of riots among prison populations (Sarat and Kearns 1992). Additionally, situations of real or perceived self-defense are considered appropriate for violent behavior. The celebrated Goetz case (described on page 30) is a telling illustration of the extent of public approval of violence perpetrated in one's own defense (Hindelang, Gottfredson and Garofalo 1978; Rubin 1986). A final example of the sanctioning of violence in our society is the sports industry as a whole, which both thrives on and fosters a culture of violence. Contact sports such as boxing, ice hockey and football explicitly legitimize violence, and even noncontact sports such as basketball and baseball sometimes break out in violent episodes that audiences seem to enjoy.

Finally, the social values involved in homicide and aggravated assault among intimates are quite similar to that of nonviolent persons. A study of violence among intimates shows that people assault, and sometimes kill, for the same reasons people live—pride, preservation of honor, the blotting out of shame, the avengence of one's self, the settlement of an argument or as a reaction to an insult (Mulvihill, Tumin and Curtis 1969). Persons who do not use violence utilize other methods to deal with such important values. Increasingly, we are seeing a turning to processes of peacemaking and mediation in place of violence (Pepinsky and Quinney 1991).

Societal Reaction and Legal Processing

The middle and upper socioeconomic groups of most societies have codified legal rules that prohibit the use of violence. Generally, the criminal laws and courts do not recognize the existence of separate subcultural norms among certain groups that deem legitimate the use of force to settle disputes. However, the courts have permitted rare exceptions to this. Although these same groups would generally not approve of murder, at the same time, in sanctioning violence that may lead to murder, there is an inconsistency in their value system. Middle- and upper-class persons (those in positions of social and political power) react strongly to the use of violence as seen in the severe legal penalties for murder, manslaughter, rape and child molestation.

Such offenses as murder, rape and aggravated assault are punished severely not because they constitute a serious threat to the larger political and economic order; rather, the punishment is severe because of the injury to the individual. Severe punishment is thought to work as a deterrent to help avoid retaliation by relatives and friends of the victims, and serves to reinforce the religious beliefs and secular values held by many in the larger society about the sanctity of life and the sexual conduct of individuals.

Penalties in the law generally do not recognize the close relationship between criminal homicide and aggravated assault. In some jurisdictions, while aggravated assault may result in a short prison sentence or even probation, if the victim dies the penalty may be death or at least life imprisonment (which usually results in serving a minimum of between 9 and 15 years—far greater than for any other criminal offense, with the possible exception of statutory rape). Serial killers and mass murderers are most likely to receive the death penalty in those states where it is a legal sanction. Murderers are less likely than nonmurderers to have been incarcerated previously for any type of crime. Because of the nature of murder and the way the public and law enforcement officials react to it, a murder is more likely to be committed by a first offender than are other crimes. A study of 621 North Carolina offenders in prison for murder and a control group of nonmurderers showed this to be the case generally, and the difference was maintained when controlled for race, age and intelligence (Waldo 1970). In fact, an inverse relationship was found between the seriousness of the offense (first-degree murder, second-degree murder, manslaughter and negligent manslaughter) and having no record of previous incarceration. "From the data presented in this study, it would seem that the incarcerated murderer has a lower 'criminality level,' and upon his release offers no more threat to society—perhaps less—than other incarcerated offenders" (Waldo 1970, 20).

Likewise, manslaughter and forcible rape are normally punished by an unusually long period of imprisonment. Forcible rape carries long prison sentences; in some states, it may be punished with a possible death sentence. The last year anyone was executed in the United States for rape was 1964; the number executed for rape that year was 6. Since 1930, 455 persons have been executed for rape in the United States; 405 of them were black (U.S. Dept. of Justice, Bureau of Justice Statistics, *Correctional Populations in the United States* 1991). Penalties for all offenses against underage females are much harsher than laws prohibiting essentially the same offense with adults. This is because this population is seen as the most vulnerable and defenseless.

Regarding social reaction to and legal processing of violent crime there has been deep frustration: "At a time when fear of crime pervades American life, there is deep discontent with the criminal justice system and its inability to stem the tide of violence. But no consensus exists about the best way to come to grips with the problem" (Public Agenda Foundation 1993, 3).

As we have seen earlier in this chapter, contrary to popular thinking, murderers, assaulters and forcible rapists generally are not career criminals. They do not conceive of themselves as being real "criminals"; they seldom identify with crime; and criminal behavior is not a significant part of their life organization. Rather than being a unique individual phenomena, the basis of most acts of violence lies in subcultural definitions derived from social class, neighborhood, ethnic group, sex, and so forth. In these terms, with the exception of rape, the victim in many instances provokes the assault. In spite of this, the legal penalties for murder, manslaughter and forcible rape are much more severe than for other crimes.

References

*Amir, Menachem (1971). *Patterns in Forcible Rape.* Chicago: University of Chicago Press.

Archer, Dane, and Rosemary Gartner (1984). *Violence and Crime in Cross-National Perspective.* New Haven: Yale University Press.

Armstrong, Troy L., and David M. Altschuler (1982). "Conflicting Trends in Juvenile Justice Sanctioning: Divergent Strategies in the Handling of the Serious Juvenile Offender," *Juvenile and Family Court Journal* (November): 15-30.

*Athens, Lonnie H. (1989). *The Creation of Dangerous Violent Criminals.* New York: Routledge.

Bart, Martha R. (1980). "Cultural Myths and Supports for Rape." *Journal of Personality and Social Psychology* 38:217-230.

Bedau, Adam, ed. (1982). *The Death Penalty in America.* New York: Oxford University Press.

Beirne, Piers, and James Messerschmidt (1991). *Criminology.* New York: Harcourt Brace Jovanovich.

Blau, Judith, and Peter Blau (1982). "The Cost of Inequality: Metropolitan Structure and Violent Crime." *American Sociological Review* 47 (1): 114-129.

Brearley, Harrington Cooper (1932). *Homicide in the United States.* Chapel Hill, NC: University of North Carolina Press.

Brennan, Patricia, Sarnoff Mednick, and Richard John (1989). "Specialization in Violence: Evidence of a Criminal Subgroup." *Criminology* 7 (3): 437-453.

Brown, Richard Maxwell (1969). "Historical Patterns of Violence in America." *Violence in America.* A Staff Report to the National Commission on the Causes and Prevention of Violence, prepared by H.D. Graham and Ted R. Gurr. Washington, DC: U.S. Government Printing Office.

*Browne, Angela (1987). *When Battered Women Kill.* New York: Free Press.

Browne, Angela, and Kirk R. Williams (1989). "Exploring the Effect of Resource Availability and the Likelihood of Female-Perpetrated Homicides." *Law and Society Review* 23 (1): 75-94.

*Brownmiller, Susan (1975). *Against Our Will: Men, Women, and Rape.* New York: Simon & Schuster.

Cheatwood, Derral, and Kathleen J. Block (1990). "Youth and Homicide: An Investigation of the Age Factor in Criminal Homicide." *Justice Quarterly* 7 (2): 265-292.

Clinard, Marshall B., and Robert F. Meier (1992). *Sociology of Deviant Behavior.* 8th ed. New York: Harcourt Brace Jovanovich.

Clinard, Marshall B. (1978). "Comparative Crime Victimization Surveys: Some Problems and Results." *International Journal of Criminology and Penology* 6 (3): 221-231.

Coser, Lewis A. (1966). "Some Social Functions of Violence." *The Annals* 364:8-18.

Currie, Elliot (1985). *Confronting Crime: An American Challenge.* New York: Pantheon Books.

Dillingham, Steven (1991). *Drugs and Crime Facts, 1990.* NCJ-128662. Washington, DC: Bureau of Justice Statistics.

Elliott, Delbert S., and David Huizinga (1983). "Social Class and Delinquent Behavior in a National Youth Panel: 1976-1980." *Criminology* 21 (2): 149-177.

Fagan, Jeffrey, Martin Forst, and T. Scott Vivona (1987). "Racial Determinants of the Judicial Transfer Decision: Prosecuting Violent Youth in Criminal Court." *Crime and Delinquency* 33 (2): 259-286.

Federal Bureau of Investigation (1988). *Uniform Crime Reports, 1987.* Washington, DC: U.S. Government Printing Office.

Federal Bureau of Investigation (1991). *Uniform Crime Reports, 1990, Preliminary Data.* Washington, DC: U.S. Government Printing Office.

Ferracuti, Franco, Renato Lazzari, and Marvin Wolfgang, eds. (1970). *Violence in Sardinia.* Rome: Mario Bulzoni.

Garofalo, James, and Michael J. Hindelang (1977). *An Introduction to the National Crime Survey.* Washington, DC: U.S. Government Printing Office.

Gebhard, Paul H., John H. Gagnon, Wardell B. Pomeroy, and Cornelia V. Christenson (1965). *Sex Offenders: An Analysis of Types.* New York: Harper & Row.

*Gelles, Richard J., and Murray A. Straus (1988). *Intimate Violence.* New York: Simon & Schuster.

Goffman, Erving (1967). *Interaction Ritual: Essays on Face-to-Face Behavior.* Garden City, NY: Doubleday.

Good, David H., and Maureen A. Pirog-Good (1987). "A Simultaneous Probit Model of Crime and Employment for Black and White Teenage Males." *The Review of Black Political Economy* 16 (1-2): 109-127.

Groth, Nicholas A., and Jean Birnbaum (1979). *Men Who Rape.* New York: Plenum.

Guzman, Campos (1964). *La Violencia en Colombia; Estudio de un Process Social.* Bogata, Colombia: Ediciones Tercer Mundo.

Hackney, S. (1969). "Southern Violence." *American Historical Review* 74:906-925.

*Haines, Herb (1992). "Flawed Executions, the Anti-Death Penalty Movement, and the Politics of Capital Punishment." *Social Problems* 39 (2): 125-138.

Hartung, Frank E. (1965). *Crime, Law, and Society.* Detroit: Wayne State University Press.

Haskell, Martin R., and Lewis Yablonsky (1970). *Crime and Delinquency.* Chicago: Rand McNally.

Hindelang, Michael, Michael Gottfredson, and James Garofalo (1978). *Victims of Personal Crime.* Cambridge, MA: Ballinger.

Hoff, Lee Ann (1990). *Battered Women as Survivors.* New York: Routledge.

Hood, Roger (1989). *The Death Penalty: A Worldwide Perspective.* Oxford, England: Clarendon.

*Inciardi, James A. (1986). *The War on Drugs: Heroin, Cocaine, Crime, and Public Policy.* Palo Alta, CA: Mayfield.

Jones, Ann (1980). *Women Who Kill.* New York: Holt, Rinehart & Winston.

Journal of the American Medical Association (1992). "Deaths by Gunshot in the United States" 267(2).

*Kleck, Gary (1991). *Point Blank: Guns and Violence in America.* New York: De Gruyter Press.

Land, Kenneth C., Patricia L. McCall, and Lawrence E. Cohen (1990). "Structural Covariates of Homicide Rates: Are there Any Invariances across Time and Social Space?" *American Journal of Sociology* 95 (4): 922-963.

Langan, Patrick A., and Christopher A. Innes (1990). "The Risk of Violent Crime." In *Violence: Patterns, Causes, Public Policy*, edited by Neil Alan Weiner, Margaret A. Zahn, and Rita J. Sagi. New York: Harcourt Brace Jovanovich.

Livingston, Jay (1992). *Crime and Criminology.* Englewood Cliffs, NJ: Prentice-Hall.

Luckenbill, David F. (1984). "Murder and Assault," In *Major Forms of Crime,* edited by Robert F. Meier, 19-45. Beverly Hills, CA: Sage.

Luckenbill, David F. (1990). "Criminal Homicide as a Situated Transaction." In *Violence: Patterns, Causes, Public Policy,* edited by Neil Alan Weiner, Margaret A. Zahn, and Rita J. Sagi. New York: Harcourt Brace Jovanovich.

MacIver, Robert Morrison (1965). *The Web of Government.* New York: The Free Press.

McCaghy, Charles H. (1967). "Child Molesters: A Study of Their Careers as Deviants." In *Criminal Behavior Systems,* edited by Marshall B. Clinard and Richard Quinney. New York: Holt, Rinehart & Winston.

McClintock, Frederick H. (1963). *Crimes of Violence.* New York: St. Martin's Press.

Messner, Steven F. (1980). "Income Inequality and Murder Rates." *Comparative Social Research* 3:185-198.

Millman, Marcia (1991). *Warm Hearts and Cold Cash: The Intimate Dynamics of Families and Money.* New York: Free Press.

Minow, Martha, Michael Ryan, and Austin Sarat, eds. (1992). *Narrative, Violence, and the Law: The Essays of Robert Cover.* Ann Arbor, MI: University of Michigan Press.

Moore, Thomas (1988). "The Black-on-Black Crime Plague." *U.S. News and World Report* (August 22): 49-55.

*Mulvihill, Donald J., Melvin M. Tumin, and Lynn A. Curtis (1969). *Crimes of Violence.* A Staff Report to the National Commission of the Causes and Prevention of Violence, Volume 12. Washington, DC: U.S. Government Printing Office.

National Commission on the Causes and Prevention of Violence (1969). *To Establish Justice, To Insure Domestic Tranquility.* Washington, DC: U.S. Government Printing Office.

New York Times (1992). "10 Slain; 22 Wounded In New York Over Holiday." July 6, Metro Section.

Newton, George D., and Franklin E. Zimring (1969). *Firearms and Violence in American Life.* A Staff Report to the National Commission on the Causes and Prevention of Violence, Vol. 7. Washington, DC: U.S. Government Printing Office.

Pepinsky, Harold E., and Richard Quinney, eds. (1991). *Criminology as Peacemaking.* Bloomington, IN: Indiana University Press.

Peterson, Richard A, David J. Pittman, and Patricia O'Neal (1962). "Stabilities in Deviance: A Study of Assaultive and Non-Assaultive Offenders." *Journal of Criminal Law, Criminology and Police Science* 53:44-49.

Pokorny, Alex D. (1965). "Human Violence: A Comparison of Homicide, Aggravated Assault, Suicide, and Attempted Suicide." *The Journal of Criminal Law, Criminology and Police Science* 56:497.

Public Agenda Foundation (1993). *Criminal Violence: What Direction Now for the War on Crime?* New York: McGraw-Hill.

Quinney, Richard (1966). "Structural Characteristics, Population Areas, and Crime Rates in the United States." *Journal of Criminal Law, Criminology and Police Science* 57:45-52.

Randall, Susan, and Vicki McNickle Rose (1984). "Forcible Rape." In *Major Forms of Crime,* edited by Robert F. Meier. Beverly Hills, CA: Sage.

Rao, S. Venugopal (1968). *A Pilot Study of Urban Patterns with Particular Reference to the City of Delhi.* New Dehli: Government of India.

Reid, Sue Titus (1988). *Crime and Criminology.* New York: Holt, Rinehart & Winston.

Reiman, Jeffrey H. (1990). *Justice and Modern Moral Philosophy.* New Haven: Yale University Press.

Riches, David, ed. (1986). *The Anthropology of Violence.* New York: Basil Blackwell.

*Riedel, Marc, and Margaret A. Zahn (1985). *The Nature and Patterns of American Homicide.* Washington, DC: U.S. Government Printing Office.

Rosenfeld, Richard, and Steven F. Messner (1991). "The Social Sources of Homicide in Different Types of Societies." *Social Forum* 6 (1): 51-70.

Rubin, Lillian (1986). *Quiet Rage: Bernie Goetz in a Time of Madness.* New York: Farrar, Straus & Giroux.

*Sarat, Austin, and Thomas R. Kearns, eds. (1992). *Law's Violence.* Ann Arbor, MI: University of Michigan Press.

Short, James F., Jr., and Marvin E. Wolfgang, eds. (1972). *Collective Violence.* Chicago: Aldine-Atherton.

Siegel, Larry J. (1992). *Criminology: Theories, Patterns, and Typologies.* New York: West.

Sismondi, Mario (1970). *Dati Su Ottanta Casi Di Omicidio.* Serie Ricerche Empiriche No. 5. Dipartimento Statistico-Metematico, Universita Degli Studi Di Firenzi: Firenzi, Italia.

Skolnick, Jerome H. (1969). *The Politics of Protest.* New York: Simon & Schuster.

Sourcebook of Criminal Justice Statistics (1990). Timothy J. Flanagan and Kathleen Maguire, eds. Washington, DC: U.S. Government Printing Office.

Thornberry, Terence, and Margaret Farnworth (1982). "Social Correlates of Criminal Involvement: Further Evidence on the Relationship between Social Status and Criminal Behavior." *American Sociological Review* 47 (4): 505-518.

Tien, James, and Thomas Rich (1990). *Identifying Persons, Other than Felons, Ineligible to Purchase Firearms.* NCJ-123050. Washington, DC: Bureau of Justice Statistics, U.S. Government Printing Office.

*Toch, Hans, and Kenneth Adams (1989). *The Disturbed Violent Offender.* New Haven, CT: Yale University Press.

United Nations (1986). *Demographic Yearbook, 1984.* New York: United Nations, Department of International Economic and Social Affairs, Statistical Office.

U.S. Department of Health and Human Services (1984). *National Study on Child Neglect and Abuse Reporting.* Denver, CO: American Humane Association.

U.S. Department of Justice, Bureau of Justice Statistics (1982). *Criminal Victimization in the United States, 1978-1980.* Washington, DC: U.S. Government Printing Office.

U.S. Department of Justice, Bureau of Justice Statistics (1990). *Capital Punishment, 1989.* NCJ-124545. Washington, DC: U.S. Department of Justice.

U.S. Department of Justice, Bureau of Justice Statistics (1990). *Felony Defendants in Large Urban Counties, 1988.* NCJ-122385. Washington, DC: U.S. Department of Justice.

U.S. Department of Justice, Bureau of Justice Statistics (1990). *Violent State Prisoners and Their Victims, Special Report.* NCJ-124133. Washington, DC: U.S. Government Printing Office.

U.S. Department of Justice, Bureau of Justice Statistics (1991). *Correctional Populations in the United States, 1989.* NCJ-130445. Washington, DC: U.S. Government Printing Office.

U.S. Department of Justice, Federal Bureau of Investigation (1989). *Crime in the United States, 1989.* Washington, DC: U.S. Government Printing Office: 190-192.

Voss, Harwin, and John Hepburn (1968). "Patterns in Criminal Homicide in Chicago." *Journal of Criminal Law, Criminology and Police Science* 59:501.

Waldo, Gordon P. (1970). "The 'Criminality Level' of Incarcerated Murderers and Non-Murderers." *Journal of Criminal Law, Criminology and Police Science* 61:60-70.

Walker, Gillian A. (1990). *Family Violence and the Women's Movement: The Conceptual Politics of Struggle.* Toronto: University of Toronto Press.

Warr, Mark (1988). "Rape, Burglary and Opportunity." *Journal of Quantitative Criminology* 4:275-288.

*Weiner, Neil Alan (1989). "Violent Criminal Careers and 'Violent Criminal Careers': An Overview of the Research Literature." In *Violent Crime, Violent Criminals,* edited by Neil Alan Weiner and Marvin E. Wolfgang. Newbury Park, CA: Sage.

Weiner, Neil Alan, and Marvin Wolfgang (1990). "The Extent and Character of Violent Crime in America, 1969 to 1982." In *Violence: Patterns, Causes, Public Policy,* edited by Neil Alan Weiner, Margaret A. Zahn, and Rita J. Sagi. New York: Harcourt, Brace Jovanovich.

Weiner, Neil Alan, Margaret A. Zahn, and Rita J. Sagi, eds. (1990). *Violence: Patterns, Causes, Public Policy.* New York: Harcourt Brace Jovanovich.

Wildeman, John, and Barbara Treen (1986). *Out of the Kitchen and into the Prison: Toward Sound Social Policy on Domestic Violence.* Paper presented at the 38th Annual Meeting of the American Society of Criminology.

Williams, Kirk R., and Robert Flewelling (1988). "The Social Production of Criminal Homicide: A Comparative Study of Disaggregated Rates in American Cities." *American Sociological Review* 53 (3): 421-431.

Wilson, Anna V., ed. (1993). *Homicide: The Victim/Offender Connection.* Cincinnati: Anderson.

*Wolfgang, Marvin (1958). *Patterns of Criminal Homicide.* Philadelphia: Pennsylvania University Press.

Wolfgang, Marvin (1961). "A Sociological Analysis of Criminal Homicide." *Federal Probation* 25:55.

Wolfgang, Marvin and Franco Ferracuti (1967). *The Subculture of Violence: Towards an Integrated Theory in Criminology.* London: Tavistock Publications, Social Science Paperbacks.

Wolfgang, Marvin, and Margaret A. Zahn (1983). "Homicide: Behavioral Aspects." In *Encyclopedia of Crime and Justice* Vol. 2, edited by Sanford H. Kadish, 849-855.

*Wright, James D., Peter H. Rossi, and Kathleen Daly (1983). *Under the Gun: Weapons, Crime, and Violence in America.* Hawthorne, NY: Aldine.

Yllo, Kersti, and Murray A. Straus (1981). "Interpersonal Violence Among Married and Cohabiting Couples." *Family Relations* 30:341-352.

Chapter 3

Occasional Property Criminal Behavior

As we have seen in the first chapter, the characteristics of a fully developed career criminal include identification with crime and a conception of the self as a criminal. There is group support for criminal activity in the form of extensive association with other criminals and with criminal norms and activities. Criminality progresses to the use of more complex techniques, the employment of more sophisticated technology and ever more frequent offenses. Ultimately, crime may become a sole means of livelihood. Those with such highly developed careers in crime generally engage in some type of theft of cash or other valuable commodities, such as, for example, jewels, drugs, electronic equipment or negotiable notes.

Occasional property criminals are the opposite of criminals who make a career out of crime. While they may commit offenses similar in type to those committed by career criminals, they do so only infrequently and on an irregular basis. Items may be taken, checks forged and automobiles stolen, but in a comparatively crude manner. It has been estimated that three-fourths of all check forgeries are committed by persons with no previous patterns of such behavior; and an even larger proportion of shoplifting is committed by noncareer offenders. Similarly, the destruction of public or private property through vandalism is a sporadic, age-specific offense; one could hardly visualize a person making a career out of vandalism or graffiti drawing.

Consequently, we do not consider in this chapter those who organize their lives around criminal activities such as the production of counterfeit access devices, forged credit cards, computer fraud, faked antiques and other works of art, forged manuscripts, forged insurance claims, stocks and bonds, letters of credit, business licenses, and so on (Bradford 1992). Nor do we consider gift certificate and gift voucher fraud, which increasingly sophisticated copying technology has made most lucrative to criminals and very costly to retailers (Hoggan 1991). Personal computer (PC) forgery, also a serious threat, will not be addressed in this chapter. With a good printer and the right software, the PC is a powerful publishing instrument that can be used to produce checks, professional-looking brochures and business forms. However, banking authorities do not classify computer forgery as a crime distinct from conventional forgery and they do not keep separate statistics on it (Churbuck 1989). Some of these illegal activities are done occasionally on an individual basis, but usually they represent a career pattern.

Legal Aspects of Selected Offenses

Any offender who steals or damages the property of another on an occasional basis may be classified as an occasional property offender. Among the occasional property offenses that have been researched extensively are check forgery—the so-called "naive (unsophisticated) check forger," shoplifting by adults, vandalism and some types of vehicular theft.

Legally, forgery is the false signing of a legal instrument that creates a liability. Under the old common law of England, forgery was "the fraudulent making, or altering, of a writing to the prejudice of another's rights." In medieval times the clerical class had a virtual monopoly on writing, so other people used seals to authenticate documents. This practice is still in use in Japan. Forgery of the seals of other persons still is an offense. Forgery can take many forms, such as forgery of wills and other documents, check forgery and counterfeiting. The banking industry lists eight different types of check forgery alone: (1) personal checks, (2) certified checks, (3) payroll checks, (4) traveler's checks, (5) government checks, (6) third-party checks, (7) blank checks (rarely accepted), and (8) money orders (Anonymous 1992). Whatever kind of check is received, the following details are to be closely scrutinized: bank, date, amount paid, legibility, spelling and limit. Customer identification may consist of driver's license, automobile registration, charge card, government or building pass, or identification issued by the armed forces, a civil service agency or a company.

For many banks, a troublesome aspect of check technology and its use arises from the need to process huge volumes of checks at a reasonable cost without exposing the bank to excessive losses due to forgery (Greco 1991). Check forgery is extensive in the United States. It seldom involves the formerly popular methods of changing the value of the check, carefully working out facsimile signatures or the manufacture of false negotiable instruments. Checks are widely used today and are cashed outside of banks, often with only perfunctory methods of identification. Rather than checks being written on someone else's account, they may be written on a nonexistent account with a nonexistent name or on one's own account without sufficient funds in the bank. The practice of "kiting" is writing a check drawn on one's own depleted account in anticipation of a future deposit. For these reasons, most check forgery is quite simple and is executed by unskilled persons rather than by professionals.

The number of checks written in the United States has grown at a steady rate. Accompanying this rapidly expanding volume have been increased opportunities for forgery. By industry estimates, more than 500 million forged checks are negotiated every year with direct losses of some $625 million a year to the industry alone. Though new high-speed, automated equipment has lowered the cost per item cleared, this also has limited the ability of institutions to detect irregularities such as forgeries. There are three major categories of forgery-fraud involving checks—all readily available to the unsophisticated occasional property offender: forged drawers' signatures, forged endorsements and material alterations (Reha 1990). When a forged check is paid, any mistake by the bank will result in the bank's bearing the loss unless the forger can be found and successfully prosecuted. The Uniform Commercial Code adopts this rule (Brocato 1990; Violano 1989; Yen 1989).

Most shoplifting and employee thefts, which are closely related in nature, involve the stealing of relatively small and inexpensive articles; professionals, on the other hand, may steal things like furs, jewelry or leather clothing. The total value of shoplifting and employee thefts may be quite large. According to government surveys, most large retail establishments estimate their overall shrinkage due to shoplifting and employee theft at 1 or 2 percent. Among the 47 percent of neighborhood businesses having a high rate of loss, 60 percent placed it at less than 2 percent and another 28 percent estimated they had lost between 2 and 6 percent (President's Commission, Task Force Report 1967). However, we may be sure this constitutes an underestimate due to lack of reporting for fear of increased insurance rates. Here, as always when dealing with crime rates, we are most likely looking at the proverbial "tip of the iceberg."

According to studies spanning the years from 1960 through 1980, crimes against small businesses, including shoplifting, employee theft, check forgery and vandalism, have cost the nation's retail industry and civil society billions of dollars a year. A field survey published in 1972, for example, reported that the total of property crime against all business in 1967-68 was $3 billion. The smaller the business, the greater the impact of losses measured as a percent of business receipts. Stores in inner-city areas of large cities suffered the greatest losses, rural stores the least. In all, shoplifting and employee theft alone accounted for $885 million that year (Small Business Administration 1972). Federal Bureau of Investigation studies found that shoplifting increased by 221 percent from 1961 through 1970 and by 73 percent from 1967 through 1972. The FBI further estimated that retail losses resulting from shoplifting escalated by 20 percent each year from 1970 through 1980 (Francis 1980). In 1993 the Stores Protective Association estimated the annual losses from shoplifting at $2 billion to $4 billion nationwide.

One study of the problem of employee theft defined it as ". . . the unauthorized taking, control, or transfer of money and/or property of the formal work

organization that is perpetrated by an employee during the course of occupational activity" (Caplan 1980; Hollinger and Clark 1983, 2). The same study reported estimates of losses due to employee theft, vandalism, shoplifting and forgery
ranging from a minimum of $10.5 to $16 billion a year. Simple shoplifting is
apparently not an uncommon practice among young people and adolescents.
For example, a nationwide self-report study of students who would graduate
from high school in 1990 found that 40 percent of the males and 26 percent of
the females reported that they had "taken something from a store without paying for it" anywhere from one to five or more times (Bachman, Johnston and
O'Malley 1986).

Legally, vandalism involves "malicious mischief" or the willful destruction,
damage or defacement of public or private property; it can be committed by a
juvenile or an adult, although most of it is perpetrated by juveniles and youths.
Juvenile vandalism can be defined as the deliberate defacement, multilation or
destruction of private or public property by a juvenile or group of juveniles not
having immediate or direct ownership in the property so abused. It is said that
the term "vandalism" was used in 1794 by a writer who, attempting to cast
blame for the willful destruction of works of art during the French Revolution,
likened such destruction to the behavior of the Vandals who sacked Rome in the
fifth century (Idzerda 1954).

Vandalism is widespread in the United States. It constitutes one of the
largest categories of juvenile delinquency offenses, although it can be committed by persons of all ages. It is associated with affluence in industrialized societies, for it rarely occurs in less developed countries, where the willful destruction of goods in limited supply is inconceivable except during riots, civil wars or
demonstrations. It is also, to a great extent, one of the few crimes that the poor
and disenfranchised segments of affluent societies can easily inflict on the more
affluent with relative impunity.

Studies of complaints made by citizens and public officials reveal that hard-
ly any property is safe from this form of aggression. Vandalism in the United
States is widespread against schools (Ban and Ciminillo 1977; Williams and
Venturini 1981), parks, libraries, public transportation facilities, telephone and
electric company facilities, religious structures (U.S. House Committee on the
Judiciary 1985), housing, and traffic department equipment and directional signs
(Perkins 1986). School property constitutes a primary target for vandals. One
study reports that the cost of window replacement alone amounts to 69 percent
of the total vandalism budget of primary and secondary schools (Weiss 1974).
Fires also pose a major and prevalent vandalism problem.

Public property of all types appears to offer peculiar allurement to children
bent on destruction. Parks, playgrounds and highway signs frequently are
defaced or destroyed. Trees, shrubs, flowers, benches, and other equipment suf-

fer in like manner. Automobilists are constantly reporting the slashing or releasing of air from tires, the breaking of windows and the theft of accessories. Golf course owners complain that benches, markers, flags and even expensive and difficult-to-replace putting greens are defaced, broken or uprooted. Libraries report the theft and destruction of books and other equipment. Railroads complain of the destruction of freight car seals, theft of property, willful and deliberate throwing of stones at passenger car windows and tampering with rails and switches. Vacant houses seem to be the particular delight of young people seeking outlets for destructive instincts; windows are broken and plumbing and hardware is stolen, destroyed or rendered unusable. Gasoline station operators report that pumps and other service equipment are stolen, broken or destroyed. Theater managers complain of the slashing of seats, willful damaging of toilet facilities, even the burning of rugs, carpets, and more.

The law generally distinguishes two types of vehicular theft. One is where there is intent to deprive the owner of the car permanently, in which the car is either kept, sold or "stripped" in what is called a "chop shop." The individual body and motor parts are then sold. The other type is borrowing the car for a "joyride" in which the car is eventually returned to the owner, although in many cases it is damaged. In many inner-city areas cars are stolen or "borrowed" in order to do "doughnuts" or spin-outs in a 360 degree circle for the entertainment of one's adolescent peers. In this case it is regarded simply as a game. Since the latter legal category usually involves no intent to deprive the legal owner permanently of the vehicle, the offense is usually designated as "operating a motor vehicle without the owner's permission." The penalty for regular auto larceny is generally about 10 years in most jurisdictions; for operating without the owner's permission, it is one year or less (McCaghy, Giordano and Henson 1977). The Federal Bureau of Investigation received well over 1.6 million reports of vehicular theft in 1990, totaling a loss of over $8 billion. It appears that the majority of the "joyride" category of auto theft is by adolescent (or preadolescent) males, and the majority of the more serious kind is by males over 21 years of age. Because cars are such an integral part of American culture and so vital for transportation in the absence of any well-developed systems of public transportation, vehicular theft is widespread. Deviance often strikes at the heart of a society.

Criminal Career of the Offender

Strictly speaking, the occasional property offender has no criminal career, nor is he or she a career criminal. A criminal behavior pattern is rooted in three main variables: (1) the distinction between people who commit crime and those who do not, (2) the individual's frequency of offending, and (3) termination of offending. Consequently, ". . . onset, persistence, and desistance are distinct aspects of the criminal career" (Barnett et al. 1992, 139). Furthermore, different factors may influence these three facets of a criminal career.

Most property offenders in this category commit only an occasional theft of some kind. Such criminal behavior is incidental to their way of life. The offenses are so infrequent that offenders in no way make a living out of crime. Occasional property offenders do not identify with crime or conceive of themselves as criminals. Their offenses show little sophistication in the techniques of crime. Most of them have little real knowledge about criminal activities or of the argot or vocabulary of crime, nor do they have contact with other offenders.

Adult occasional shoplifters or pilferers (referred to as "snitches" in the literature, as contrasted with "boosters" or professional shoplifters) do not, in general, define themselves as criminals. They often are what one classic study called "respectable" employed persons or "respectable" housewives (Cameron 1964). Some studies have pointed out the role of shame as a deterrent to such persons (Braithwaite 1989). Another early study of the occasional or "naive" check forger showed that such persons perceive their offenses as relatively minor acts of crime because large sections of the public do not think they fit the "criminal" stereotype. Check forgery has low visibility as a crime because of the peculiar interaction with the victim who accepts the check. As one criminologist has pointed out, forgery for them emerges "as behavior which is out of character or 'other than usual' for the persons involved" (Lemert 1953).

Naive check forgers may commit such offenses in the face of a financial problem when other alternatives are blocked. The offense is a product of (1) occasional difficult social situations in which the offender finds himself or herself, (2) a certain degree of social isolation, and (3) a process of "closure" or "constriction of behavior alternatives subjectively held as available to the forger" (Lemert 1953, 297).

> Assuming we have established situational isolation as the more general prerequisite for the commission of naive check forgery, it is still necessary to factor out more specific situational factors conducive to the crime. These we believe are found in certain dialectical forms of social behavior—dialectical in the sense that the person becomes progressively involved in them. These behaviors are further distinguished in that they make imperative the possession of money or money substitutes for their continuance or fulfillment. They are objective and identifiable and once a person is committed to them the impetus to "follow through" with them is implicit. A quick example is that of a man away from home who falls in with a small group who have embarked upon a two- or three-day or even a week's period of drinking and carousing. The impetus to continue the pattern gets mutually reinforced by interaction of the participants, and tends to have an accelerated beginning, a climax and a terminus. If midway through such a spree a participant runs out of money, the pressures immediately become critical to take such measures as are necessary to preserve the behavior sequence. (Lemert 1953, 302)

These same forces seem to be at work with the nonprofessional or amateur adult shoplifter, who steals largely for his or her own pleasure.

> Amateur shoplifters or "snitches" steal amounts of property which vary in cost, so that some steal petty items and others steal quite costly merchandise. Amateur shoplifters also vary in terms of crime skills, some of them employing "booster bags" and other criminal paraphernalia, while others exhibit only rudimentary techniques of crime. Further, these offenders vary in their degree of involvement in crime, for some steal only once or twice and others are caught up in recurrent acts of deviance. The distinguishing mark of the amateur as contrasted to the professional "booster" is that the former steals merchandise for his own use. The "booster," on the other hand, converts the results of his thievery into cash by selling the stolen goods to other persons. (Gibbons 1968)

During holiday periods in which gift-giving is customary, retailers commonly display vast quantities of commodities in conspicuous view in order to stimulate sales. It comes as no surprise, then, that during these periods, shoplifting—particularly of the snitch, amateur variety—is most prevalent (Baumer and Rosenbaum 1984). In this sense it may be argued that the retailers bring about their own inventory losses, for a culture founded on commercialism activates its own peculiar brand of deviance. This is particularly true in countries such as the United States, where there exists a wide range between the wealthy and the impoverished, and where television displays the same commodities for all to desire equally.

As mentioned previously, vandalism is an offense associated with the affluence of the more developed, industrialized countries. It has become customary to differentiate between wanton vandalism, predatory vandalism and vindictive vandalism (Martin 1961). *Wanton vandalism* is associated with the purely "ornery," nonutilitarian offenses of juveniles, primarily of the lower classes (Cohen 1955). This variety of offense is normally sporadic, occasional, time-bound and associated with what criminologists call "techniques of neutralization" or psychological defense mechanisms activated to deflect blame for what are usually minor offenses (Matza and Sykes 1961). *Predatory vandalism* is economically oriented, but rarely constitutes a criminal career; this includes offenses such as breaking into parking meters or public telephones for small change. Offenders in this category are usually involved in other petty crimes of a nonviolent nature, though they can hardly be described as having careers in crime. Finally, there is *vindictive vandalism,* or what has come to be labeled as "hate crime" (Herek and Berrill 1992). These are offenses directed against the property of, and occasionally the persons of, people of a different race, religion, ethnicity, social class or sexual preference.

A large proportion of those who commit vandalism are likely to have a non-criminal view of themselves and their actions. The fact that often nothing is stolen during acts of wanton or vindictive vandalism tends to reinforce the vandal's conception of self as prankster rather than delinquent or criminal. On the whole, therefore, acts of vandalism are committed by persons who have no special criminal orientation toward themselves or what they do. Some writers consider this a distinguishing characteristic of the vandal when compared with other property offenders. Property destruction does function for the adolescent in that he or she considers it entertaining, rebellious and exciting, as well as a protest against his or her role and status in the social structure of class society. Very often the type of vandalism found in urban inner-city areas is characterized by the attitude, "Why not? We got nothin' to lose." Much of what has been said with regard to vandalism is equally applicable to the "joyriding" of the occasional car thief.

Joyriding is not a career type of offense. It is usually done only by teenagers and the offenses committed are sporadic in nature. The usual patterns are quite simple—either stealing a car that has readily accessible keys, using a duplicate key, or jumping or hot-wiring the car. With the sophisticated modern anti-theft devices installed in many cars, however, this is becoming progressively more difficult. The theft of a car is more like "borrowing" it and does not involve techniques commonly associated with conventional career offenses, such as selecting a special type of car, finding fences for the sale of the car or its parts, or stripping the car. Moreover, the occasional car thief, or joyrider, does not usually progress in techniques and skills.

Of particular significance among occasional offenders is their ability to rationalize their criminal behavior. Adult department store pilferers, for example, tend to take relatively inexpensive items of merchandise just a little above the level of that which they would purchase; therefore, they view their acts as somewhat reprehensible but not "really criminal." Other rationalizations may include the thought that "department stores are rich" or that many other people also steal small items. For example, research has shown that many occasional property offenders would not even consider stealing from a mom-and-pop store, while the large, chain franchises like Sears, J.C. Penney or Walmart are fair game (Smigel 1970).

Group Support of Criminal Behavior

The occasional property offender generally has little group support for his or her criminal behavior. Occasional property crimes need relatively little group or peer support, because they are relatively easy to pull off (in the sense that few skills are called for and a social network of facilitators is not necessary). One study has found that the influence of delinquent peers on delinquency is mediated by three factors: (1) the offender's emotional attachment to his or her peers, (2) the amount of time actually spent with them, and (3) the extent to which the peers present definitions favorable to delinquency and reinforce it: "A measure of association with peers who engage in minor delinquency, however, is not conditioned by (these) variables" (Agnew 1991, 47). In other words, these three factors are not necessary ingredients for most occasional property offenses.

All of this suggests the relative unimportance of criminal associations in crimes of this type. Most persons in their everyday lives have occasion to cash personal checks and need no one's help to do so. Likewise, the present-day mass display of merchandise in stores makes training in techniques of theft largely unnecessary. To some who illegally "borrow" an automobile, it involves no more than driving away an unlocked car. Naive check forgeries generally are committed by persons who have had no previous criminal record and no previous contact or interaction with delinquents and criminals. The offenders in these crimes are characteristically much older than most property offenders, being in their late twenties or thirties. This type of offender generally does not come from an area with a high delinquency rate.

Similarly, most adult shoplifters have had no present or sustained contact with a criminal subculture. In a classic study, approximately 92 percent of the women who were officially charged with shoplifting had never been convicted of an offense (Cameron 1964). Some may have had such associations when they were younger, however. The behavior of adult shoplifters after arrest frequently indicates just how little association with a criminal subculture they have had.

> Pilferers had no knowledge of arrest procedures, and they had clearly given little or no forethought to the consequences of their arrest. They appeared to have thought about being "caught," but not about being arrested. Not understanding that they would be searched, for example, many attempted to give fictitious names (for a woman, usually her maiden name) while at the same time carrying a billfold or pocketbook with complete identification papers. (They did not realize that arrest implied search). . . . Not infrequently pilferers confessed some of their past thefts to store detectives, detailing the time, place, and objects stolen. Some of these past thefts had been memorable events arousing and continuing to arouse strong feelings of guilt. (Cameron 1964, 170)

Naive check forgery is also usually carried out alone. Shoplifting by adults is generally done alone as well. Shoplifting by juveniles is generally a group activity, although not group-coordinated beyond setting up a lookout. More typically, a group of adolescents will disperse throughout a store, meeting later at another location to see who has stolen the most goods and the most valuable commodities. Afterwards, what has been shoplifted is either used, sold or thrown away. In contrast, generally there are several individuals involved in acts of simple wanton vandalism, but what takes place is more the result of the collective interaction of the moment than the product of a criminal subculture or subculture of vandalism.

> Acts of vandalism seldom utilize or even require prior sophisticated knowledge. They grow out of collective interaction of the moment; few are deliberately planned in advance. Participation in acts of vandalism gives status and group interaction to each member; through direct involvement the individual avoids becoming a marginal member of the group. Vandalism is spontaneous behavior and the outgrowth of social situations in which group interaction takes place. Each interactive response by a participant builds upon the action of another participant until a focus develops and the group act of vandalism results. In the typical act of vandalism there are usually five stages: (1) waiting for something to turn up; (2) removal of uncertainty about what to do, resulting in an "exploratory gesture" to the act (3) mutual conversion of each member of the group to participation; (4) joint elaboration of the vandalism; and (5) aftermath and retrospect. (Wade 1967, 268)

The functional mutual excitation or group contagion is of particular importance in vandalism. A primary function of this element is the tendency for the individual to lose his or her feeling of self-identity in the prevailing group interaction. This temporary loss of identity is especially significant because it helps make possible the participation in vandalism and any resulting elaboration of the act. The very fact that property destruction is generally a group act functions to reduce individual feelings of fear and guilt. The dilution of such feeling in the peer association operates as a sort of "guilt insurance." The peer group inadvertently furnishes a sense of security in numbers, which functions to reduce feelings of individualiity and responsibility. Further, the belief is that when the act is committed by a group, the authorities will find it difficult, if not impossible, to single out the specific instigators. The feeling of security is enhanced by the additional belief that vandalism is one of the less serious delinquencies. This is particularly the case when the adolescent interprets his or her destructive behavior as a prank or "just being mischievous." This interpretation also functions as an attempt to neutralize whatever guilt feelings the offender may have from participation in vandalism.

Correspondence between Criminal and Legitimate Behavior

Most conforming behavior is evaluated and judged from the rational choice perspective. Research has shown, however, that occasional property offenses such as petty theft and vandalism are not sufficiently explained by the rational choice model (Paternoster 1989). (The same research found that marijuana use and underage drinking are not explained by this model either.) The same may be said with regard to public support for this form of criminal behavior: Occasional property offenders find little similarity in their criminal behavior to the legitimate behavior patterns of society. In general, all of the offenses represent a violation of the values placed on private property in capitalist society. In most cases, offenders are attempting to obtain something that they consider to be necessary and important, but which they are unable to obtain through legitimate channels. One study of 1,575 randomly selected citizens in Chicago concluded that most Americans obey most of the laws most of the time because they think that the legitimate authorities should be respected and because most law-abiding people want to think of themselves as moral persons (Tyler 1990). This being the case, it is not difficult to see the lack of fit between criminal and legitimate behavior in the case of occasional property offenses: While these offenders tend to be committed to the general goals of society, at least in their own minds their behavior stands in occasional contradiction to this self-image.

Occasional property offenders tend to be committed to the general goals of society. Naive check forgers "appear to have acquired normal attitudes and habits of law observance" (Lemert 1953, 298). Adult department store pilferers are generally "respectable" citizens with little or no contact with criminal groups (Cameron 1964, xii). It is only in their criminal acts that there is little correspondence between the offender and the nonoffender.

The extent to which occasional property crime represents a rejection of legitimate behavior patterns, as incorporated in what are conventionally called "middle-class" norms, is open to question. Much destruction of property through vandalism seems to occur as a way of challenging the complex of values associated with the emphasis placed on private property in the United States. In many other cases vandalism appears to be an attempt merely to have some fun. For example, graffiti—which is a form of vandalism in many cases—has been variously interpreted as "street art," "people's art" or "spraycan art" (Chalfant 1987). It has also been defined as malicious destruction of public property by irresponsible adolescents, as an attempt to call public attention to oneself or one's cause, and as simply having some fun. Perhaps it is all of these things. Increasing evidence seems to indicate that "middle-class" legitimate behavior patterns are not equally internalized by all persons and groups and that many law violators are relatively isolated from the behavior patterns of the dominant power segments of American society (Bursik 1988; Lieberman and Smith 1986; Van Voorhis et al. 1988). Others theorize that both delinquent and middle-class legal norms are internalized and that delinquency is a product of the delinquent's relations with an inconsistent and vulnerable legal code (Matza and Sykes 1964).

With all forms of vandalism, shoplifting, forgery, and so on, the behaviors that may become defined as criminal are pursued for a wide variety of reasons, with variations occurring according to the location of the participants in the social structure. In the last analysis, the study of criminal behavior must be kept as objective as possible. That is, the criminologist must be extremely careful not to impute his or her own motives and values to those that underlie the behavior of the offenders. This awareness demands a constant effort on the part of the observer and analyst.

Societal Reaction and Legal Processing

Societal reaction toward occasional property crime often is not severe. Because the offender is unlikely to have any (or at most a minor) previous criminal record, and because these types of offenses do not represent a serious personal threat to the average person, the charge is often likely to be dismissed or the offender given probation, a fine or a suspended sentence or warning. In the case of minor property crimes, the penal law may result from the political process itself, which incorporates and protects the interests of various interest groups over time and political jurisdictions (Lindquist 1988). These interest groups may be considerably more successful in getting laws passed than they are in getting effective enforcement of these laws.

In most cases the illegal behavior is carried out in isolation from the supporting values of a criminal subculture or group, and largely in a system of non-criminal relationships. The criminal behavior of the occasional offender is likely to be unstable, and when confronted with legal action in the form of an arrest, which defines the behavior as actually being "criminal," the offender is usually deterred from continuing such activity.

The effect of this societal reaction generally holds true whether it is shoplifting, simple check forgery or vandalism. Persons can behave, for example, as thieves without defining themselves as thieves. Arrests by store detectives or the police are crucial in helping to redefine a shoplifter's conception of his or her behavior as being merely "antisocial" or "bad" to being "criminal." Considerable leniency is allowed the occasional property offender by law enforcement and judicial agencies because such offenders are not likely to progress into a criminal career.

There are several reasons why relatively few shoplifters are turned over to the police and prosecuted. There is difficulty in getting court action; the suspect often will refuse to "fess up"; the thefts are not usually of large, expensive items; and often the suspects are "respectable, middle-class women" and the companies do not wish to appear to be "picking on" the individual. One final consideration looms large: the more shoplifting losses a retail outlet reports to the police, the higher go its insurance rates.

One study of one of this nation's largest corporations employing over a quarter of a million people in almost 300 stores across the country found that there was a *private* justice system, one complete with investigative, adjudicatory and sentencing powers to deal with shoplifters. No need here to turn the suspect over to the public police or to risk higher insurance rates. This study found that among the factors determining private justice for shoplifters were such variables as the retail value of the item taken, and the neighborhood, social class and degree of physical resistance of the suspect (Davis, Lundman and Martinez 1991).

A final element in the moderate reaction to occasional property crime is the fact that the offenders often come from the same classes that are responsible for the enforcement of the law (and in some cases, from higher classes). In many localities the offenders are an integral and important part of the community. In such cases much of the criminal behavior of residents is ignored by the local law enforcement agencies. This is one reason for strong objections to the "federalization" of law enforcement. Through their own legal agencies, local communities are able to establish and make viable the limits to which they will tolerate certain forms and amounts of deviance.

References

Agnew, Robert (1991). "The Interactive Effects of Peer Variables on Delinquency." *Criminology* 29 (1): 47-72.

Anonymous (1973). "A Counter-Attack on Vandalism." *American School and University* (June): 43-44.

Bachman, Jerald G., Lloyd Johnston, and Patrick O'Malley (1986). *Monitoring the Future, 1986.* Ann Arbor, MI: Institute for Social Research, University of Michigan. In *Sourcebook of Criminal Justice Statistics, 1990,* table 3.56.

Ban, John R., and Lewis M. Ciminillo (1977). *Violence and Vandalism in Public Education: Problems and Prospects.* Danville, IL: Interstate Printers & Publishers.

Barnett, Arnold, Alfred Blumstein, Jacqueline Cohen, and David Farrington (1992). "Not All Criminal Career Models are Equally Valid." *Criminology* 30 (1): 133-140.

*Baumer, Terry L., and Dennis P. Rosenbaum (1984). *Combating Retail Theft: Programs and Strategies.* Boston: Butterworth.

Bradford, Michael (1992). "Thieves Sting Banks with High-Tech Forgeries." *Business Insurance* 26 (9): 14-15.

Braithwaite, John (1989). *Reintegrative Shaming: A New General Theory of Crime?* Cambridge, MA: Cambridge University Press.

Brocato, Thomas L. (1990). "Avoiding the Loss on Forgeries." *Texas Banking* 79 (7): 12-14.

Bursik, Robert J., Jr. (1988). "Social Disorganization and Theories of Crime and Delinquency: Problems and Prospects." *Criminology* 26 (4): 519-551.

Cameron, Mary Owen (1964). *The Booster and the Snitch: Department Store Shoplifting.* New York: Free Press.

Caplan, Marc H. (1980). *Retail Security: A Selected Bibliography.* NCJ-67519. National Institute of Justice, Washington, DC: U.S. Government Printing Office.

Chalfant, Henry (1987). *Spraycan Art.* New York: Thames and Hudson.

Churbuck, David (1989). "Desktop Forgery." *Forbes* 144 (12): 246-254.

Clinard, Marshall B., and Andrew Wade (1958). "Toward the Delineation of Vandalism as a Sub-Type in Juvenile Delinquency." *Journal of Criminal Law, Criminology and Police Science* 48 (1): 493-499.

Cohen, Albert K. (1955). *Delinquent Boys: The Culture of the Gang.* New York: Free Press.

Davis, Melissa G., Richard J. Lundman, and Ramiro Martinez, Jr. (1991). "Private Corporate Justice: Store Police, Shoplifters, and Civil Recovery." *Social Problems* 38 (3): 395-411.

Francis, Dorothy B. (1980). *Shoplifting, The Crime Everybody Pays For.* New York: Elsevier/Nelson Books.

Gibbons, Don C. (1968). *Society, Crime and Criminal Careers.* Englewood Cliffs, NJ: Prentice-Hall.

Gottfredson, Michael, and Travis Hirschi (1988). "Science, Public Policy, and the Careeer Paradigm." *Criminology* 26:37-56.

Greco, Thomas J. (1991). "When Automation Endorses Check Fraud." *ABA Banking Journal* 83 (3): 93-94.

Greenbert, David (1991). "Modeling Criminal Careers." *Criminology* 29:17-46.

*Herek, Gregory M., and Kevin T. Berrill (1991). *Hate Crimes: Confronting Violence Against Lesbians and Gay Men.* Newbury Park, CA: Sage.

Hoggan, Karen (1991). "Retailers Under Threat from Fraud." *Marketing (UK)* (Jan. 10): 2-3.

Hollinger, Richard, and John Clark (1983). *Theft by Employees.* Lexington, MA: Lexington Books.

Idzerda, S. J. (1954). "Iconoclasm during the French Revolution." *American Historical Review* 60:13-26.

Lemert, Edwin M. (1953). "An Isolation of Closure Theory of Naive Check Forgery." *Journal of Criminal Law, Criminology and Police Science* 44:290-310.

Lieberman, Louis, and Alexander B. Smith (1986). "Crime Rates and Poverty—A Reexamination." *Crime and Social Justice* 25:166-177.

Lindquist, John H. (1988). *Misdemeanor Crime: Trivial Criminal Pursuit.* Newbury Park, CA: Sage.

Martin, John M. (1961). *Juvenile Vandalism: A Study of Its Nature and Prevention.* Springfield, IL: Charles C Thomas.

Matza, David, and Gresham Sykes (1961). "Juvenile Delinquency and Subterranean Values," *American Sociological Review* 26(5), 712-719.

*Matza, David, and Gresham Sykes (1964). *Delinquency and Drift.* New York: John Wiley & Sons.

McCaghy, Charles, Peggy Giordano, and Trudy Knicely Henson (1977). "Auto Theft." *Criminology* 15:3267-3281.

Murphy, J.P. (1954). "The Answer to Vandalism May Be Found at Home." *Federal Probation* 18.

Paternoster, Raymond (1989). "Decisions to Participate in and Desist from Four Types of Common Delinquency: Deterrence and the Rational Choice Perspective." *Law & Society Review* 23 (1):9-40.

Perkins, David (1986). *Manual on Countermeasures for Sign Vandalism.* U.S. Department of Transportation, Federal Highway Administration. Washington, DC: U.S. Government Printing Office.

President's Commission on Law Enforcement and the Administration of Justice (1967). *Task Force Report: Crime and Its Impact—An Assessment.* Washington, DC: U.S. Government Printing Office.

Reha, John F. (1990). "Fighting Check Fraud." *Bank Management* 66 (12): 52-59.

Small Business Administration (1972). "Crime Against Small Business." In *Combating Crime Against Small Business,* edited by Richard S. Post. Springfield, IL: Charles C Thomas.

*Smigel, Erwin (1970). *Crimes Against Bureaucracy.* New York: Van Nostrand Reinhold.

*Tyler, Tom R. (1990). *Why People Obey the Law.* New Haven, CT: Yale University Press.

U.S. House Committee on the Judiciary: Subcommittee on Criminal Justice (1985). *Crimes Against Religious Practices and Property.* Washington, DC: U.S. Government Printing Office.

Van Voorhis, Patricia, Francis Cullen, Richard Mathers, and Connie Garner (1988). "The Impact of Family Structure and Quality on Delinquency: A Comparative Assessment of Structural and Functional Factors." *Criminology* 26 (2): 235-61.

Violano, Michael (1989). "The High-Tech Future of Foiling Fraud and Forgery." *Bankers Monthly* 106 (4): 34-40.

Wade, Andrew L. (1967). "Social Processes in the Act of Juvenile Vandalism." In *Criminal Behavior Systems: A Typology,* edited by Marshall B. Clinard and Richard Quinney. New York: Holt, Rinehart and Winston.

Weiss, Norbert J. (1974). "Vandalism: An Environmental Concern." *N.A.S.S.P. Bulletin* 58 (379): 6.

Williams, Robert B., and Joseph L. Venturini (1981). *School Vandalism: Cause and Cure.* Saratoga, CA: Century Twenty One.

*Wolfgang, Marvin, Terence Thornberry, and Robert Figlio (1987). *From Boy to Man, from Delinquency to Crime.* Chicago: University of Chicago Press.

Yen, Elizabeth C. (1989). "Examination for Forged Signatures: What Constitutes 'Ordinary Care'?" *Banking Law Journal* 106 (2): 184-187.

Chapter 4

Public Order Criminal Behavior

No one knows for certain which crimes are committed with the greatest frequency, but with the possible exception of fraud, crimes falling into the category of public order crimes are the most numerous. Public order crimes include prostitution, homosexual acts, drunkenness, the use of controlled substances, gambling, traffic offenses, disorderly conduct, vagrancy and exhibitionism.

In one sense, all public order crimes are similar in that they all break some penal law. In another sense, each individual crime is unique in time and space. The same may be said of all crimes that fall into one criminal behavior system: in many ways they share similarities, while in other ways they are unique. There are obviously some striking differences in the behavior systems of the more important public order offenses of prostitution, homosexual behavior, public drunkenness and use of controlled substances. Still, because of the many similarities, all the offenses in this group will be discussed together under each of the five dimensions: legal aspects, criminal careers, group support, correspondence between criminal and legitimate behavior and societal reaction/legal processing. In each case, when pertinent and reliable data exist, the differences between these types of offenses will also be indicated and discussed.

Legal Aspects of Selected Offenses

Many of these so-called "public order" crimes do not involve any real injury to another person or persons. Rather, they disturb the moral sense of some members of the community, as in the case of prostitution, homosexual acts and drunkenness, or they may be judged to be injurious to the individual engaging in them, as in drunkenness, or abuse of controlled substances. Since the partners in homosexual behavior are willing, often loving, associates, and the act of using controlled substances is—outside of addiction—a voluntary act, one writer has used the term "crimes without victims" (Schur 1965). The same might be said for acts of prostitution in which both parties are willing partners who stand to gain something from the exchange. Penal laws that criminalize these acts fail to recognize the absence of any bond between the acts themselves and any real harm to others. So, we can say that acts involved in crimes against public order are quite different in nature from crimes committed against persons or their property, such as murder, rape or theft and destruction of another's property—crimes by which real and unwanted suffering is inflicted upon one person by another.

Prostitution

The history of prostitution in the western world is characterized by a history of ambiguity. This remains true today. In the Middle Ages prostitution was widespread and regarded as a necessary evil; it was not usually considered a criminal act. The demand for prostitution, "the world's oldest profession," from all social classes was great; therefore, in Europe it was often not simply tolerated but even protected and regulated by law and was a source of public revenue. In some areas of Europe the Catholic Church was involved in the maintenance of houses of prostitution, particularly in France. The Protestant Reformation, with its extreme concern for personal morals, initiated a reaction against extramarital relations of any type. At the same time, many were concerned about the increasing spread of venereal diseases such as syphilis, thought to have been brought from the New World, in which prostitutes were heavily involved. As a result, statutes enacted against prostitution in the fifteenth and sixteenth centuries were enforced to a considerable degree. In England, when prosecution passed from the ecclesiastical courts to the common law after 1640, prostitution was not regarded as a criminal offense but rather as a public nuisance.

From its beginnings in France and Germany, state regulation of prostitution spread across Europe, and in 1871 at the International Medical Congress in Vienna an international law was proposed to make regulation uniform throughout the world. The goal was social reform and improved health conditions. Prostitution itself was not questioned. In England the Contagious Diseases Acts were implemented between 1864 and 1869. The crusade of one courageous middleclass Victorian woman of Liverpool, England, was to radically change the way people thought about prostitution. Josephine Butler engaged in rescuing young girls and women from prostitution on the Liverpool docks. "To Josephine Butler, the Contagious Diseases Acts formalized and legalized the sexual enslavement of women" (Barry 1984, 15). She eventually built her campaign from a single-city movement to a national, and then international, crusade against statecontrolled and state-protected prostitution (Butler 1976). Butler was among the first to recognize prostitution as male domination and exploitation of females. All 50 states today have laws criminalizing prostitution, variously targeting pimps, procurers, patrons and prostitutes themselves. Most of this legislation draws a clear distinction between females under and over certain ages.

Prostitution takes a variety of forms: (1) the "call girl," (2) the common "streetwalker," (3) those working in organized houses of prostitution, and (4) the independent professional with her own stable clientele. Recently a social movement has arisen in the United States that challenges the traditional definitions of prostitution as a social problem, as sinful, or as activity needing state regulation. Centered around an organization called COYOTE (an acronym for "Call Off Your Old Tired Ethics"), the campaign seeks to sever prostitution from its historical association with sin, crime and illicit sex, and "place the social problem of prostitution firmly in the discourse of work, choice, and civil rights" (Jenness 1990, 403).

Homosexual Behavior

Homosexual behavior refers to sexual relations with those of one's own sex. The term is derived from the Geeek word, ομοσ (pronounced "homos"), meaning "same." Homosexuality or being homosexual is not a crime. It is rather an orientation toward sexual and love relations with members of one's own sex. Only certain homosexual acts have been defined as criminal, as indeed in some jurisdictions have been certain heterosexual acts.

Laws forbidding homosexual behavior are widely thought to be rooted in ancient Hebrew sex codes that were formalized by the Christian church over the centuries into the ecclesiastical laws that governed much of medieval Europe and later provided the basis for English common law. As a result of a variety of historical forces, the Christian church gradually came to view sexual behavior as virtuous and permissible only when it was engaged in for the purpose of human reproduction. It was not until the thirteenth century that the canon law of the Church systematically condemned homosexual intercourse, as well as certain heterosexual acts even within marriage. The Fourth Lateran Council in the year 1215 was the first to create clear boundaries between "them," referring to homosexual people, heretics and infidels, and "us," the faithful. Thus began a process of regulation, surveillance and documentation of sexual misconduct, both homosexual and heterosexual. By this time the doctrine of clerical celibacy was firmly, if not universally, in place (Brundage 1988), a fact that makes the Church's negative attitude toward sex easier to understand.

For hundreds of years homosexual acts were commonly punished by the religious authorities of Europe with death or torture. As late as the mid-eighteenth century, homosexual people were publicly burned at the stake in Paris. Liberalization of legal attitudes came to Europe with the Enlightenment, the French Revolution and later the Code Napoleon, which left homosexual acts out of the legal structure, a standard that still exists in most European countries. Many of these laws, however, were later changed to permit homosexual acts only between consenting adults over 21 years of age. In most European countries today, homosexual acts between consenting adults, engaged in privately, are not considered to be criminal matters.

In England homosexual acts first became a matter of the secular courts in 1533, when a statute (with religious implications) making sodomy punishable by death was introduced under Henry VIII. It so remained until the nineteenth century when the penalty was reduced to life imprisonment. An act passed in 1861, which remained in force until 1956, provided life imprisonment for sodomy by two men or by a husband and wife. Efforts to gain equal rights for homosexual people in Great Britain have been largely successful since 1950. Since 1950, conditions have generally improved, especially following the 1967 decriminalization of some aspects of homosexual behavior. This trend toward greater tolerance, however, was somewhat reversed under the Thatcher government of the 1980s (Jeffery-Poulter 1991).

The legal effects of the French Revolution did not reach the largely Protestant, puritanical United States. While imposition of penalties for homosexual acts is extremely rare today, most states have misdemeanor laws covering homosexual acts. In addition, some states have sexual deviance laws by which a homosexual offender may be committed for so-called "treatment" in excess of the period provided by the criminal statutes. What this actually represents is usually holding a person in custody, and most of these laws reflect the thinking that homosexual people are "sick" and in need of change-oriented treatment. These laws and the thinking behind them are currently under legal challenge in the courts.

Drunkenness

Under English common law, intoxication itself was not a crime; it was tolerated, whether in a public place or not, unless it resulted in some breach of the peace or disorderly conduct charge. It was not until 1606 that intoxication in public first became a criminal offense. Intoxication in public still remains a criminal offense, at least on the books, in most jurisdictions of the United States.

Laws against public drunkenness have their origin in religious values and attitudes (particularly Protestant) toward personal morality, that is, ideas about the individual's lack of moral control and his or her inability to carry out effectively the "will of God" in his or her work and family relationships. Another facet is the protection of citizens from bothersome disorderly public behavior. Laws against public drunkenness reflect the power structure in that lower-class persons are most likely to be drunk in public places, having few resources to protect their private behavior from public view.

According to the FBI, more than .5 million United States citizens were arrested in 1989 for public drunkenness alone, excluding drunken driving offenses and other alcohol-related crimes. Drunkenness is a crime punishable under a variety of statutes and ordinances. Some are worded "drunk in a public place," while others say "unable to care for his own safety." Others use laws stating that drunkenness that causes a breach of peace is punishable, while still others deal with drunkenness under a disorderly conduct provision. Although the laws provide maximum jail sentences ranging from five days to six months, generally it is 30 days or a fine. Some states punish habitual drunkenness as a felony with a two-year sentence of imprisonment. Drunkenness under certain conditions, such as while operating a motor vehicle, is severely punished in most other countries (notably the Scandinavian countries and Japan), where not only may the offender be fined and imprisoned, but his or her driver's licence will almost certainly be revoked for a year or even permanently (and this is generally with even the *slightest* amount of alcohol in the blood.)

Use of Controlled Substances

In past editions of this book we have used the phrase "drug use," when what was actually meant was use of controlled substances. Drug use in the United States and other countries is pervasive. This includes the use of drugs that have been "controlled" by the state and the use of certain kinds of drugs that have not been criminalized by penal law. By far the greatest costs to a nation in economic and health terms accrue from the use of noncontrolled drugs: the use of nicotine, (defined in *Webster's International Dictionary* as "a poisonous alkaloid. It is a colorless, oily, acrid liquid") in tobacco, the use of caffeine in coffee, and the use of alcohol in alcoholic beverages such as beer, wine or "hard liquor." Of all forms of addiction, alcohol addiction is the drug problem that affects the largest number of humans, yet it is not a "controlled substance" in the United States. However, for the sake of brevity, "drug use" will continue to be used here since it a less awkward phrase than "use of controlled substances."

The term *drug abuse,* also referred to as chemical or substance abuse, is the willful misuse of either legal or illegal drugs for recreation or convenience. *Drug misuse,* on the other hand, is the unintentional or inappropriate use of either prescribed or "over-the-counter" drugs (Gossop 1987). There are many different kinds of controlled substances that are commonly abused. There are six classes of these: narcotics, depressants, stimulants, hallucinogens, cannabis and organic solvents. The principle narcotics are opium, morphine, heroin and methadone. They cause high physical and psychological dependence. The principle depressants are barbiturates, methaqualone, and benzadiazepines. Known popularly as tranquilizers, downers or sleeping pills, these range from moderate to high in physical and psychological dependence. The principle stimulants are cocaine and its derivative "crack," amphetamines and phenmetrazine; these drugs cause possible physical dependence and high psychological dependence. The principle hallucinogens are LSD, mescaline, peyote and phencyclidine (PCP or "angel dust"). Very little is known of the physical or psychological dependence they cause. The most important cannabis drugs are marijuana, hashish and hash oil. These cause moderate psychological dependence, and an unknown degree of physical dependence. Finally there are the organic solvents that are inhalants: model airplane glue, hairspray, spray paint, rubber cement and paint thinner. Aside from the last category, all of the above drugs have been designated as controlled substances by various pieces of federal legislation from the 1914 Harrison Act through the Anti-Drug Act of 1988 (U.S. Dept. of Justice, Drug Enforcement Administration 1989).

During the eighteenth and nineteenth centuries in this country the sale and use of uncontrolled patent medicines flourished widely. Any legislation regarding these medicines was concerned solely with protecting the secret, patented ingredients, which ranged from alcohol, through opium, morphine and cocaine, to heroin. An accumulating series of historical/social forces gradually led to the dawning of a new consciousness in the country, to the effect that patent medicines were often ineffective, frequently harmful and usually led to addictive dependence. A series of articles in *Collier's* magazine in 1905, under the title "The Great American Fraud," alerted the general public to the abuse of patent medicines. These articles coined the term "dope fiend" from "dope," which was an African word meaning "intoxicating substance" (Witters, Venturelli and Hanson 1992, 60). The American Medical Association quickly joined in the attack. With regard to the smoking of drugs, Nevada became the first state, back in 1877, to criminalize retail sales of smokable opium, "the Chinese scourge."

The first real milestone in federal regulations controlling the marketing of drugs was the Pure Food and Drug Act of 1906, concerned mainly with addiction to patent medicines. This was followed by the 1912 Sherley Amendment, which criminalized false or fraudulent claims on drug labels. However, the history of true drug abuse laws on the federal level began in 1914 with the Harrison Act, actually a tax bill that sought to control the dispensing of and dealing in narcotics. Unfortunately, the Harrison Act was principally the result of the anti-Chinese sentiment of the times. There followed the Narcotic Drugs Import and Export Act of 1922, the Heroin Act of 1924, the Federal Narcotics Hospitals Act of 1928, the Marijuana Tax Act of 1937, the Opium Poppy Control Act of 1942 and the Narcotic Drug Control Act of 1956. The effect of these acts was to impose stiff penalties for the importation, sale, distribution, possession and/or use of what eventually came to be known as controlled substances. The Comprehensive Drug Abuse Prevention and Control Act of 1970 established a series of education, research and rehabilitation programs, and divided drugs into five "schedules" according to their actual or relative potential for abuse (Morgan 1981). The so-called "war on drugs," declared by President Ronald Reagan, resulted in the severely repressive drug enforcement-oriented Anti-Drug Abuse Act of 1988 advocated by the Bush administration.

As for regulation on the state level, historically the states were the first to pass laws regulating the abuse or misuse of drugs. Federal legislation usually followed.

> Today, state law enforcement of drug statutes does not always reflect federal regulations, although for the most part, the two statutory levels are harmonious. For example, marijuana in small amounts for personal use is only considered an act of minor misconduct in Alaska or Oregon but is considered a Schedule I substance by federal regulatory agencies. Consequently, as long as this substance is used inside the state boundaries . . . for personal use only, there is little likelihood of prosecution. However, the more severe federal laws are invoked whenever use of this illicit substance involves interstate issues. (Witters, Venturelli and Hanson 1992, 90)

Criminal Career of the Offender

Many public order offenders do not regard their behavior as criminal *per se,* nor do they believe that criminal behavior is part of their life organization. The ambivalence of general social norms toward much of this behavior accounts, in part, for the fact that most offenders do not have a clearly defined criminal career. These empirical generalizations, however, differ greatly depending upon the public order offenses we are referring to. For example, the drug user/abuser or prostitute is more likely to regard his or her behavior as criminal. It is less likely that the alcoholic or problem drinker would, except with regard to the offenses he or she commits while under the influence of alcohol. Gays and lesbians are least likely to define their behavior as criminal. Again, it is most important that we make the distinction between the status of *being* a certain kind of person and the acts of *doing* certain things.

Prostitution

Prostitution is defined as sexual intercourse or the rendering of other sexual "services," such as oral sex, usually with emotional detachment, on a promiscuous and mercenary basis. Both males as well as females may be prostitutes, though it is an offense largely dominated by females. In some countries, as well as in some of our states, prostitution itself is legally not a criminal offense;

rather, the prostitute is punished for soliciting. Mere sexual experiences do not make a person a prostitute, but the cash nexus does. Historically, persons who enter prostitution have lived in local communities, such as inner cities or definitely delineated physical boundaries, where sexual promiscuity has been approved or at least condoned. For example, in Tokyo today there still exists a district that was surrounded by a moat during the Edo period, where prostitution is publicly accepted and condoned. The various houses even have advertisements and various prices displayed on marquees out front. Among other cities, Amsterdam also has a delineated "red light district."

Prior to entering into professional prostitution most people have had personal contact with someone professionally involved in such activities: pimps, other prostitutes or those seeking sexual activities in exchange for payment. A sort of "quasi-prostituting" experience may lead to prostitution as in the case of waitresses who accept money from customers in return for sexual intercourse. The actual mechanics of developing a career in prostitution generally involve a series of progressive stages: entrance into the career, apprenticeship under other prostitutes or pimps, and the cultivation and development of a stable clientele. Training and the establishment of contacts are essential elements in building a career in prostitution as is the learning of the requisite emotional distancing from clients. This is why a subculture must be entered into, one that provides the proper milieu for learning, practicing and executing the behaviors necessary for success as a prostitute (Bryan 1965). Less training, skill and apprenticeship experience are required for the relatively simple role of streetwalker, than for that of call girl or independent professional. On the other hand, the nonverbal skills required of a call girl are not as complex as those required of a streetwalker. "The tasks of avoiding the police, soliciting among strangers for potential customers, and arrangements for the completion of the sexual contract not only require different skills on the part of the the streetwalker, but are performances requiring a higher degree of professional 'know-how' than is generally required of the call girl" (Bryan, 296). Prostitutes of all types develop an argot (a distinct professional language), a repertoire of special acts and services, and patterns of bartering with customers and establishing impersonal relationships with them. Rationalizations for their activities are facilitated by the entertainment media, which is prone to depict the prostitute's life as a sort of fairy tale, an exotic, exciting and socially valuable life; films like *Pretty Woman* or the classic *Never on Sunday* are examples of this misleading genre.

It is difficult to generalize about the self-attitudes of prostitutes. Because the prostitute encounters a duality of social values, there is a tendency to justify or rationalize commercial sex behavior by emphasizing certain legitimate values of society, such as financial success or taking care of persons who are financially dependent on them. One study found that the stated ideology of those who had been call girls for an average length of 27 months includes the beliefs that customers are exploitative, that other women are hypocrites about the use of sex to gain advantages, that prostitution provides a valuable social service by providing necessary sexual outlets and psychological comfort to customers, and that call girls' relationships are close and honest (Jackman, O'Toole and Geis 1963). However, when the individual opinions of prostitutes were studied, many of the ideologies were generally not supported. The conclusion is that, although professional ideology is learned and may serve a function during the apprentice period of prostitution, it does not remain of equal importance throughout a call girl's career. For the apprentice the ideology is important in counteracting a negative self-image and reducing moral conflict during the initial period of prostitution. Once the person enters into and fully recognizes the brutal reality of the life, these defenses quickly collapse.

There are a number of ways to get out of prostitution. The aging process, if nothing else, eventually ends a person's career as a prostitute (and prostitutes tend to feel their age rapidly as a result of the hardships of the trade). In addition, there are many social agencies, both public and private, religious as well as secular, available to reach out and offer rehabilitation and alternatives to those seeking a new lifestyle. Sometimes it happens that a person engaged in prostitution eventually marries a former customer, but this is rare. Some financially successful prostitutes—those who have been able to achieve and maintain a high standard of living—eventually establish their own business. These "madams" then employ others either in houses of prostitution or in a complex call girl network or "escort service."

Previous arrest records, however, may make leaving the profession more difficult; and for many, some of whom are eventually affected by AIDS or other sexually transmitted diseases, alcoholism and drug addiction, the end is a derelict life, punctuated more or less regularly by arrests and jail sentences. From there it seems to be an easy step to petty stealing, street corner drug sales and shoplifting. Because the illegality of prostitution forces prostitutes into a world of police, courts and correctional institutions—thus keeping them from leaving the profession—law enforcement efforts generally fail to reduce prostitution. Contacts with legal authorities often become complicated by arrests for alcoholism, drugs and petty theft, bringing back the very same way of life the person more than likely left behind to enter into prostitution. The individual's position makes her or him vulnerable to blackmail by the police and other political and legal forms of corruption. Often the person is forced by the police into the highly dangerous role of an informer on thefts and drug dealing.

Homosexual Behavior

Sex is but one aspect of a person's total life. Generally, it is not independent of a total life pattern and seldom is it the dominating one. Thus the term "homosexual" is somewhat misleading. Labeling a person a homosexual or a lesbian tends to make a single aspect of that person's life (i.e., sexual relations) cover their entire life pattern. These are "global" terms in that they identify the totality of the person with only one aspect of his or her social reality. We are unlikely to speak of a nonhomosexual as a "heterosexual." There are homosexual and lesbian people in all walks of life, in business and the professions and in lower, middle and upper socioeconomic positions.

Homosexual men have come to refer to themselves as "gay," while homosexual women generally prefer the term "lesbian" (etymologically derived from the word "Lesbos," an island in the Aegean Sea known in Greek legend for the reputed sensuality of its people). These self-designations have passed into mainstream terminology in public discourse and the media, so in what follows we will use the terms *homosexual, gay* and *lesbian* interchangeably. Until recently, researchers generally have estimated the male homosexual population to be about 5 percent. Research reported in 1993 lowered this percentage to about 2 percent. In one research estimate, between 3 and 6 percent of adult females were reported as exclusively lesbian, although many women have had homosexual encounters during the course of their lives (Hunt 1974).

Sex roles are learned roles; sexuality may be understood within three concepts: sex role adoption, sex role preference and sex role identification. People may, for various reasons, usually of a pragmatic nature, simply adopt the sex-role characteristics of one sex or the other; or they may prefer one sex role over another as more desirable; finally, they may organize their lives around one sex role or another, independently of their actual biological/physiological characteristics. Most persons who engage in homosexual behaviors are not homosexuals in the full sociological sense in that they have consciously and deliberately chosen a sex role identification in variance with their actual physical makeup. They are called *primary deviants* rather than *secondary deviants*. Secondary deviants in this case seek sexual gratification predominantly and continually with members of the same sex. They develop a self-concept and play a homosexual role in connection with these acts. Such persons come to have the *feeling* of being gay or lesbian and accept that reality. In his classic essay on stigma, Goffman limited the term *homosexual* to "individuals who participate in a special community of understanding wherein members of one's own sex are defined as the most desirable sexual objects and sociability is energetically organized around the pursuit and entertainment of these objects" (Goffman 1965).

The learning of the social roles deemed to be gay or lesbian results from having been socialized into the gay or lesbian subculture. One must recognize oneself as homosexual and enter into the stream of homosexual life. In contemporary terms we would say such a person has "come out of the closet" or simply "come out." This self-conception as gay or lesbian is derived in part from the reaction of others, which results in the individual's seeking further associations with the gay or lesbian subculture.

Homosexual identity may also grow in part out of participation in single-sex environments rather than public labeling. Pressures from society tend to push individuals along a four-stage progression, although some individuals do not progress beyond the second stage and others become members of homosexual groups without losing interest in other activities in the mainstream community. The first stage, normally between the ages of 15 and 25, is a period when the individual finds interests other than pursuing the opposite sex with the intention of eventually marrying. The person may or may not be conscious of homosexual tendencies and has yet to come to terms with them. At the second stage, the person is gradually excluded from or withdraws from the company of heterosexuals and may begin to regard himself or herself as an outsider, as different. This is normally a lonely, anxious conflicted and frustrating period in the person's life. The third stage finds the young person meeting others like himself or herself and going to their gathering places and joining in their social activities. At this point, there is no longer a need to conceal one's inner feelings, identifications and inclinations. Most people feel a sense of freedom and relief at this stage, while others may continue to try to hide their true identity from family members or heterosexual friends. At the fourth stage the gay or lesbian person's lifestyle comes to monopolize his or her interest, time and energy. No longer does the person find it necessary to try to reconcile or resolve the conflicts between the outside world and the homosexual lifestyle (Schofield 1965, 181).

It is at this final stage that many gays and lesbians become involved in political activity advocating homosexual causes such as social equality and AIDS research. One such politically influential organization is ACT UP, an acronym for AIDS Coalition To Unleash Power, formerly Action Coalition To Unleash Power; another is the Gay and Lesbian Alliance Against Defamation. These organizations and many of their activities are in opposition to *homophobia,* the extreme negative reaction to (or fear of) homosexuality and/or homosexual people, rooted for the most part in religious taboos and traditions. One national public opinion survey found that 54 percent of those surveyed consider homosexuality an unacceptable lifestyle, presumably for themselves as well as for others. On the other hand, the same survey, however, found that 60 percent approved of gay or lesbian people entering law enforcement, governmental service or the career of an elected official (*Newsweek* 1989). Today's politicians can no longer afford to snub the gay and lesbian community.

For some persons the homosexual relationship may be quite stable; the sexuality is integrated among such "married" couples into long-standing affectionate, personal and social patterns. Many such couples (lesbian for the most part) are currently involved in court cases seeking to adopt children. Most homosexuals, however, tend to be quite promiscuous; the relationships of such people are short-lived and relatively anonymous. Many become acquainted—"encounter one another" is a better phrase—in public places such as public toilets, gay bars, parks, clubs, beaches and movie theaters (Hoffman 1968). A large part of these sex relations are highly impersonal and may be carried out in a "tearoom," a public toilet in which homosexuals meet for sex (Humphreys 1970). It is not unusual in these situations for a third person to act as both voyeur and lookout.

Married persons may engage in both homosexual and heterosexual relations. Sometimes marriage may serve as a "cover-up"; in other cases, both types of sex relations may be enjoyed. Many such persons, while periodically engaging in impersonal homosexual relations, cannot be called "homosexuals" in the sociological sense. The Humphreys study of those who engage in "tearoom trade" showed that the largest group (38 percent) were married or previously married men, largely blue-collar or clerical workers.

Drunkenness

Alcoholism is not a crime, but public drunkenness and drunken driving are crimes. Extreme use of alcohol sets the stage for arrest for public drunkenness and drunk driving. Alcohol has both short-term and long-term effects. Among the former are disinhibition, or the loss of conditioned reflexes due to depression of inhibitory centers of the brain, and the "hangover," the morning-after effect of fatigue, nausea, upset stomach, headache and ill temper. Among the long-term effects are hallucinations, tremors, muscle (heart) disease, and cirrhosis of the liver, which often leads to death (U.S. Department of Health and Human Services 1987).

There is a significant difference in the drinking patterns of men and women in the Unites States as a result of our cultural biases. American culture in general does not allow much room for heavy drinking or alcoholism on the part of women. Women, largely still role-defined as wives and mothers, are seen as society's moral agents and family sustainers. Thus, women who drink excessively are defined by the public as promiscuous and unfit for their traditional female roles. As a result, the social response to women alcoholics has traditionally been silence and there are fewer resources for treatment of females with serious drinking problems.

There is a plethora of literature about wives of alcoholic husbands, but very little about husbands of alcoholic wives. In addition, whereas a man can go to a bar or tavern and have "a drink or two with the guys," women are frequently not allowed as much leeway. As a result, women are under much more pressure to drink alone in the home, and drinking alone is taken as a sign of alcoholism

(Ridlon 1988). But for better or worse, times are changing. In the late 1980s and early 1990s a new class of liquor advertisements began to appear: "She made Law Review. And she drinks Johnnie Walker," brags one man to another at a bar. Or, "Now that you're bringing home the bacon, don't forget the Chivas." Thus speaks America. Moreover, a new ingredient has been added to the picture: Fetal Alcohol Synrome (FAS). Medical researchers have recently found that infants born to drinking mothers run a high probability of being afflicted with FAS, an ailment characterized by facial deformities, growth deficiencies and mental retardation. The severity of FAS seems to be related to the amount of alcohol the mother has consumed during the pregnancy.

There is considerable evidence that a large proportion of those arrested for drunkenness are alcoholics with a long history of prior drunkenness arrests. Recidivism runs very high among this group of offenders; becoming the virtual "career alcoholic," some individuals are arrested for drunkenness up to 20 times a year. In 1989 on the national level, of the 3,170,932 arrests for alcohol-related offenses, 1,326,995 were for driving under the influence, 500,963 were for liquor law violations, 645,137 were for drunkenness, and 674,722 were for disorderly conduct or vagrancy (U.S. Dept. of Justice, *Sourcebook of Criminal Justice Statistics* 1991). The majority of these arrests, particularly of those arrested for driving under the influence, were repeat offenders.

Drunk driving is the most common form of "violent crime" in America, accounting for some 2 million collisions annually, over 700,000 personal damage injuries, over 25,000 deaths, and around $21 billion in property damage (Giesbrecht et al. 1989; National Highway Traffic Safety Administration 1983; Wilson and Mann 1990). Drunk driving is the most frequently prosecuted offense in the lower criminal courts; second and third offenders typically do more time behind bars than do robbers, burglars and larcenists. Attorneys as well as social scientists have called attention to the startling contrast between the surprisingly rapid institutionalization of the anti-drunk driving movement (e.g., MADD, "Mothers Against Drunk Driving") on the one hand, and on the other, the incredibly ambivalent and tolerant nature of public opinion and law enforcement with respect to drinking and driving (Jacobs 1989).

Religious values appear to play a complex role in alcohol use. Drunkenness is seen as a lack of moral strength, willpower and devotion to the goals of personal discipline and work. Religious communities differ in their attitudes and teachings with regard to the use of alcohol. Some religions take an abolitionist stand against alcohol, prohibiting its use altogether. These are known as "proscriptive" religions. Other religious groups permit the use of alcohol, sometimes even in their liturgy. These are known as "nonproscriptive religions." A 1990 study of 8,652 persons, 18 years or older, taken from the General Social Surveys from 1972 to 1986 concluded that "individuals changing from proscriptive to nonproscriptive religions increase their use of alcohol in predictable ways, (while) those changing from nonproscriptive to proscriptive religions moderate their alcohol use" (Beeghley, Bock and Cochran 1990, 275). Of course, antecedent variables are also at work here.

Societal reaction to drunkenness may be expressed through the spouse, employer, work associates, parents, friends, neighbors or church members. Repeated arrests and incarcerations for drunkenness may actually serve to reinforce the deviance rather than correct it (Pittman and Gillespie 1967). Finally, excessive drinking and alcoholism may be perceived by others as extreme deviation. Excessive drinkers may eventually come to think of themselves as problems, and even as alcoholics, but not as criminals even though their drinking may result in frequent arrests. They may well come to refer to themselves as "drunks" and "drunken bums" but not as criminals; increasingly, the more persistent excessive drinkers come to conceive of themselves as alcoholics or persons with an illness calling for medical and psychotherapeutic intervention, whether they actively seek help or not.

Use of Controlled Substances

Drug addiction is learned just as any other behavior is learned, primarily from association with other addicts or through knowledge of its use. An addict must learn the techniques of drug use, how to acquire the drug and how to recognize and appreciate its effects. The use of drugs is one thing; addiction is another. Addiction, as a generic term, is defined as "a condition consisting of periodic or chronic dependence on a drug or several drugs; an insatiable desire to use drugs contrary to legal and/or social prohibitions" (Witters, Venturelli and Hanson 1992, 478). Under closer inspection, the term has a variety of meanings. It is often used to refer to dependence, whether physiological or psychological, or it may be used synonymously with the term *drug abuse*. The traditional addictive drugs are the opiate narcotics: opium, morphine, codeine and heroin. Many people use these drugs over extended periods of time and do not become addicted; others become addicted in a very brief time. Addiction to the narcotics class of drugs is a product of the physical qualities of the drugs and the recognition of the association of the drug with the distress that accompanies sudden cessation of its use.

The elements of drug dependence or addiction generally follow a pattern. If the initial drug experience is unrewarding or aversive, there normally is no further use. A rewarding experience, on the other hand, leads to many trials and consequent positive reinforcement, resulting in primary psychological dependence. Next comes intermittent and chronic abuse of the potent psychoactive drugs: the stimulants—cocaine and its derivative crack, and amphetamines; the hallucinogens—LSD, marijuana or mescaline; the depressants—alcohol, barbiturates or the opium derivatives, heroin and morphine.

In becoming an addict, the individual changes his or her conception of self and of the behavior he or she must engage in as a "drug addict." The more the individual associates with other drug addicts and the drug subculture, the more he or she withdraws from prior social and family relationships. Moreover, the more the person finds that it is impossible to free himself or herself from drug dependence, the more he or she comes to adopt the self-concept and play the social role of an addict (Lindesmith 1968).

In arriving at an empirically grounded answer to the general question "Why do people use heroin and other drugs?" Stephens has developed a "general role theoretic explanation of heroin use." The theory is composed of five propositions from which seven hypotheses are drawn. The propositions are as follows:

Proposition 1. There is a subculture of street addicts.

Proposition 2. Within this subculture, a master (or central) role exists, the components of which are organized about the expected use of heroin.

Proposition 3. This master role, called the street addict role, is an ideal type. That is, no one individual exactly meets all of the role requirements so as to be the consummate street addict. However, this master role is highly valued by members of the subculture, and the more one's behavior approximates the role, the higher one's status is in the subculture.

Proposition 4. The street addict role provides meaningful social and personal rewards to those who play it.

Proposition 5. There are a number of secondary roles in the subculture that are organized around the master role of street addict. These other roles (such as dealer, tout, steerer, etc.) function to maintain the subculture, especially the status of the master role. (Stephens 1991, 42)

Stephens claims that "street addicts" (addicted to heroin) are "rational actors" in that most of them have chosen to become street addicts and to take on the role appropriate to their way of life (Stephens 1991). These addicts are products of those areas where there is little chance to develop successful lives in the outside world. People living in such neighborhoods look upon heroin use as an expressive lifestyle that gives dignity and a sense of belonging and success to many alienated and disenfranchised individuals. He calls such a role a "cool cat syndrome," a favorable attitude toward conning or trickery and an antisocial attitude toward the outside world. The "cool cat" shows little concern or even guilt for his or her actions. Instead, he or she values signs of material success, such as possessing heroin and other drugs. He or she admires and practices an ability to communicate easily in street language and to experience its excitement. The role consists of not believing in long-range planning, in condemning snitching and in minimizing the use of violence. Since the role is modeled on the street addict culture, the addict places a high premium on an ability to con or trick others into providing drugs, cash, food or lodging. Finally, the street addict role involves feelings of persecution in a world largely peopled by persons who cannot be trusted. Such a view of heroin addiction consistently contradicts the widely held position that heroin addiction comes from individualistic physiological or genetic factors, or personality adjustment problems.

Addicts may engage in serious larceny, burglary, petty theft or prostitution in order to support their habit. Even when criminal activities become associated with securing funds to maintain the drug habit, crime does not become an end in itself. Those addicts, juvenile or adult, who engage in other crimes do so chiefly to obtain funds with which to purchase illicit drugs. There is little evidence to indicate that crimes of violence are associated with obtaining drugs. This is in contrast to crimes of violence that are committed while under the influence of one or more drugs. Violence is rampant, however, among competing groups of illegal drug sellers, street gangs and organized crime groups.

Heroin or crack addicts from the lower segments of society live in a world where most drugs are generally acceptable and easily obtainable, and where one's peers typically use more than one drug. This situation differs considerably from that of college and university students who have ready access to marijuana and have peers who use this drug exclusively, except for the addition of some form of alcoholic beverage. Once addicted to a drug like heroin or cocaine, an individual must depend upon a continuous supply; this demand usually becomes the most important single aspect of the person's daily life. While these addicts originally took the drug for pleasure or an effect, most of them soon take it to ward off the pain of withdrawal symptoms. As tolerance is built up and larger and more frequent dosages are needed, the cost may be as high as $100 or $200 a day to support the addiction. Such a daily expenditure involves finances that are greater than most addicts earn or have legitimate access to, which forces the addict to engage in theft or other crimes simply to maintain an adequate supply. Many such addicts begin street corner dealing to support their habits, thus "hooking" still others. And so the cycle grows exponentially. In the case of the street corner dealer and other low-echelon suppliers, it is a common practice to "step on" the drug, that is, dilute it with a neutral substance like milk sugar before selling it down to the next in line. A serious problem arises here. Many street buyers assume the drug is "stepped on," and adjust their dose accordingly. Sometimes, however, it has not been so diluted, and the user winds up overdosing. According to figures released by the New York State Office of Alcoholism and Substance Abuse Services, hospital emergency rooms in the greater New York metropolitan area treated 4,300 people for cocaine abuse in the third quarter of 1991, up from the 3,100 treated in the third quarter of 1990; they treated 2,000 people for heroin abuse in the third quarter of 1991, up from 1,000 treated in the third quarter of 1990 (*New York Times* 1992). This barometer indicates a large increase in cocaine and heroin abuse as a result of a variety of factors, one possibility being the rapid decrease in the street price of these substances.

Use of marijuana requires availability; and there must be testimony as to its positive values as well as an ability to maintain situations for its use without detection by social control agencies. In modern America these preconditions are easily met. A person using marijuana for pleasure must learn to think of the drug as something that can produce pleasurable sensations. For most persons, the first use of marijuana is unrewarding; it is a learned high (Becker 1953). The individual must learn three things: (1) to smoke the drug in a way that will produce certain effects, (2) to recognize the effects and connect the drug with these effects; and (3) to enjoy the felt sensations. When people first use marijuana they do not ordinarily get high. This may be because they do not know the proper technique of drawing on the joint and holding the smoke in the lungs. Even after learning the technique they do not always form an immediate conception of the smoking as being related to pleasure. Even though there are pleasurable sensations, the first-time marijuana user may not be sufficiently aware of the specific nature of the sensations to become a regular user. People learn to feel the sensation of being high as defined by others. With more frequent use, they begin to appreciate the drug's sensations. Finally, a further step is necessary to continue the use of marijuana. The person must learn to enjoy the sensations being experienced. Feeling dizzy, being thirsty, misjudging distances, getting "the munchies" or finding ordinary objects and conversations very amusing may not of *themselves* be pleasurable experiences. The person must learn to define these sensations in this way. Associations with other marijuana users help to turn sensations that were perhaps initially frightening into something pleasurable and to be looked forward to. In a general way it is like learning to define the medicinal taste of whisky as a pleasant tasting beverage.

Marijuana use is closely related to age. Only 4 percent of people who first use it during their twelfth and thirteenth years continue to use it throughout their lives. Lifetime use rates climb sharply higher in successive age groups: 15 percent among the 14- to 15-year-old first users, 30 percent among the 16- to 17-year-old first users, and 64 percent of those who first use it from age 26 to 29. From this peak, lifetime use rates steadily decline until only 8 percent of those who first use marijuana at age 50 or beyond continue using it throughout the remainder of their lives (National Institute on Drug Abuse 1990). The irony here is that, in general, the younger someone experiments with marijuana, the less likely he or she will continue using it for any significant period of time.

Most drug users, whether of hard drugs or marijuana, do not think of themselves as criminals, for they deny the validity of drug laws and consider as wrong the punishment of what should be a matter of individual choice. Widespread support for their views is found among fellow users of the drug and even among segments of the population of nonusers, particularly in the case of marijuana. Persons who use the opiates seldom think of themselves as real criminals because they tend to regard themselves as being in a unique situation when under the influence of a drug. They feel it is because of necessity that they violate the law by using the controlled substances or committing offenses to "support" their habit.

Group Support of Criminal Behavior

Public order offenses such as homosexual behavior, prostitution and drug use grow out of and are deeply immersed in clearly defined deviant subcultures. Others, such as drunkenness, have group support in the drinking patterns of certain social classes and ethnic groups and in the general norms of society that support the drinking of alcoholic beverages.

Prostitution

One method of classsifying prostitutes is according to their methods of operation. As we have seen, there are (1) individual streetwalkers (often referred to as "hookers," a name derived from the camp followers of Union General "Fighting Joe" Hooker during the Civil War) and their pimps, (2) organized houses of prostitution, variously known as brothels, bordellos, red-light houses or massage parlors, (3) "bar girls," known as "B-girls," (4) "call girls" or escort services, and (5) independent prostitutes who may operate out of their own homes. In each of these cases there is an elaborate network of support systems and personnel to teach, foster and nourish the proper values, attitudes and techniques, to provide a steady supply of customers and to collect and equitably distribute the fees. In many cases there is also the need for go-betweens to pay off local law enforcement officials.

In the earlier years of the twentieth century, prostitution was mainly conducted in organized houses. Since prostitution is a business wherein money is made illegally and its practitioners and operators are not likely to go to the police for aid and assistance, these houses were vulnerable targets for extortion by organized crime bosses. Organized crime syndicates (e.g., the Mafia) controlled most of the brothel trade at that time, moving the prostitutes from house to house and city to city as the market dictated. The term "white slave trade" came to be used to designate this practice. Since the 1960s, however, this organizational form was gradually abandoned, and was replaced by the call girl and streetwalker *modus operandi*. Because this form of the trade is extremely decentralized, organized crime found extortion costly and ceased to view prostitution as a major income-generating business.

Prostitution, as any business enterprise, has a continual turnover of workers as prostitutes grow old, contract diseases, drop out of "the life" or move away to new locations. As a result, new girls and women are constantly being recruited. New personnel recruited to work in an organized house of prostitution must be gradually introduced to the rules and regulations, and each new worker soon learns various sex techniques during what amounts to a probationary period. She* learns how to handle large numbers of customers without running the risk of losing them as patrons, how to deal with different types of customers, and above all, how to protect herself against AIDS and other venereal diseases. The call girl, a step higher in the status system, usually depends upon others for recruitment of her patrons. Although she may operate independently and have her own list of patrons who call for her services directly, this is not a common arrangement. More frequently, patrons are secured through the intermediary services of hotel personnel, taxi drivers or other agents who give the potential customer the telephone number used by the prostitute and/or arrange for a hotel or motel room. These people then get their cut of the fee. In the case of "escort service" prostitutes, advertisements may be run in local newpapers and listed in telephone directories, thus giving the business an air of legitimacy. Most forms of prostitution are associated with agents, panderers or pimps who solicit for the prostitutes and live off their earnings. These characters are notorious for their sometimes harsh and violent treatment of the women in their "stables."

Some prostitution is not strictly organized as such, but is knowingly permitted and may even be encouraged through legitimate, but often shady, businesses such as massage parlors, burlesque shows, strip joints, night clubs or amusement parks. At one time there were also "taxi-dance halls," which afforded opportunities for the dime-a-dance girls to make engagements if they wished with their patrons, either in a room hired for the occasion or in the dancer's own room or apartment.

Prostitutes are often indoctrinated into the profession by someone closely associated with it. Usually coming from lower-class backgrounds, they seldom develop a high degree of organization within their occupational group. Its very nature is competitive, each prostitute attempting to build and maintain her own clientele; hence, the personal group solidarity that does exist is mainly for protection from the police or from others who threaten their occupation and income.

---

*For the most part, these are girls and women, but not always, for there are also male prostitutes.

Homosexual Behavior

How an individual becomes a gay or lesbian person in sexual orientation has been the object of an enormous number of theories and empirical studies over the years. Theoretical approaches or "schools" and clinical/empirical research abound. Among the former, there is psychoanalytic theory, based for the most part on the work of Freud (Fine 1985; Freud 1905); neo-Freudian theory (Sternlicht 1987); behaviorist theory (Woolfolk and Richardson 1984); psychobiological theory (Meyer-Bahlburg 1984); and gender role theory (Maffeo 1982; Stoller 1985). Close scrutiny has been given to the childhood period of psychosexual development as well as the adolescent period. Equal attention has been paid to the roles of the family, peers and the community.

Studies of nonclinical homosexual samples indicate that most homosexual people are satisfied with their choice of lifestyle (Bell and Weinberg 1978). A review of the literature demonstrates that there are no clear-cut or identifiable causes of people's sexual object choice (Sultan, Elsner and Smith 1987). Homosexual object choice, however, seems to most frequently coexist with a normal and healthy psychological adjustment (Lewes 1988, 214). A significant portion of homosexuals are satisfied with their homosexuality, show no significant signs of pathology and can function well (Spitzer 1973).

Homosexual experience in and of itself does not make one a homosexual; many adult heterosexual men and women had one or more homosexual experiences as children. The channeling of sexual expression into homosexual patterns must come through some cultural or subcultural definitions, just as do heterosexual relations and behavior patterns. Consequently, our concerns here are with the social and cultural structures that organize and are the focal point of the lives of gays and lesbians.

It appears that younger gay men do not initially identify with each other and are reluctant to have many gay friends, associate with gay couples or enter into emotionally intimate relationships with one another. Many of these people are unconvinced by the rhetoric of the visible gay community and are ambivalent about their social commitments to this community (Harry and DeVall 1978, 49). This hesitancy in becoming socially integrated into the gay community and network makes them outsiders in a community of outsiders, deprived of the potential support and nurturing of like-minded people: "Such gay men are in the community of male homosexuals but not of it, because they hold at a distance other gays as a reference group" (Harry and DeVall, 51). Most juvenile gay males stay in a social and psychological closet until well into adolescence. It is only when they attain the freedom of adulthood that they are able to cast off and reject the heterosexual expectations that society imposes upon them, to "come out" and fashion a lifestyle that is consistent with their sexual identity. The confusion and anxiety of the pre-adult "closet stage" may take anywhere from a year to a lifetime to overcome.

"Marriages" between gay men, as the term is defined in the gay subculture, are highest among men between the ages of 30 to 39 (49 percent) and lowest among the over-40 age group (15 percent). Thirty-six percent of those between 18 and 29 are married. Single gay men in the 18-29 age group constitute 55 percent of all gay men; singles in the 30-39 age group constitute 35 percent of all gay men; and of those over 40 years old, 10 percent are single (Fullerton 1977; Harry and DeVall 1978; Warren 1974).

The existence of a clearly defined gay and lesbian argot has been documented (Farrell 1972; Hayes 1981; Rodgers 1972; Stanley 1970). Homosexuality exists everywhere, but only in certain cultures and under certain conditions does it become structured into a subculture and forced into the official institution of a segregated and oppressed community. For this reason, a homosexual slang has grown out of these ostracized subcultures. As is the case with all specialized language shared by members of a subculture, the linguistic form serves as a group-integrating mechanism, fostering and supporting group solidarity, cohesion and support. Examples of this argot may be seen in words such as the following: *camp, dyke, faggot, drag queen, cruising, come out, closet, straight, butch, femme, basket, clone, rough trade, O.F., panic hour,* and so on (Dynes 1990). Some of this language is absorbed into the larger carrier culture, while some goes unrecognized outside the gay/lesbian community. Also serving a similar subcultural integrating function are many elaborate clothing signals adopted in gay and lesbian communities, ranging from the various displays of a colored bandana to the way in which one laces his or her shoes or in which ear an earring is placed. One student of gay and lesbian life has collected a series of studies and reflections on the subject of gay/lesbian communications systems and titled it *Gayspeak* (Chesebro 1981).

While many homosexual people have chosen to live their lives scattered throughout straight society, others prefer not to. Consequently, the gathering places, neighborhoods of homosexual concentration, social functions and meeting places wherein gays and lesbians live and carry on their lives are multifold (Harry and DeVall 1978). New York city's annual "Halloween Parade" and "Gay Pride Parade" and its West Greenwich Village are well-known examples of homosexual social functions and living places. There exist similar functions and living places in all the major cities in the United States. Knowledge of these events, opportunities and relatively bias-free zones and locales serve the subculture well as both protection from the larger society, much of which is infected with homophobia, and as mechanisms for passing on the subculture from generation to generation.

The Mattachine Society was among the pioneering organizations of homosexual people in the United States devoted to advancing gay liberation and gay rights. Perhaps more than any other single development, the genesis and spread of infection with HIV (the human immunodeficiency virus) and the AIDS epi-

demic in this country has advanced this tradition and fostered solidarity and con-
certed political action in gay and lesbian communities. Advocacy organizations
such as ACT UP (AIDS Coalition to Unleash Power), ACT NOW (AIDS Coalition to Network Organize Win), WIC/MAC (Women's Caucus/Majority Actions
Committee) and others have become part of what is widely referred to as the
Gay Liberation Movement (Goodman 1983). As a result, programs of gay and
lesbian studies have been established in many colleges and universities (Saalfield and Navarro 1991) and a host of gay and lesbian publications—newspapers, newsletters, magazines and scholarly journals—have been produced that
are dedicated solely to homosexual themes, concerns and interests. One of the
most respected of such publications is the *Journal of Homosexuality,* first published in the Fall of 1974 by Hawthorne Press. With a minimum of effort, there
is no gay or lesbian person in the United States who cannot avail himself or
herself of group support and access to a wide variety of homosexual networks
involved in social and political activities.

Drunkenness

There is a very high level of group support for drinking in the United States.
A promotional campaign designed to urge Americans to drink more alcohol
appeared in the early years of the 1990s in popular magazines across the land.
"Isn't it funny," ran one of the blurbs, "how so many of the places we find
Smirnoff, feel like home." Pitches like "This Bud's for you—for all you do," "It
can't get any better than this," "Bass helps you get to the bottom of it," "When
you're having more than one" and other alcohol advertisements in the media
thunder in on the average American. One writer on the role of law enforcement
in alcohol-related crises referred to this as "a barrage of commercial propaganda" (Garner 1979). There is evidence that excessive drinking and alcoholism are
associated with a culture where there is conflict over its use, where children are
not introduced to it early in life and where drinking is largely done outside meals
for personal reasons and not as part of a ritual, ceremony or family celebration.
Such use of alcoholic beverages characterizes a great deal of American behavior.

Earlier studies of "skid row" alcoholics and chronic drunks and "winos"
called attention to the social forces leading to excessive drinking patterns
(Bogue 1963; Kackson and Connor 1953; Peterson, Maxwell and Maxwell
1958; Rubington 1958; Wallace 1968). One researcher commented:

> The major function of these drinking groups . . . is in providing the context,
> social and psychological, for drinking behavior. In reality we have subcommu-
> nities of inebriates organized around one cardinal principle: drinking. The fan-
> tasies concerning the rewards of the drinking experiences are enforced in the

interaction of the members, who mutually support each other in obtaining alcohol and mutually share it. (Wallace 1968)

This observation can no longer be thought of as true only for social derelicts, bums and "bottle gangs." It applies equally to drinking groups such as college students, business associates, professional gatherings and backyard barbecues. In short, this quotation describes mainstream behavior in the United States. The degree of group support for drinking among college students is such that, according to one through-time study of 139 college students, drinking and driving are not deterred very much by the threat of legal punishment (Lanza-Kaduce 1988). Another study of 1,000 randomly selected United States drivers showed the impact of socialization to group norms, especially among beer drinkers, to be so powerful that ". . . perceived risk of arrest and knowledge of the law had no apparent effect on inhibiting drinking-driving violations" (Berger and Snortum 1986, 151).

There has not been a great deal of research on the question of differential drinking patterns among different segments of the American population. It is known, however, that group associations determine the kind of beverage and the amount used, the circumstance under which drinking takes place, the time of drinking and the individual's attitude toward excessive drinking. In the United States, heavy drinking is more common among men than among women, and among Protestants than among Catholics or Jews (Biegel and Chertner 1977; Snyder 1958). Drinking patterns vary by ethnic group: for example, there is less heavy drinking among Italian-Americans than among Irish-Americans (Lolli et al. 1958; Stivers 1976). Excessive drinking appears to be generally higher among African-Americans (Lex 1985), Hispanics (Caetano 1989) and Native Americans (Lemert 1982) than among European Americans. Asian-Americans have the lowest rates of heavy drinkers and alcoholics (Klatsky et al. 1985). Bear in mind, however, that (as is usually the case with these types of generalizations) a series of antecedent variables is at work mediating the conclusions. Nevertheless, there is a very high degree of group support for drunkenness and all that the term implies, both among certain subsets of the American population as well as in the general culture, the media and the alcoholic beverage industries and their advertisers.

Use of Controlled Substances

When we consider the nature and degree of group support for the use of the more widely used illicit drugs of marijuana and cocaine, we find that it is overwhelming, powerful and resistant to change from the outside. Perhaps no other form of criminal behavior has the same intense degree of group support. This generalization is true not only of the disenfranchised segments of American society, but of the financially more fortunate segments of society as well. In fact, this is one of the most frequently advanced arguments for the decriminalization of certain drugs that are currently controlled. Laws making the use of certain drugs a crime, the argument goes, make it more difficult to obtain those drugs, thus throwing those who do use them into a highly bonding mutual dependency in order to obtain them.

These studies reinforce what has been suspected for a long time, namely that the use of drugs is learned primarily from association with others who also use drugs. Most persons are initiated into the use of controlled substances by friends, siblings, significant adult role models and marital partners. In these close relationships people not only learn how to use drugs and appreciate them but they also learn a series of positive beliefs about the benefits of drugs—beliefs that others help to reinforce constantly. Perhaps most important of all from a practical viewpoint, they learn how to *obtain* the controlled substances in the first place—at the lowest risk. ("There's a great little bodega down on X street where they have great stuff for a dime, and you're never hassled.")

What Goode reported some time back, regarding the use of marijuana as a group activity lending itself to friendships and participation in a group setting, remains as true today as it did when he wrote it:

> 1) It is characteristically participated in in a group setting; (2) the others with whom one smokes marijuana are usually intimates, intimates of intimates, or potential intimates, rather than strangers; (3) one generally has long-term con-tinuing social relations with the others; (4) a certain degree of value consensus will obtain within the group; (5) a value convergence will occur as a result of progressive group involvement; (6) the activity maintains the circle's cohesion, reaffirms its social bonds by acting them out; (7) participants view the activity as a legitimate basis for identity—they define themselves, as well as others, partly on the basis of whether they have participated in the activity or not. (Goode 1969, 54)

One study of 1,222 young adults at three different points in time—adoles-cence, young adulthood and adulthood—found strong support for cultural deviance theory, that is, deviant individuals are very similar to nondeviants in their social relationships and have strong ties with members of their friendship networks. "Few differences were found in the characteristics of friendship net-works of illicit drug users and nonusers. Where differences were observed, the frequent users tended to have *more* intimate friendships than other young adults, which supports the cultural deviance perspective" (Kandel and Davies 1991, 441). The study also revealed that use of controlled substances, ranging from marijuana to heroin, predicts substantially higher levels of intimacy among males, where intimacy is defined both in terms of confiding in or interacting with friends. The policy conclusion is that these strong and mutually supportive social ties make it very difficult to develop effective intervention strategies. In addition, the careless interchange of needles in heroin use is a major mode of transmitting the HIV virus.

A Detroit field study of 15 street-level heroin dealers uncovered the group nature and social relationship that develops over time between adult syndicate executives in illicit drug distribution bureaucracies and their young street operatives. With the development of the "runner system," a series of close, mutually interdependent relationships is fostered between minors and adults involved in the drug trade. The runner system is an organized, cooperative strategy for selling heroin in public places (e.g., curbsides and areas in front of small grocery stores, take-out food operations, playgrounds, parks, schoolyards, etc.). It is designed to market heroin through the use of individual participants who are organized into a rational system of division of labor. In the course of this cooperative interaction, in accordance with accepted rules, not only is heroin sold relatively risk-free, but mutual dependencies and support networks are fostered (Mieczkowski 1986). In the course of operating this distribution network, not only are minors introduced to the use of various, multiple controlled substances, but they find that they can make a great deal of money as well.

An Arizona study of drug use and sibling influence among 135 brother pairs, 142 sister pairs and 141 mixed-sex pairs found a high degree of group support for use of controlled substances, principally marijuana, between siblings and their friends. Specifically, siblings are embedded in a common friendship network. Sibling mutual interaction characterized by warmth and frequency of contact with mutual friends was found to condition the behavioral resemblance of the younger and older sibling, especially with regard to the use of controlled substances. The study found that same-sex siblings who have "a greater frequency of contact with mutual friends were more alike than other siblings in delinquency and substance use" (Rowe and Gulley 1992, 231).

A study based on data drawn from the "Monitoring the Future" project, which uses large, nationally representative samples of high school seniors surveyed annually by the University of Michigan's Survey Research Center, addressed the role of racial and ethnic differences in adolescent drug use and the impact of background and lifestyle. Here again, the force of group support emerges as a powerful factor. It found that several lifestyle factors—educational values and time spent in peer-oriented activities—strongly relate to drug use and help to explain subgroup variations in drug use by adolescents. It concluded that "the most powerful lifestyle predictors [current frequencies of truancy and of evenings out for fun and recreation], are . . . both causes and consequences of drug use. [They] are not, however, nearly as closely related to drug use as the most proximal lifestyle variables such as peer drug use and perceived risk" (Wallace and Bachman 1991, 348).

In the United States the role of advertising drugs in the electronic and print media provides further evidence of powerful group support for drug use, if not necessarily for the use of *controlled* drugs. But people are not always acutely conscious of the distinctions and differences between the two types of drugs: over-the-counter (OTC) drugs and illegal drugs. Pushing one subtly fosters use of the other. The media are literally saturated with advertisements for OTC drugs that promise relief from whatever illness or discomfort the audience may experience. We are inundated with ads for drugs that will induce sleep or stave off sleep, for treating indigestion, headaches, tension, constipation, diarrhea, depression, energy levels, and so on. The message here is clear but subtle, thus making it all the more insidious: if you are experiencing some undesirable physical or emotional symptoms, taking drugs is acceptable. Furthermore, studies have found that most youthful drug users are from homes and families in which OTC drugs (coffee, tobacco, analgesics, diet aids, skin products, allergy remedies, stress tabs, medicinal syrups, vitamins, tablets, "night-caps," etc.) are used frequently and plentifully (Coombs 1988).

We will be looking at the illegal drug industry more closely under the headings of other criminal behavior systems later in this book, but for now, in connection with group support of drug use, it is useful to bear in mind that the illegal drug trade in this country alone has been estimated to be a $90 billion a year industry, ranking second in yearly earnings to Exxon and just above General Motors and Mobile Oil. This fact in and of itself serves as proof of the extensive, albeit illegal, support of the use of controlled substances in America. It is a system wherein addicted persons as well as casual users continually recruit new members in order to both sell and obtain drugs. There are also defensive communication systems with their own argot for drugs, suppliers and drug users and various warning systems by which addicts and sellers are protected by others. The support of drug habits requires a complex distribution network of controlled substances. This is what the so-called "Panama Connection" involving the Noriega government and many officials in our own government is about: getting the goods to the consumer. Controlled substances can be imported or produced domestically, either in the clandestine laboratory on in the open field. This import-domestic, production-wholesale distribution industry is largely run through both legitimate and illegitimate groups—organized crime syndicates as well as other highly organized and legitimate structures. This constitutes group support at the highest level, for it is a support system that provides the user with that which he or she uses. A crack cocaine street dealer in St. Louis, Missouri speaks: "They're not winning the drug war. There's never a shortage of cocaine in this city. They could lock up a thousand brothers, even 10,000 brothers. There's always going to be someone new out here selling. . . . There's nothing else to do: no type of recreation, no work, nothing" (Treaster 1992b).

Correspondence between Criminal and Legitimate Behavior

It is difficult to differentiate the goals and general life orientations of homosexual and heterosexual people except in the means of sex gratification. Likewise, except for those who are highly involved in their way of life, prostitutes, users of illegal drugs and excessive drinkers are probably not much different in their attitudes toward the general goals of society from those who are not so engaged. Where the behavior becomes more fully an important part of the individual's life organization and there is a degree of isolation from conventional society, however, such offenders may become more committed to the goals of a deviant subgroup, such as the subculture of drug addicted or homosexual people, and less to more conventional values.

Most of the behavior of public order offenders is consistent with legitimate behavior patterns. The prostitute's behavior is a commercial occupation with the same goal of most other occupations: making money. Homosexual people, while deriving satisfaction in a different way, are engaging in what is widely practiced sex behavior. Such a person is involved in a local community of friendships. A drunken person is participating in the generally approved behavior for adults, that is, the drinking of alcoholic beverages.

The use of drugs such as heroin, cocaine and marijuana, while legally and officially disapproved of, has its counterparts in the frequent use of legitimate drugs such as alcohol, tobacco, tranquilizers for relaxation, barbiturates for sleeping and relaxation, and other minor drugs such as aspirin. Coffee and tea are also drug stimulants that can have considerable effect when consumed regularly in large quantities. Some idea of the widescale use of the more accepted drugs is indicated by the fact that well over 1 million pounds of barbiturate derivatives are manufactured each year in the United States, or the equivalent of 24 half-grain doses for each person in the country, enough to kill each person twice over. Years ago criminologist George Vold indicated that in many of these public order offenses, as in the United States, there are economic and cultural considerations common to the general society (Vold 1958). In such offenses as drunkenness, narcotic addiction and prostitution, commercial gain plays a prominent role. Prostitution is an economic commodity: the sale of sex. A huge economic interest enters the production and sale of alcoholic beverages and tobacco, and there are large financial gains resulting from the illegitimate sale of narcotics. The illegal behavior represents an occupation for many of the offenders in this group. Prostitution is a "job" as much as any other. There are even opportunities to develop a degree of professional skill with resulting status among one's associates, i.e., a career pattern.

In sum, it may be argued very plausibly that the forms of behavior we have been discussing in this chapter are but phantom images, or a subterranean acting-out of what we like to call "normal" behavior. As such, public order criminal behavior is not all that different from "what the rest of us do" than we would like to think. This will be discussed further when we consider the issue of decriminalization of public order offenses at the end of this chapter.

Societal Reaction and Legal Processing

As was pointed out at the beginning of this chapter, public order offenses are numerous. They constitute behavior defined by law as contrary to the system of morals or the standards of proper conduct for an individual. Yet for the most part the condemnation is not strong. Prostitutes, when arrested, normally are booked, held overnight and released the following day with a small fine. Only when specific interest groups press for the enforcement of the law are they driven from an area. Anti-homosexual laws are seldom enforced unless there is organized pressure resulting from what some in the community regard as a "public nuisance," and penalties are seldom severe. With the exception of drunk driving, drunkenness is widely tolerated and in the event of an arrest, the penalties are mild. The media uses the theme of "the drunk" to entertain us. And drug addiction is no longer thought of as calling primarily for a law enforcement response, but rather for medical/psychotherapeutic intervention. The use of marijuana, or even cocaine, for recreational purposes is seldom a matter for individual arrest and prosecution. The possession or sale of substantial amounts of drugs, and the combination of drug use and the commission of other, more serious, crimes, however, does call down a strong public and law enforcement response.

Times change and our values and moral standards change with them. The behavior involved in public order offenses reflects, in part, the changing definitions of what is and what is not proper behavior and also the extent to which the political state can rightfully and effectively intervene to support the morals and practices of some and condemn the morals and practices of others. As Vold has pointed out, blasphemy and heresy were once condemned in the interest of private and public morality and were severely prosecuted as criminal offenses. "Both of these have disappeared from the categories of crimes calling for police control in the world of today, though both types of behavior persist in the community. But ideas and events in the world at large have changed and we no longer seek to make men religious by law and police action. Could it be that we may be in the process of a similar transformation in the matter of control of personal habits and morality represented by these categories of petty crime, as they appear in the American world of today?" (Vold 1958, 148). In other parts of the modern world many of these public order offenses are not considered to be crimes, while in yet other cultures they are severely punished. For example, the blasphemy of invoking the name of "Allah" or desecrating the sacred Koran merits death in some countries.

Public order crimes represent efforts to control certain moral and personal behavior through laws, often without attempts to mold public opinion to support the legislative and police activity. Undoubtedly, only a small proportion of those who commit these offenses are actually ever apprehended. Indeed, there is a dilemma regarding criminal action against such behavior as prostitution, drunkenness, drug use and homosexual behavior. And there is the further question of economics. Many argue persuasively that the costs of criminalization are two-fold: first is the tremendous cost incurred by the state in enforcing laws that seek to control these behaviors; and second is the loss of tax revenues that would occur if selected controlled substances were de-criminalized and a tax levied on their purchase.

Prostitution

The practice of commercializing sex—using sex to sell commodities—is deeply ingrained in American culture. However, the the practice of *selling* sex (that is, prostitution) summons up a deep ambivalence. Attitudes toward prostitution have varied historically, and today they differ widely by country and region of country. Some persons in the United States are willing to tolerate it as necessary. These people feel that if certain urban areas were set aside specifically for prostitutes, they could be regularly inspected for AIDS and other sexually transmitted diseases. In fact, the relatively recent explosion of the AIDS epidemic, and the positive HIV testing that signals the eventual onset of this disease, have created an unprecedented amount of caution on the part of those who regularly seek the services of prostitutes. To many supporters of the movement for women's equality, prostitution is but one more symbol of women's enslavement to men. Prostitution is opposed because of (1) the degradation of the women who engage in it; (2) the effect on general law enforcement through police protection; (3) the effect on marital relations where recourse is had to prostitutes, and the consequent fear of infection with HIV; and (4) the patronage of prostitutes by young persons and its effect on national values, a nebulous and ambiguous phrase.

A Toledo, Ohio, study of public attitudes toward prostitution found a wide degree of tolerance. The study was based on a random sample of 413 adults drawn from the Greater Toledo Survey by the Population and Society Research Center at Bowling Green State University (McCaghy and Cernkovich 1991). The median age of the sample was 38 years; whites constituted 92 percent of the sample; 66 percent were women. The study found that the respondents' views regarding prostitution are consistent with those that have been found by other surveys. That is, the majority does not define the offense as serious enough to warrant harsh sanctions, and sizable minorities at least would consider alternatives to supression. With regard to outright suppression as a policy alternative, 69 percent of the respondents disagreed that the law should severely punish prostitutes and 54 percent disagreed that the law should severely punish customers. As for toleration, 43 percent agreed that the police should enforce laws against prostitution only if it is a nuisance to a neighborhood. The statement "prostitution should be legal but under government control with special health and licensing requirements" was agreed with by 44 percent of the respondents, but 95 percent disagreed with the proposition that "Prostitution should be legal like any other business with no special government controls." Of course, it is important to note that there is no business that is *not* subject to some government controls.

A historical case study of the politics of prostitution in America throws light on the links between the prostitution economy, gender ideology and labor markets. The study shows "how essentially contested prostitution policy has been over the last century and a half, and . . . [that] the differences go to the heart not only of a society's organization of class and gender but also of the state's role in regulating morals and markets" (Hobson 1988, 3). What is of note also is the fact that those who supported reform in the past included middle-class women who considered prostitution to be an expression of class and gender inequalities. For them, the problem was male dominance and the appropriate response was controlling male sexual behavior and protecting women. "Beyond that, some see prostitution as a way to economic independence and a means for women to control their own sexuality, while others see it as sexual slavery" (Tilly 1989, 491).

Another study gives us a historical overview of the interrelationship of class, culture and campaigns against prostitution and other forms of vice in American cities in the latter part of the nineteenth century (Beisel 1990). The argument is that moral reform movements are a form of class politics. Indeed, it was normally the upper classes that initiated and supported these anti-vice movements.

The prostitute frequently is arrested as the result of solicitation by the police or a "lure" provided by the police. Sometimes informers are used to locate the rooms being used. In order to "buy" her way out of an arrest a prostitute may offer to serve as an informant in the apprehension of her pimp or a drug dealer. Even the threat of a "quarantine hold" for medical examination is used to control the behavior of a prostitute during arrest and to provide sources for apprehending more serious criminals. All these tactics, plus the periodic "crackdowns," are to the prostitute what being laid off temporarily is to other workers.

In several revised state penal codes, with Illinois, Wisconsin and New York leading the way, the patrons (or "johns") as well as the prostitutes have been made subject to criminal prosecution. A study in New York City showed, however, that of 508 convicted dispositions only 0.8 percent were for patronizing a prostitute (Roby 1969). The police generally ignored the patrons; when they were arrested their names were rarely made public in the print or electronic media. Most arrests were of streetwalkers. The high-priced call girls and their patrons were also generally ignored. It appears that streetwalkers and their customers are not only the most visible and vulnerable, but also rank lowest in social prestige.

Homosexual Behavior

As in the case of prostitution, public attitudes toward homosexual people and their way of life have differed from one period in history to another and from one culture to another. Homosexual behavior was prevalent, for example, in ancient Greek and Roman societies. It was more or less taken for granted and of no special note. In some societies homosexual practices were related to certain religious rites. In fact, among the armed forces of ancient Athens and Sparta not to have a male lover was widely regarded as traitorous, for such male bonds were looked on as fostering an increase in group loyalty: one sacrifices one's life in battle for a lover more readily than for a comrade in arms. A great deal of the negative attitudes in parts of Western society toward homosexuality can be explained by certain aspects of the Christian tradition (Bailey 1955). The early Christian hierarchy preached that homosexual behavior was a sin, and in the Middle Ages the ecclesiastical courts imposed harsh penalties, including torture and death. Much of contemporary public opposition to homosexual acts stems from a belief that they are "unnatural" in the sense that they contradict the law of the creator, whose sole intent in giving human beings sexual organs was that they should be used for procreation only.

Today in the United States people's reactions to homosexuality are conditioned by subcultural and situational factors. The processes by which people come to be defined as homosexuals are contingent upon the varying interpretation of others and the treatment as a result of this definition. Interpretation of homosexuality may result in several different societal reactions by heterosexuals. These may be: (1) explicit disapproval and immediate withdrawal of relationships, (2) explicit disapproval and subsequent withdrawal, or (3) a "live and let live" response.

In addition, the reaction may be homophobic and violent. Frequently social institutions play leading roles in suppressing discourse on gay and lesbian issues and supporting violence against them. Data gathered from police reports, media reports and surveys done by various organizations like the National Gay and Lesbian Task Force show that "[p]erpetrators are not only predominantly male and white, but just as likely, or even more likely, to be middle class . . . good in their classes, popular, friendly, and sociable" (Comstock 1991, 106). The ambivalence of institutions such as the family, the criminal justice system and the churches toward lesbians and gays has contributed to their vulnerability to physical violence. Furthermore, patriarchy has been singled out by some as causative factors in "gay bashing." Here the argument is that homosexuality constitutes a threat to male sex hegemony.

In reality, very few people are taken into custody for homosexual acts, and courts and juries tend to be lenient toward the few offenders who are. In most segments of American society considerable reliance is placed on the shame or stigma that will result from the apprehension. Apprehension is difficult in any case because there is generally no complaining witness and because such acts occur largely in private. There are vigorous police enforcement campaigns now and then where the acts (e.g., public solicitation) become more visible. For example, a secret police videotape surveillance operation over a 10-day period at a highway rest area in Michigan resulted in the arrest of 42 men for homosexual acts (Barlow 1990, 375). Perhaps more than punishing the behavior and the homosexual persons involved, the long-term result of such operations is to show other homosexuals where to go for contacts. Even with felony statutes in effect in most states under the general aegis of sodomy laws, most criminal justice officials handle these offenses under misdemeanor charges, perhaps because of leniency and tolerance or because misdemeanor laws are easier and cheaper to apply (Weinberg and Williams 1975).

As with prostitution, but even more strongly with homosexuality, the AIDS epidemic has prompted greater attention to homosexuality. One representative study of 301 gay men found that the proportion reporting unsafe sexual practices had decreased, largely as a result of public education. Still, an uncomfortable 36 percent of these men claimed that they had had more than one sexual partner during the past month (Barlow 1990).

The political activity of the police in the form of raids on gay bars or other homosexual groups, or in arrests for sex acts in public places like parks or toilets, only tends to unify homosexual people; and homosexual advocacy groups give maximum coverage to police harassment in their publications. This potential threat of harassment is real to homosexual people even though not carried out often. It has a chilling effect on their lives. The threat of exposure has also been a source of blackmail of homosexual people in high places, such as political figures, church leaders and leading professionals.

Drunkenness

Although the consumption of alcohol may bring pleasure and relaxation to millions, its social role is perceived by different observers as a blessing or a curse. In spite of the vast amount of research that has shown the involvement of alcohol in countless injuries, diseases and crimes, the precise nature of the relationship remains problematic and quantitatively unpredictable. In research dealing with diseases, accidents or criminal violence, all that is known for certain is that only in a variable proportion of cases is alcohol involved. The proportion of involvement is often quite high, however.

Of further consideration here is the empirical evidence that there are important cross-national, regional and situational variations in the role of alcohol in casualties. Different sectors of any population run different risks of alcohol-related casualties. Studies have shown that young adult males have a high proportion of drinking-related accidents and violent crime; older people have drinking and falls; chronic heavy drinkers have drunken driving accidents; middle-aged men and women have suicides. But the relative risk based on the frequency of the activity in relationship to consumption of alcohol may show different findings. As has been stated, these relationships are complex, dynamic and non-linear (Roizen 1982).

If excessive drinking is continued over long periods of time the individual may increasingly become involved in difficulties that arise from the drunkenness itself. People may lose spouses and jobs. They may be ostracized by neighbors and friends. The Protestant ethic may play an important role in the attitudes of others because drunkenness is regarded as a lack of moral strength, of devotion to the goals of personal discipline, of willpower and of dedication to work. The excessive drinker who becomes an alcoholic is sometimes the chronic drunkenness offender before the courts. Such a person may, with increasing frequency, be arrested and jailed. The irony is that drinking may become a way of getting away from the societal reaction to problems caused by the drinking itself: problems caused by drinking can be faced only through more excessive drinking, which in turn leads to more arrests for public order disturbances. Final rejection is taking up a life of social ostracism.

Drunkenness offenders are usually brought before a judge or magistrate the morning following arrest, often appearing with groups of 15 to 20 or more others. There are few due process safeguards and the arrestees are hurried through the court process. Persons arrested and held for prosecution for drunkenness alone almost never have legal representation; according to FBI statistics over the years, they are almost always found guilty, normally as a result of entering a guilty plea.

Since most drunkenness offenders receive short sentences, they are simply fed, sheltered and given some recreation; there is little or no treatment within the context of the criminal justice system. After serving the sentence, the drunken offender, most often an alcoholic and in some cases also a mentally ill person, simply returns to his or her former haunts with no money or job and is often rearrested within days, perhaps even hours (Spradley 1970). It is a relatively uncontested proposition, particularly among law enforcement personnel, that the criminal justice apparatus is not an effective way to control either drunkenness or the involvement of alcohol in crimes of violence.

The administration of public intoxication laws does not affect most middle- and upper-class excessive drinkers and alcoholics who have a home and can drink in private and semiprivate conditions without disturbing others. Law enforcement in this case discriminates against the homeless and the poor. Evidence also suggests that some persons in the lower class feel the brunt of the law more than do others.

Use of Controlled Substances

The societal reaction and legal processing of drug suppliers and drug users may be summed up in one bellicose phrase: the "war on drugs." In this "war," which was launched under the Reagan administration in the 1980s, cocaine eradication has received top priority, but cocaine is by no means the only target drug. In the 10-year period between 1978 and 1988 the United States experienced the largest cocaine "epidemic" in history, an epidemic related to a whole range of antisocial and criminal activities. This "get tough" stance and all the slogans, from the simplistic "Just Say No" to "This Is Your Brain on Drugs" (a favorite of the alcohol and tobacco industries' assault on controlled substances), reflect the perspective of a citizenry and its political leadership that has been victimized by escalating drug-related crime and personally touched by drug tragedies in families, in the workplace or among friends (Witters, Venturelli and Hanson 1992). The "war on drugs" resulted in the Anti-Drug Abuse Act of 1988. By 1990 the entire program directed by the Office of National Drug Control Policy had an estimated budget of $6.5 billion (Halloway 1991).

According to a 1990 Law Enforcement Management and Administrative Statistics (LEMAS) report, more than 16,000 local police and sheriffs' officers and over 2,000 state police officers nationwide were assigned full-time to special drug units. Further, it was reported that about half of local police and sheriffs' departments with primary drug enforcement responsibilities were taking part in a multiagency drug enforcement task force. These 6,500 agencies had assigned nearly 10,000 officers full-time to such task forces. Two out of every three state police departments and two out of five local police and sherrifs' departments reported that at least some of the persons they arrested were required to take a test for illegal drugs (Reaves 1990).

Extreme measures have been employed in this effort through the 1980s into the early 1990s, but the effort has been seen as a failure by many experts in the field. The entire arsenal of weapons has been thrown into the fight: eradication of marijuana and cocaine crops in Colombia and Bolivia through aerofumigation with the deadly pesticide paraquat and other chemical herbicides; border interdiction of illegal drug shipments to the United States from foreign countries; seizure of assets ranging from yachts to automobiles wherein even as little as one marijuana "roach" (butt) is found; the involvement of Immigration and Customs officials; the use of United States troops to assist and train antinarcotic forces in Bolivia, Mexico and Colombia; and even a war on the small nation-state of Panama in order to bring General Noriega to trial in the United States on the charge of drug trafficking. The frenzy of these efforts has led some critics to label the "war on drugs" a transnational crime of broad scope that can be called *ecobiogenocide* (del Olmo 1987).

Legal sanctions for those involved in the international drug traffic are severe. So are sanctions for importers, distributors and sellers of controlled substances within the territorial borders of the United States harsh and unyielding. As a result, the demand for more and more prison cells has exploded across the country. For example, in New York State alone, according to figures released by the New York State Department of Correctional Services, the percent of overcapacity of its prisons rose dramatically from 6.1 percent overcapacity in 1984 to 19.6 percent overcapacity in 1991. The percentage of all inmates convicted on drug charges rose correspondingly from 15.3 percent in 1984 to 44.7 percent in 1991 (*New York Times,* February 1992).

The Fourth Amendment to the Constitution deals with the rights of people to be secure in their persons, houses, papers and effects "against unreasonable searches and seizures." Such searches and seizures can be legalized only through the issuance of a warrant if the searches involved "probable cause." The latter, in the enforcement of drug laws, often goes well beyond the real legal interpretation to illegal search and seizure (Chevigny 1969). Some of these involve frequent routine searches on the street and the search of private premises. In fact, in 1970 Congress adopted a "no knock" provision to facilitate drug apprehension. Intrusions may be made to gain evidence for prosecution procedures; sometimes they are made for investigation, harassment or the collection of contraband.

At the street level of distribution, various methods have been and continue to be used to entrap drug sellers: the use of other drug users and prostitutes as informants, various "inside" and "outside" buying situations and strategies, "stake-out" operations and the use of marked money (Skolnick 1966). By being informants individuals protect their own drug supplies or avoid arrest. Entire police precincts and departments are being corrupted with drug money as a result of these and other strategies. Again, informed critics and authorities have by and large declared these low-level tactics a failure in reducing the flow of drugs to an increasingly eager and lucrative market.

Decriminalization of Public Order Offenses

The problem of public order crimes has become so difficult that there has been serious discussion of eliminating or "decriminalizing" public drunkenness, gambling, the use of controlled substances, homosexual offenses and prostitution on the grounds that these crimes constitute an "overreach of the criminal law." These offenses however would remain crimes if committed against persons under a certain age, if more than a certain quantity of drugs were possessed (presumably for sale) and if an injury to someone has taken place in connection with intoxication. However, there is ongoing debate over these points. It is not as if the decriminalization of certain behaviors is a new concept or action in the history of the United States. The two best known instances—the decriminalization of the manufacture, sale and use of alcoholic beverages, known as the 1934 repeal of Prohibition, and the decriminalization of abortion by the *Roe v. Wade* decision in 1973—both resulted from intensive organizing and political pressure by activist groups. The repeal of Prohibition was widely acclaimed for a variety of reasons, not the least of which was that it reduced corruption of police and high-level political officials. One decriminalization was the result of legislative action on the federal level and the other was the result of a judicial decision handed down by the Supreme Court.

In reality, the decriminalization of selected controlled substances has already occurred, albeit in a piecemeal fashion. As far back as 1973 the state of Oregon began to treat marijuana possession as a misdemeanor punishable by a small monetary fine, and by 1984, 10 other states had followed Oregon's example (Goode 1984). In the 1980s some segments of the conservative intelligentsia joined forces with many liberals to argue that prohibitive drug laws are no match for the law of supply and demand, and that the government should stop trying to impose the moral beliefs of some upon others (Gravely 1988). The legalization of heroin has been urged on the grounds that it is less destructive physically, socially and psychologically than is alcohol (Reiman 1984).

The decriminalization of consensual homosexual acts has been forcefully advanced on the grounds of the constitutional right to privacy. The case for decriminalization of prostitution has been argued on the grounds that "the criminalization of prostitution appears to be an illegitimate vindication of unjust social hatred and fear of autonomously sexual women, and their rights to define and pursue their own vision of the good" (Richards 1982, 121). Three alternatives to criminalization of prostitution are licensing; regulations of place, time and methods; and the elimination of all regulations.

The arguments for the elimination of public order offenses can be summarized as follows: (1) such acts should not be the concern of the state, (2) the interference of the political state makes matters worse, for "where the supply of goods and services is concerned, such as narcotics, gambling, and prostitution, the criminal law operates as a 'crime tariff' which makes the supply of such goods and services profitable for the criminal by driving up prices and at the same time discourages competition by those who might enter the market were it legal" (Morris and Hawkins 1970), (3) little is accomplished by such crime control because it is ineffective against the behavior of people who are favorably disposed to the behavior, and (4) the legal processing of the offenses seriously interferes with a justice system that is already insufficient and intolerably overburdened almost to the point of collapse. According to estimates by the Federal Bureau of Investigation, the estimated number of arrests in 1989 for public order crimes in the United States was 3,074,300 (U.S. Dept. of Justice, Federal Bureau of Investigation 1990). Arrests for public order crimes in this context include: prostitution and commercialized vice, drug abuse violations, gambling, homosexual acts, public drunkenness and violations of liquor laws. All this effort has proven largely impotent in the elimination of such behaviors. In fact, it may even be counterproductive.

Many authorities and groups have recommended that drug addiction be regarded as a medical or social problem, as it is in some other countries. If providing affordable treatment for drug users and devising more creative legal solutions to drug problems is successful, addicts would not have to turn to crime to get their drugs (Trebach 1987). It has been suggested that greater controls on currently legal drugs such as alcohol and tobacco, be put in place and that such measures be replicated in the control of drugs that are currently illegal. There also has been a fairly strong movement for the legalization of marijuana use.

The inclusion of public order offenses in the criminal code has other important consequences of a negative nature. Many persons are driven into associations with others who are already well-established in the subculture of criminality. It is particularly in the areas of prostitution, controlled substances and gambling that police and political officials are corrupted. Organized crime gains enormous profits from drugs in particular, and to a lesser extent, from gambling and prostitution.

The public debate over criminalization versus decriminalization of public order crimes is a healthy exercise, and it is certain to continue well into the future. The real changes will come about only when there is sufficient public pressure and political pressure brought to bear on the courts and the legislative bodies (elected officials) across the country to effect change. The sooner some changes in existing criminal law are effected, the sooner our criminal justice system will become more efficient and less subject to the temptations of corruption and the sooner the range of personal choices will be expanded.

References

Associated Press (1991). "Alcohol Deaths Stopped Declining." *Boston Globe* (January 27): 8.

Bailey, David S. (1955). *Homosexuality and the Western Christian Tradition*. New York: David McKay.

Barlow, Hugh D. (1990). *Introduction to Criminology*. Glenview, IL: Scott, Foresman.

*Barry, Kathleen (1984). *Female Sexual Slavery*. New York: New York University Press.

*Becker, Howard S. (1953). "Becoming a Marijuana User." *American Journal of Sociology* 59:235-242.

*Beeghley, Leonard, W. Wilbur Bock, and John K. Cochran (1990). "Religious Change and Alcohol Use: An Application of Reference Group and Socialization Theory." *Sociological Forum* 5 (2): 261-278.

Beisel, Nicola (1990). "Class, Culture, and Campaigns Against Vice in Three American Cities, 1872-1892." *American Sociological Review* 55 (1): 44-62.

Bell, A.P., and Martin S. Weinberg (1978). *Homosexualities*. New York: Simon & Schuster.

*Berger, Dale E., and John R. Snortum (1986). "A Structural Model of Drinking and Driving: Alcohol Consumption, Social Norms, and Moral Commitments." *Criminology* 24 (1): 139-153.

Biegel, Allan and Stuart Chertner (1977). "Toward a Social Model: An Assessment of Social Factors Which Influence Problem Drinking and Its Treatment." In Kassin, Benjamin, and Genri Geglieter, eds., *Treatment and Rehabilitation of the Chronic Alcoholic*. New York: Plenum Press, 197-233.

Bogue, Donald (1963). *Skid Row*. Chicago: University of Chicago Press.

Brounstein, Paul J., H. Hatry, David M. Altschuler, and L. Blair (1989). *Patterns of Drug Use and Delinquency among Inner-City Adolescent Males*. Washington, DC: Urban Institute Press.

Brundage, James A. (1988). *Law, Sex, and Christian Society in Medievel Europe*. Chicago: University of Chicago Press.

Bryan, James H. (1965). "Apprenticeships in Prostitution." *Social Problems* 12 (4): 287-296.

Butler, Josephine E. (1976). *Personal Reminiscences of a Great Crusade*. Westport, CT: Hyperion Press.

Caetano, Raul (1989). "Drinking Patterns and Alcohol Problems in a National Sample of U.S. Hispanics." In *The Epidemiology of Alcohol Use and Abuse among U.S. Minorities*. National Institute of Alcohol Abuse and Alcoholism. Washington, DC: U.S. Government Printing Office.

Centers for Disease Control (1985). "Morbidity and Mortality." *Weekly Report*, October 11: 613-618.

Chesebro, James W. (1981). *Gayspeak: Gay Male and Lesbian Communication*. New York: Pilgrim Press.

Chevigny, Paul (1969). *Police Power: Police Abuses in New York City.* New York: Vintage Books, Random House.

Cochran, John K., Leonard Beeghley, and E. Wilbur Bock (1988). "Religiosity and Alcohol Behavior: An Exploration of Reference Group Theory." *Sociological Forum* 3:256-276.

*Comstock, David Gary (1991). *Violence against Lesbians and Gay Men.* New York: Columbia University Press.

*Coombs, R.H., ed. (1988). *The Family Context of Adolescent Drug Use.* New York: Haworth.

Davis, Sally (1982). "Driving under the Influence: California Public Opinion, 1981." *Abstracts & Reviews in Alcohol & Driving* 3:3-8.

del Olmo, Rosa (1987). "Aerobiology and the War on Drugs: A Transnational Crime." *Crime and Social Justice* 30:28-44.

Dynes, Wayne, ed. (1990). *Encyclopedia of Homosexuality.* New York: Garland.

Farrell, Ronald A. (1972). "The Argot of the Homosexual Subculture." *Anthropological Linguistics* 14:97-109.

Fine, Reuben (1985). *The Meaning of Love in Human Experience.* New York: John Wiley.

Freud, Sigmund (1905). *Three Essays on Sexuality.* In *Male and Female Homosexuality: Psychological Approaches,* edited by Louis Diamant. Washington, DC: Hemisphere, 1987.

Fullerton, Gail (1977). *Survival in Marriage.* Hinsdale, IL: Dryden Press.

*Fuss, Diana (1991). *Inside/Out: Lesbian Theories, Gay Theories.* New York: Routledge.

Gallup Poll (1990). "Alcohol Use and Abuse in America." (October): Report 265. Princeton, NJ: Gallup.

Garner, Gerald W. (1979). *The Police Role in Alcohol-Related Crises.* Springfield, IL: Charles C Thomas.

Giesbrecht, Norman, et al., eds. (1989). *Drinking and Casualties: Accidents, Poisonings and Violence in an International Perspective.* New York: Routledge, Chapman, and Hall.

*Goffman, Erving (1965). *Stigma: Notes on the Management of Spoiled Identity.* Englewood Cliffs, NJ: Prentice-Hall.

Goode, Erich, ed. (1969). *Marijuana.* New York: Atherton Press.

*Goode, Erich (1984). *Drugs in American Society.* New York: Alfred A. Knopf.

Goodman, Gerre (1983). *No Turning Back.* Philadelphia, Pennsylvania: New Society.

Gossop, M. (1987). *Living with Drugs.* 2nd ed. Aldershot, England: Wildwood House.

Gravely, Eric (1988). "Building the Case against America's Narcotic Jihad." *In These Times* (December) 3, 10.

Halloway, M. (1991). "Rx for Addiction." *Scientific American,* March, 95-103.

Harris, L.S., ed. (1988). *Problems of Drug Despondence.* Washington, DC: U.S. Government Printing Office.

*Harry, Joseph, and William B. DeVall (1978). *The Social Organization of Gay Males.* New York: Praeger.

Hayes, Joseph J. (1981). "Lesbians, Gay Men, and Their 'Languages.'" In *Gayspeak: Gay Male and Lesbian Communication,* edited by James W. Chesebro, New York: Pilgrim Press.

*Hobson, Barbara Meil (1988). *Uneasy Virtue: The Politics of Prostitution and the American Reform Tradition.* New York: Basic Books.

Hoffman, Martin (1968). *The Gay World: Male Homosexuality and the Social Creation of Evil.* New York: Basic Books.

Humphreys, Laud (1970). *Tearoom Trade: Impersonal Acts in Public Places.* Chicago: Aldine.

Hunt, Morton (1974). *Sexual Behavior in the 1970's.* New York: Dell Books.

Jackman, Norman R., Richard O'Toole, and Gilbert Geis (1963). "The Self-Image of the Prostitute." *Sociological Quarterly* 4 (2): 150-161.

*Jacobs, James B. (1989). *Drunk Driving: An American Dilemma.* Chicago: University of Chicago Press.

*Jeffery-Poulter, Stephen (1991). *Peers, Queers & Commons: The Struggle for Gay Law Reform from 1950 to the Present.* New York: Routledge, Chapman, and Hall.

Jellinek, E.M. (1952). "Phases of Alcohol Addiction." *Quarterly Journal of Studies on Alcohol* 13:637-84.

Jenness, Valerie (1990). "From Sex as Sin to Sex as Work: COYOTE and the Reorganization of Prostitution as a Social Problem." *Social Problems* 37 (3): 403-417.

Kackson, Joan K., and Ralph Connor (1953). "The Skid Row Alcoholic." *Quarterly Journal of Studies on Alcohol* 14:471-479.

Kandel, Denise, and Mark Davies (1991). "Friendship Networks, Intimacy, and Illicit Drug Use in Young Adulthood: A Comparison of Two Competing Theories." *Criminology* 29 (3): 441-467.

Klatsky, A.L., A.B. Siegelaub, C. Landy and G.D. Friedman (1985). "Racial Patterns of Alcoholic Beverage Use." *Alcoholism: Clinical and Experimental Research* 7:372-377.

*Lanza-Kaduce, Lonn (1988). "Perceptual Deterrence and Drinking and Driving among College Students." *Criminology* 26 (2): 321-341.

Lemert, Edwin M. (1982). "Drinking Among American Indians." In Gomberg, Edith Lisansky, Helene Raskin White and John A. Carpenter, eds., *Alcohol, Science and Society Revisited.* Ann Arbor: University of Michigan Press.

Lewes, Kenneth (1988). *The Psychoanalytic Theory of Male Homosexuality.* New York: Simon & Schuster.

Lex, B.W. (1985). "Alcohol Problems in Special Populations." In Mendelson, J.H., and N.K. Mello, eds., *The Diagnosis and Treatment of Alcoholism,* 2nd ed. New York: McGraw-Hill.

Lindesmith, Alfred (1968). *Addiction and Opiates.* Chicago: Aldine.

Lindesmith, Alfred, and John Gagnon (1964). "Anomie and Drug Addiction." In *Anomie and Deviant Behavior: A Discussion and Critique,* edited by Marshall B. Clinard. New York: Free Press.

Livingston, Jay (1992). *Crime and Criminology.* Englewood Cliffs, NJ: Prentice-Hall.

Lolli, Giorgio, Emilio Serianni, Grace M. Golder and Pierpalo Luzzato-Fegis (1958). *Alcohol in Italian Culture.* New York: Free Press.

Maffeo, P. (1982). "Gender as A Model for Mental Health." In *Gender and Psychopathology,* edited by Ihsan Al-Issa. New York: Academic Press.

McCaghy, Charles H., and Stephen A Cernkovich (1991). "Research Note: Polling the Public on Prostitution." *Justice Quarterly* 8 (1): 107-120.

Meyer-Bahlburg, H.L. (1984). "Psychoendocrine Research on Sexual Orientation: Current Status and Future Options." *Progress in Brain Research, Sex Differences in the Brain.* Vol. 61. New York: Elsevier.

*Mieczkowski, Thomas (1986). "Geeking Up and Throwing Down: Heroin Street Life in Detroit." *Criminology* 24 (2): 645-666.

*Morgan, Howard Wayne (1981). "The Therapeutic Revolution." *Drugs in America: A Social History, 1800-1980.* Syracuse, NY: Syracuse University Press.

Morris, Norval, and Gordon Hawkins (1970). *An Honest Politician's Guide to Crime Control.* Chicago: University of Chicago Press.

National Highway Traffic Safety Administration (1983). *Facts on Alcohol and Highway Safety.* Washington, DC: U.S. Department of Transportation.

National Institute on Drug Abuse (1990). *Capsules: Facts about Teenagers and Drug Abuse.* January, No. 17. Rockville, MD: NIDA.

Newsweek (1989). "Homosexuality and Politics: A *Newsweek* Poll." September 25, 19.

New York Times (1992). "Under Lock and Key: Drug Offenders and Overcrowding." February 17.

Peterson, W., Jack Maxwell, and Milton A. Maxwell (1958). "The Skid Row 'Wino.'" *Social Problems* 5 (1): 308-316

*Pittman, David J., and Duff G. Gillespie (1967). "Social Policy as Deviancy Reinforcement: The Case of the Public Intoxication Offender." In *Alcoholism,* edited by David J. Pittman, New York: Harper & Row.

Raschke, Carl A. (1990). *Painted Black: From Drug Killings to Heavy Metal—An Alarming True Story of How Satanism Is Terrorizing Our Communities.* New York: Harper & Row.

Reaves, Brian (1990). "Drug Enforcement by Police and Sheriffs' Departments, 1990." *Bureau of Justice Statistics Special LEMAS Report.* Washington, DC: U.S. Government Printing Office.

*Reiman, Jeffrey (1984). *The Rich Get Richer and the Poor Get Prison.* New York: John Wiley.

Richards, David A.J. (1982). *Sex, Drugs, Death, and the Law: An Essay on Human Rights and Overcriminalization.* Totowa, NJ: Rowman and Littlefield.

*Ridlon, Florence V. (1988). *A Fallen Angel: The Status Insularity of the Female Alcoholic.* Lewisburg, PA: Bucknell University Press.

Roby, Pamela A. (1969). "Politics and Criminal Law: Revision of the New York State Penal Law on Prostitution." *Social Problems* 17:83-109.

Rodgers, Bruce (1972). *The Queens' Vernacular: A Gay Lexicon.* San Francisco: Straight Arrow.

Roizen, J. (1982). "Estimating Alcohol Involvement in Serious Events." *Alcohol and Health Monograph.* Lexington, MA: Lexington Books.

*Rowe, David C., and Bill L. Gulley (1992). "Sibling Effects on Substance Use and Delinquency." *Criminology* 30 (2): 217-233.

Rubington, Earl (1958). "The Chronic Drunkenness Offender." *The Annals* 315 (1): 65-72.

Saalfield, Catherine, and Ray Navarro (1991). "Shocking Pink Praxis: Race and Gender on the ACT UP Frontlines." In *Inside/Out: Lesbian Theories, Gay Theories,* edited by Diana Fuss, 341-396. New York: Routledge.

Schofield, Michael (1965). *Sociological Aspects of Homosexuality: A Comparative Study of Three Types of Homosexuals.* Boston: Little, Brown.

*Schur, Edwin M. (1965). *Crimes without Victims.* Englewood Cliffs, NJ: Prentice-Hall.

Seevers, M.H. (1968). "Psychopharmacological Elements of Drug Dependence." *Journal of the American Medical Association* 206 (6): 1263-1266.

Skolnick, Jerome H. (1966). *Justice without Trial: Law Enforcement in Democratic Society.* New York: John Wiley.

Snyder, Charles R. (1978). *Alcohol and the Jews.* Carbondale, IL: Southern Illinois University Press (originally published 1958).

Special Issue (1988). "Drugs—The American Family in Crisis." *Juvenile and Family Court* 39: 45-46.

Spitzer, Richard (1973). "A Proposal about Homosexuality and the APA Nomenclature: Homosexuality as an Irregular Form of Sexual Behavior and Sexual Orientation Disturbance as a Psychiatric Diosorder." *American Journal of Psychiatry* 132:1214-1216.

Spradley, James P. (1970). *You Owe Yourself A Drunk: An Ethnography of Urban Nomads.* Boston: Little, Brown.

Stanley, Julia P. (1970). "Homosexual Slang." *American Speech* 14 (1&2): 45-59.

Sternlicht, Manny (1987). "The Neo-Freudians," In *Male and Female Homosexuality: Psychological Approaches,* edited by Louis Diamant. Washington, DC: Hemisphere.

*Stephens, Richard C. (1991). *The Street Addict Role: A Theory of Heroin Addiction.* Albany: State University of New York Press.

Stivers, Richard (1976). *A Hair of the Dog: Irish Drinking and American Stereotype.* University Park, PA: Pennsylvania State University Press.

Stoller, R.J. (1985). "Gender Identity Disorders in Children and Adults." In *Comprehensive Textbook of Psychiatry,* edited by H.I. Kaplan, and B.J. Sadock. Baltimore, MD: Williams & Wilkins.

Sultan, Faye, Denise Elsner, and Jaime Smith (1987). "Ego-Dystonic Homosexuality and Treatment Alternatives," In *Male and Female Homosexuality: Psychological Approaches,* edited by Louis Diamant. Washington, DC: Hemisphere.

Tilly, Louise A. (1989). Book Review of Barbara Hobson, *Uneasy Virtue: The Politics of Prostitution and the American Reform Tradition in American Journal of Sociology* 95 (2): 490-491.

Treaster, Joseph B. (1992a). "Hospital Visits by Drug Users Rise Sharply." *New York Times* July 9, 1B.

Treaster, Joseph B. (1992b). "Some Think the 'War on Drugs' Is Being Waged on Wrong Front." *New York Times* July 28, A1.

*Trebach, Arnold S. (1987). *The Great Drug War.* New York: Macmillan.

U.S. Department of Health and Human Services (1987). *Sixth Special Report to the U.S. Congress on Alcohol and Health.* Rockville, MD: NIAAA.

U.S. Department of Justice, Drug Enforcement Administration (1989). *Drugs of Abuse, 1989 Edition.* Washington, DC: U.S. Government Printing Office.

U.S. Department of Justice, Federal Bureau of Investigation (1990). *Crime in the United States, 1989.* Washington, DC: U.S. Government Printing Office.

U.S. Department of Justice, Office of Justice Programs (1991). *Sourcebook of Criminal Justice Statistics—1990.* Table 4.33. Washington, DC: U.S. Government Printing Office.

Vold, George (1958). *Theoretical Criminology*. New York: Oxford University Press.

*Wagenaar, Alexander C. (1983). *Alcohol, Young Drivers, and Traffic Accidents*. Lexington, MA: Lexington Books.

*Wallace, John M., and Jerald G. Bachman (1991). "Explaining Racial/Ethnic Differences in Adolescent Drug Use: The Impact of Background and Lifestyle." *Social Problems* 38 (3): 333-357.

Wallace, Samuel E. (1968). "The Road to Skid Row." *Social Problems* 16:102-103.

Warren, Carol (1974). *Identity and Community in the Gay World*. New York: John Wiley.

Weinberg, Martin S., and Colin J. Williams (1975). *Male Homosexuals: Their Problems and Adaptations*. Baltimore, MD: Penguin Books.

Wilson, R. Jean, and Robert E. Mann, eds. (1990). *Drinking and Driving: Advances in Research and Prevention*. New York: Guilford Press.

*Witters, Weldon, Peter Venturelli, and Glen Hanson (1992). *Drugs and Society*. Boston, MA: Jones and Bartlett.

Woolfolk, A.L., and Richardson, F.C. (1984). "Behavior Therapy and the Ideology of Modernity." *American Psychologist* 39:777-786.

Chapter 5

Conventional Criminal Behavior

Our previous chapters have dealt with *noncareer* criminals. Normally, people do not construct careers around assaulting, murdering or raping other people. Nor do they ordinarily make careers out of shoplifting, vandalism, sporadic check forgery or stealing cars for personal enjoyment. But people *do* build criminal careers around behaviors that will enable them to have a somewhat steady and predictable income. Therefore, there are three types of criminal behavior systems that are characterized by a definite career pattern: *conventional* crime, *organized* crime and *professional* crime. These three types of career criminal behaviors are different, but they have four very important characteristics in common.

First, people engaged in career crime pursue crimes of gain, mostly property crimes. Career criminals either supplement an existing income—be it legitimate or illegitimate—through property crime or, as with organized criminals and professional criminals, make a living solely from their criminal activity. In comparison to people in legitimate occupations, career criminals make part or all of their living by pursuing activities that have been defined as illegal. One of the occupational hazards for the career criminal, however, is the risk of being arrested and subsequently convicted. But since only a small percentage of all property offenses (and only those *known* to the police) are cleared by arrest and since those cleared by arrest are for the most part bargained down to misdemeanors, the risks are not exceptionally high. For many career criminals, the oft-quoted Dostoyevskian adage that "crime does not pay" is a fiction, a myth maintained by and for law-abiding citizens.

Second, criminal activity is a part of the way of life of the career offender. A career crime involves a life organization of roles built around criminal activities, which includes identification with crime, a conception of the self as a criminal and extensive association with other criminals in what amounts to a clearly defined subculture. In career crime there is a progression in crime that includes the acquisition of more complex techniques and technologies, more frequent offenses, and, ultimately, dependence on crime as a partial or sole means of livelihood.

Third, people in career crime tend either to develop a pattern of property violations or in some cases to specialize in a particular kind of offense. A career criminal, for example, may specialize in one of a number of crimes, such as purse snatching, stealing automobile accessories, shoplifting, picking pockets, or hotel/motel theft. Career criminals also develop, over a period of time, special skills and techniques for committing offenses.

Fourth, career criminals are engaged in systematic behavior that requires both personal and social organization and careful planning. In contrast to noncareer crime, which is usually sporadic and unplanned, the violations of career criminals are not the result of the pressures of immediate circumstances. Career criminals commit their offenses only after careful planning. In other words, their behavior is both calculated and rational, oriented solely toward economic gain. Career criminals depend upon the assistance of other criminals and may be involved in an organizational network of criminals. Because of their involvement in crime, there is the prospect of a lifetime career in crime with increased isolation from legitimate work patterns.

It is important to stress here that the notions of *career crime* and *career criminals* as used in this book differ from the notion of *criminal careers* as defined and studied by Blumstein and his colleagues (Blumstein et al. 1986). This latter concept refers to the careers of hard core, repeat offenders of any type. Although most career criminals also fall into the category of those having criminal careers, not all those with criminal careers are career criminals. For Blumstein, the four key dimensions of criminal careers are: (1) participation in crime, (2) frequency, or rate of criminal activity, (3) seriousness of offenses, and (4) career length, or length of time the criminal is active.

Conventional crime as a behavior system is at the bottom of the hierarchy of career crime. The degree of development of conventional criminals and their sophistication in crime is much less than that found among organized and professional criminals. Compared to the other career criminals, conventional property criminals are less skillful in committing offenses and are not as well organized in avoiding arrest and conviction. Conventional offenders often begin their illegal activities as adolescents, and many terminate their careers before reaching the age of 30.

Conventional crime may or may not involve force or the threat of force. For example, the burglar enters what he or she hopes is an unoccupied residence or motel room in search of valuables. If, however, he or she encounters an unexpected occupant, the burglar is faced with the immediate decision of whether to simply flee the premises or to physically subdue the other. It is not infrequent that assaults and even some homicides are committed in this context. Robbery, however, by legal definition means the actual use or threat of violent force against the victim. It involves the additional element of direct confrontation between criminal and victim. In spite of this, only about 30 percent of all robberies result in actual physical injury to the victim (Cook 1986). Larceny/theft, on the other hand, with the exception of some purse snatchings, seldom involves the threat or use of physical violence.

Legal Aspects of Selected Offenses

Conventional criminals are those who commit the conventional kinds of property crime such as larceny, burglary and robbery, which have been regarded as crimes for centuries. Burglary alone, for example, accounted for approximately 17 percent of all arrests for index crimes in the United States in 1990. The arrest rate for burglary in 1989 was 178 per 100,000, down from a rate of 211 per 100,000 in 1971. Moreover, only 13.8 percent of all burglaries known to the police in 1989 were cleared by arrest (*Sourcebook 1990,* Tables 4.1, 4.23, 4.24). Thus, burglary is a fairly common crime with a relatively low risk of arrest.

Offenses against property were among the first to be punished under legal systems the world over. What has been regarded as "property," however, has differed widely according to cultures, because the importance of various forms of property have changed with developments in modes of production and social/cultural structures, such as the transition from the feudal mode of production to capitalism, and the transition from agricultural to industrial economies. In addition, because of the development of technologies, the penalties for crimes against property have also changed. Theft is the generic term we use today to encompass all property crimes, but the basic theft offense in old English common law was larceny. This act consists of taking and carrying away goods from the possession of another without the owner's consent. Originally the goods had to be in actual possession, but this concept was enlarged later to cope with the problems of industrial and commercial societies with the addition in the eighteenth century of embezzlement and obtaining money under false pretenses. Other additions have included receiving stolen property. With today's computer technology we now have the crime of theft of intellectual property and of ideas, that is, violation of certain copyright laws (Wildeman 1985). Shoplifting is also a form of larceny.

Burglary and robbery are other property crimes that involve theft and larceny with a long history under the common law. Burglary under the old common law was breaking and entering a dwelling house of another at night with intent to steal. Today it includes buildings other than houses and the night element has been eliminated. Robbery is regarded as aggravated larceny. It consists of taking property from another with an element of force, placing the victim in a state of fear and intimidation. The fear and intimidation may be induced by a gun, knife, iron pipe, fist or other instrument (even a toy gun).

Criminal Career of the Offender

It is the conventional offender whom the general public usually considers to be "the criminal." These offenders generally begin with an adolescent group or a youth gang, and their criminal activities move then to more serious and frequent adult crime. They engage in property crimes such as larceny, burglary and robbery. They rarely, however, specialize in one type of offense as do the professional criminals (discussed later). As they progress in crime they acquire increasingly sophisticated techniques and rationalizations derived partly from association with other offenders. Most of them have frequent contacts with the law, as the degree of their criminal sophistication does not enable them to avoid arrests or even imprisonment. Conventional offenders develop a definite conception of themselves as criminals. This arises because they are often isolated to a great extent from contacts with law-abiding society, they associate with others who engage in criminal activities and they are more often apprehended and severely dealt with by the law. Conventional offenders usually end their criminal careers by middle age for various reasons, such as marriage or the acquisition of a legitimate occupation, or for health reasons.

The career patterns of conventional offenders can be illustrated in a comparison of persons convicted of armed robbery with a group of other property offenders (Roebuck and Cadwallader 1961). As juvenile delinquents, the former frequently carried and used weapons, their arrest histories showing an average of 18 arrests. The armed robbers showed early patterns of stealing from their parents, in school and on the streets; truancy; street fighting; association with older offenders; and membership in gangs. Compared with other offenders, the armed robbers also had more extensive records of previous acts of violence and based their claims to leadership in gangs on superior strength and skill.

Conventional criminals begin their careers early in life as juvenile delinquents. In the United States persons anywhere from 9 years of age through 17 years of age constitute from roughly 35 to 40 percent of those arrested for burglaries, larcenies and auto theft. In 1989 in the United States, 32 percent of those arrested for burglary, 41 percent of those arrested for robbery and 41 percent of those arrested for vehicular theft were under the age of 18 (U.S. Dept. of Justice 1990). Conventional criminal behavior typically begins in adolescence. Studies have outlined typical adolescents likely to engage in conventional crime. They are from lower middle- to lower-class backgrounds, and are likely to live in areas characterized by crime and drugs. They are from broken homes or homes where no father is living. Most are white, but black adolescents are disproportionately represented in relation to the makeup of the general population. Most belong to or have belonged to gangs. The occupational aspirations of most of these youths tend to range from low to zero. Their early life histories are likely to show a pattern of truancy, destruction of property, street fighting and gang membership. Consequently, by the time they have reached young adulthood they have an extensive history of contact with the law, and possibly have had some experience in an institution or some sort of correctional facility. Life histories show that criminality proceeds from the trivial to the serious, from occasional to frequent, from game to business and from crimes committed by isolated individuals to crimes committed by tightly organized groups. The following case study narrative is typical. The narrator is 15 years old.

> We had begun to drink and smoke weed on weekends. My brothers had begun to shoplift, to "borrow" cars, and to do other "small-time" stuff . . . One weekend we were getting drunk and ran out of beer. None of us had much money, and this one guy said that he knew where we could get a lot of beer for free. It was Saturday afternoon and we waited until about 7 o'clock that night, and the three of us went and snuck behind this guy's house. I waited outside as a lookout while another guy picked the lock. We each took two six-packs of beer and one guy took a drill. Then we went back to our place and got drunk . . . About a month or so later, (one) guy said he had been to his girl's house and saw that her folks kept all this booze in the living room. He said he knew a real easy way to get in and he knew it would be no trouble. I was only 16 then, and we hadn't drunk any hard stuff, so we were really excited. We spent all day drinking beer and getting stoned, and so on Saturday night we were ready. The same three of us went out again. We got in the house and got the booze and got back out. I guess a neighbor saw us and called the police. She knew who we were and where we lived, so the police came and arrested us about a half-hour later. We were all so drunk at the time that I remember when the police came in, we just sat there and laughed. I was sent to county jail and spent two months there for theft. The other guys also went to county jail, but they did longer. (Petersilia, Greenwood and Lavin 1978, 102-103)

Conventional criminals normally begin their careers in groups in association with adolescents of similar demographic characteristics, whether these groups come to be defined as "gangs" or simply as temporary and transient configurations. For many of these adolescents, the law and its agents may simply be something that one has to reckon with in the course of living a life. Their acts are not isolated and personal, but rather are part of the way of life and norms of the local neighborhood (disproportionately an inner-city neighborhood, but sometimes a suburban neighborhood). At an early age they learn to commit illegal acts and find group support for their behavior. From early experience in such a setting they readily progress to adult criminal behavior in which thefts are more frequent, substantial and sophisticated.

A Dallas/Houston study of age-specific robbery arrests showed an overall descending rate of 293 arrests per 100,00 of people from age 15 to 19, a rate of 210 from age 20 to 24, 109 from age 25 to 29, and 100 from age 30 to 39. Broken down by race, the robbery arrest rate per 100,000 for black males aged 15 to 29 was 774; for white males aged 15 to 29 it was 171; for black males in the over-30 age group, the arrest rate for robbery was 188 per 100,000; for white males over 30, it was 37 (Chilton 1991). Whether black or white, robbery arrest rates decreased dramatically with age in these two cities. The interpretation of these statistics is, as always, problematic. Perhaps with age, people gradually learn how to avoid arrest. Or perhaps with age they find more efficient ways of earning a living.

A "gang" can be defined as "a group whose members meet together with some regularity, over time on the basis of group-defined criteria of membership and group-defined organizational structure, and some sense of territoriality" (Short 1990a, 148). Characteristics that are important, but not essential, to gang identity and behavior include specific hand signs, colors, dress, names and types of organization. The delineation of a gang's territory is extremely important, for in the case of drugs it means market hegemony. As in the case of nation states, gangs will fight to the death to maintain and expand their marketing territory.

Two extensive studies of gangs in Milwaukee, Wisconsin, and Brooklyn, New York, pay particular attention to gang structure, membership composition and activities (Hagedorn 1988). Both studies revealed the growing integration of gangs into innner-city neighborhood structures and institutions. Often this integration was achieved through force, violence and intimidation directed toward law-abiding members of the communities. Gang members had minimal opportunities for stable, legitimate employment—the kind of employment needed to raise a family—and could only look forward to downward mobility. As new gang members begin to age from adolescence through the late teens and into early and mid-adulthood, their values and goals center increasingly on crime and survival as the only roads open to the future. These conclusions reinforce a study of gangs in Philadelphia in the late 1980s and early 1990s (Anderson 1990). The major impact of the drug trade in inner-city communities seems to have created a sort of generation gap between the older gang members and the younger ones. Nevertheless, as the young members age, they remain part of the gang, having no other social group to turn to for support and membership. The gang, in fact, becomes the only real family they know.

The "aging out" process of gang members that was typical of urban gangs in the 1950s has given way to longer and longer participation in gang-related conventional crime. Both the Milwaukee and Brooklyn studies relate these processes to the larger socioeconomic processes of segmentation of the labor market, deindustrialization and job flight from the inner cities, which gained momentum during the decade of the 1980s. No longer is any hope of upward social mobility a reality for these inner-city youths. Movement up the socioeconomic ladder has grown progressively remote, resulting in a permanent underclass whose activities increasingly involve conventional crime and the sale and use of illegal drugs. With little probability of obtaining conventional jobs, youth in this predicament may become involved in large-scale organized crime involving drugs and the use of lethal weapons.

An ethnographic study of 37 street gangs of different ethnic and racial composition in Los Angeles, New York and Boston supports the conclusion that gang membership and the conventional criminal behavior that goes with it are taking on more of a career pattern. Street gangs are growing increasingly organized, rational and cohesive, indicating a change in the age structure of gang membership. Also, as a result of individuals remaining part of these gangs well into adulthood, there is a progression in conventional crime technique, violence, the acquisition and use of more lethal weapons, recruitment techniques and relations with the law-abiding community (Jankowski 1991).

A 13-year panel study in Toronto found that an important factor in explaining adolescent delinquents' transition into conventional crime as adults was the existence of negative effects on employment as an adult, which stem from involvement in an adolescent delinquent subculture. Further, these negative adult employment outcomes were conditioned by social class location. The negative adult employment outcomes were found primarily among those from working-class families (Hagan 1991). In addition, a Boston study of black inner-city males found that in spite of a rapidly expanding labor market in that city during the 1980s, the percentage of those youths who saw a higher earnings potential in crime relative to legitimate earnings increased significantly (Freeman 1987, 1991; Hagan 1992). A Philadelphia study showed a similar finding: underemployment, unemployment and the lack of proper preparation for the tasks of adulthood increase the likelihood of a transition from juvenile conventional crime to a career criminal pattern in adulthood (Thornberry and Christenson 1984). On the other hand, membership in middle- and upper-class families opens greater opportunity structures, a higher degree of community absorption and access to second chances for those who, as adolescents, became involved in delinquent subcultures. Upon reaching adulthood, these people no longer needed "street income," but could build a conventional life around a conventional career and respectable earnings (Jessor, Donovan, and Costa 1991).

When crime is pursued as a way of life, as it is with conventional career criminals, other ways of living are not readily observed, understood or desired by the offender. Furthermore, the original excitement and notoriety offered by a criminal career may seem more rewarding to the offender than the prospects offered by making a living and supporting a family in the conventional manner, especially if such prospects are only a remote possibility. A group consciousness among criminals makes movement to a law-abiding life less comprehensible and desirable, even were it to be made available. However, if by age 15 an adolescent has seen no other alternatives, if he or she sees death and desolation daily on the streets, and if his or her primary supporter is a drug addict, then a life outside of mainstream society may seem to be the only viable alternative. The youth is by this time securely penned into the "holocaust" of the American ghetto. The situation has changed somewhat from the late 1960s, when one observer could report:

Once a gang boy gets beyond the age of 18, his situation changes rather dramatically. Whether he likes it or not, he now has a choice to make about what identity system to enter. He could get married, get a job, and assume the status of a full-fledged "adult"; he could decide to postpone this decision in legitimate ways such as joining the Army and going to school at night . . . If he managed to graduate from high school, he may well decide to go on to college; but if he was expelled from high school, he may feel either bitter or reluctant about going back to night school to get the high school degree.

In short, it is at this point in his career that the "opportunities" available to him will affect his behavior, his attitudes, and the decisions he makes about his life. If there are no legitimate options open to him, options that at best would not make him suffer a sudden decrease in status and at worst would allow him not to face his ultimately dismal status-fate as an adult, then he may well decide to stay on the streets . . . He may adopt a "hustle," and he may also adopt a full-blown ideology along with it. Since he now views the conventional world as a place he is expected to enter, he tends to develop a "position" on it. Jobs become "slaves"; going to school becomes "serving time"; and in some cases, the assumptions about marriage and getting a conventional job are replaced by fantisies about the quick and big "score." . . . They have an answer to everything, and they always "know the score." (Werthman 1967)

Group Support of Criminal Behavior

Conventional crime is disproportionately the product of inner-city life, for it is in this setting that many of the preconditions exist that lead to gang membership and gang-related activities (generally drug-related). Some evidence of this is seen in the fact that the arrest rate for robbery in these areas is extraordinarily high. Offenders who commit robbery and burglary come out of these areas as well as do violent personal offenders. Large cities with a population of 500,000 and over account for about 80 percent of all robbery arrests in the United States annually (U.S. Dept. of Justice 1990, 199-201).

The inner-city areas of our large metropolitan cities are generally extremely congested. The housing is substandard, and residents lack the amenities that those who live outside these areas take for granted. Extensive poverty, poor health delivery systems and ineffective educational programs are typical. One dramatic case study of two inner-city African-American adolescent brothers struggling to grow up in Chicago graphically portrayed the overwhelming problems these adolescents face (Kotlowitz 1991). There is often inadequate plumbing, poor sanitation and poorly maintained public housing facilities. Although such inner-city areas vary from one type to another and from one city to another, the general living patterns are universal; and although these general patterns of physical characteristics are almost without exception typical of large inner-city areas, it would be a serious mistake to view them only in these terms (Suttles 1968). They actually are far more than this; they represent a way of life that sometimes continues through several generations (Clinard 1966, 3-43; Short 1978). Inner-city areas are often characterized by a high incidence of crime, juvenile delinquency, drunkenness, illegal drug use, prostitution, illegitimacy and family maladjustment. Middle-class goals of educational achievement are often lacking, and there is often a feeling of apathy and social isolation from the dominant middle-class society. Inner-city neighborhood residents have opportunities for close associations with people who engage in, or encourage them to engage in, various crimes—including the use and sale of illegal drugs. Violence is a common means of settling disputes.

Support for illegal behavior begins for many conventional offenders at an early age. Thrasher long ago noted in his classic study of juvenile and youth gangs that adolescents in play groups, in the course of fun and adventure, engage in a variety of activities that are both legal and illegal in nature (Thrasher 1927). The extent to which these groups engage in illegal behavior depends upon such factors as the organization of the neighborhood (usually minimal), family characteristics, community values and community reaction to gang activity. In most of these areas crime, delinquency and gang membership become the principle means of adjusting to the problems of growing up. The activities that become most important to the gang are normally in violation of the law. The illegal activities of the gangs are at first relatively minor. The members engage in running drugs or numbers or in a variety of conventional property offenses, such as stealing from stores, empty houses, drunks and other sources of vulnerable property. Gradually, the offenses become more like those engaged in by adults, such as burglary, armed robbery and grand larceny. As gangs increase in organization and tradition, they usually come into conflict with other gangs in the vicinity, in which case extreme violence of various forms becomes commonplace. Drive-by shootings, ride-by shootings (on bicycles) and even walk-by shootings have become common in many inner-city areas.

The role of gangs in delinquent and criminal behavior has been well-documented over the years. The landmark 1967 *Challenge of Crime in a Free Society* concluded that the "typical delinquent operates in the company of his peers, and delinquency thrives on group support. It has been estimated that between 60 and 90 percent of all delinquent acts are committed with companions. That fact alone makes youth groups of central concern in consideration of delinquency prevention" (President's Commission 1967). Most delinquents are arrested in company with others, and it can be safely assumed that those who had no companions at the time of their arrest had at least one in the beginning of their delinquency. In their early study of 5,480 Chicago delinquents, Shaw and McKay found that 81.8 percent of those brought into juvenile court had one or more companions in the delinquent act (Shaw and McKay 1931).

Vehicular theft often abounds with virtual immunity from prosecution. According to the National Crime Insurance Bureau, Newark (NJ), the city with the highest rate of car theft in the United States (with a rate of 5,398 reported thefts per 100,000 population), is an example. Some of this larceny is for profit, but much of it is simply part of an adolescent ritual of growing up in the inner city. It has become a rite of passage, a way of gaining respect among one's peers: you haven't earned respect and admiration unless you have stolen at least one car. Typically, the cars are stolen, raced, wrecked and abandoned, all for the entertainment of others. An adolescent is able to demonstrate his or her daring, skills and defiance by "doing doughnuts," a game where the youth or youths in a stolen car race down a stretch of city street and at an intersection suddenly jerk the steering wheel and fully apply the brakes, bringing the car shrieking into a 365-degree turn and leaving a doughnut-shaped patch of rubber at the intersection. Peers, lining the street and intersection, cheer and applaud and then do the same thing themselves. These and similar demonstrations are known as "car shows." This can begin with children as young as nine years of age. About 70 percent of the stolen cars are eventually recovered, although they are often damaged beyond repair. The fact that they are usually abandoned after the demonstration of driving skills is an indication of the lack of the profit motive in the larceny (*New York Times,* August 11, 1992, A1). Typical of the comments of the young thieves: "I drive, crash a couple of them, dump them and go get some more"; "It feels good. You get this feeling like you are scared, like you feel high, like you're going to top over"; "I don't want a job, I just want to have fun." One 18-year-old was quoted as saying, "I never want to hurt anybody. It's the little boys who don't know what they're doing. That makes it bad for everybody" (*New York Times,* August 11, 1992, A1).

Patterns of social interaction develop in each juvenile gang. Group solidarity and tradition develop in the course of the common experience of the members. The gang becomes of such importance to the members that they participate very little in the social and youth institutions of conventional society. More often than not these institutions are not available in any case. Adolescents become dependent upon each other for a large share of their interpersonal gratification. The social roles, traditions, values and location of the gang may remain relatively intact as members grow out of delinquency into adult crime and as new members become active. Gangs are not dependent upon their present membership for their ongoing existence. Just as any other social organization, attrition patterns must be balanced out by recruitment patterns; and juvenile gangs are able to continue in spite of the necessary fluctuations in personnel over time. Frequently the gang becomes the adult's "alma mater."

In his extensive research on delinquent gangs, Short documented several specific group processes and mechanisms that are involved in delinquency episodes. Probably the most important is:

The gamble of status v. punishment risk. In the calculus of decision making, status rewards within the group often tip the scales toward "joining the action," and therefore becoming involved in delinquency." (Short 1965)

Correspondence between Criminal and Legitimate Behavior

Conventional offenders are only partially committed to more commonly held norms and values. When there is commitment, it is usually sporadic, temporary and superficial. A fluctuation in commitment to "legitimate society," outside a delinquent or criminal subculture, is evident in much of juvenile delinquency. Sykes and Matza were the first to suggest that delinquents do not completely reject the dominant values and norms of the larger society but only neutralize the values and norms in the course of violating the law. They argued that, in fact, this is how an adolescent learns to become a criminal: he or she learns certain techniques of neutralization (Matza and Sykes 1961; Sykes and Matza 1957). But it appears that delinquents are not fully committed to any particular value system. Matza has suggested that in being uncommitted the delinquent "drifts" between a delinquent and a nondelinquent way of life.

Drift stands midway between freedom and control. Its basis is an area of the social structure in which control has been loosened, coupled with the abortiveness of adolescent endeavor to organize an autonomous subculture, and thus an independent source of control, around illegal action. The delinquent transiently exists in a limbo between convention and crime, responding in turn to the demands of each, flirting now with one, now the other, but postponing commitment, evading decision. Thus, he drifts between criminal and conventional action. (Matza 1964)

What may be called the "mid-twentieth century period" of American criminology (Quinney and Wildeman 1991) abounded with theories that attempted to explain adolescent delinquent behavior and gang delinquency. Many names come to mind: Block and Niederhoffer's theory of adolescent powerlessness and gang delinquency (Block and Niederhoffer 1948), Cohen's theory of delinquent boys as protesting against middle-class values (Cohen 1955), Miller's theory of lower-class culture as producing delinquent behavior (Miller 1958), Cloward and Ohlin's theory of delinquent behavior as linked to restricted legitimate opportunities (Cloward and Ohlin 1960), and so on. All of these theories, formulated from 1948 to 1960, turned out to be too simplistic and could not be adequately supported by empirical research. Individually, none of them could sufficiently deal with the complexities of contemporary urban society. The most likely explanation appears to be one that combines the norms and values of the local adult community with the striving for status within the gang. A delinquent gang is patterned and influenced by the neighborhood social system of which it is a part.

Problems of identity appear to be particularly pressing in contemporary society. Gang membership and delinquency are attempts to achieve identity and meaningfulness on the part of many inner-city youths. Gangs give a sense of "place" or "family" to adolescents. The question is: Why does gang delinquency and membership serve this function for some youths while other social arrangements serve this function for other youths and adolescents? The answer is most certainly related to the location of the individual in the general structure of our society, especially the wealth and opportunity distribution structures.

Finally, it is clear that conventional criminal behavior corresponds rather closely with what we call legitimate and law-abiding behavior. As Clarence Darrow, one of the most noteworthy criminal lawyers in American history, argued in his 1903 "Address to the Inmates of Cook County Jail" in Chicago, everyone does their best under the circumstances made available to them.

Societal Reaction and Legal Processing

The fact that societal reaction to the conventional crimes of burglary, theft and larceny is severe and harsh should not be surprising, for the value of personal property lies at the very core of our social system. Crime and deviance always strike at the core values of any society. We have created the powerful magic of a *criminal justice system* to severely punish those among us who transgress these laws protecting our private property. We have created a system of dealing with our young who violate these values, and we have named it our *juvenile justice system*. We comfort ourselves behind this dual bulwark of criminal justice and juvenile justice, secure that the law will stand behind us in our resolve to protect our property from those who would deprive us of it. The notion of criminal justice casts the spotlight on individual criminals and not on the injustices of the social order that lead to stealing.

The penalties for conventional crimes of the type dealt with here are best seen as reflections of the power of those in the dominant segments of society and their ability to see that such offenses of the lower orders are punished much more severely than are occupational, corporate or white-collar property offenses. In general, the differential punishment for certain criminal behavior, through the formulation and administration of criminal law, is the domain of groups in positions of power. The reality, however, is that infinitely more human suffering, violence and deprivation have been caused by corporate crime than by all of the conventional crimes throughout our history (Eitzen and Zinn 1992). Thus it is that an understanding of who defines behavior as criminal is as essential in the study of conventional crime as it is in the study of criminal behavior in general, for the powerful classes of any society have never defined their own actions as crimes.

The official processing of conventional criminal offenders results in a lengthy series of arrests and convictions. The type of offenses they commit, often without a great degree of skill, may lead to a considerable risk of apprehension and incarceration in penal institutions. In this regard they are quite different from professional criminals. Many spend a considerable part of their life in correctional institutions, possibly withdrawing from a life of crime in their late thirties or early forties. Since society generally holds imprisonment (rather than what the person actually did) against a person, those who have been imprisoned are among the most stigmatized of all offenders. Our culture provides no graduation from the status of "ex-con."

A disproportionate number of conventional crimes are committed by juvenile delinquents. The very phrase "juvenile delinquency" is, in fact, a creation of our modern industrial era. It was invented in 1816 in London with the publication of a "Report of the Committee for Investigating the Causes of the Alarming Increase of Juvenile Delinquency in the Metropolis." The creation of our modern juvenile justice system was not far behind. In New York City in the year 1819 the Society for the Reformation of Juvenile Delinquents was founded, and in 1825 the first modern juvenile institution was opened (Bernard 1992). America had begun putting its children, principally its poor children, behind bars. The offenses these poor adolescents were charged with were mainly conventional crimes of theft, burglary, larceny and the like. Many prominent people of the time were convinced that poor people were poor precisely because they were criminals, corrupt and vice-ridden. Popular thinking has not changed all that much since then.

Young males, disproportionately minorities, commit crime far in excess of what one would expect given their numbers in the total population (Hirschi and Gottfredson 1983). Juveniles between the ages of 13 and 17, while constituting some 8 percent of our total population, account for four times as many arrests for serious property crimes than would be expected, were they to be arrested at the same rate as everyone else (Strasburg 1984). Up to about 1952 juvenile arrest rates in this country were both low and stable over time. In 1951 juveniles accounted for 4.5 percent of all arrests and 14.6 percent of all arrests for serious property offenses (Teeters and Matza 1964). This has changed drastically in the last 30 years. As of 1989, juveniles accounted for 15.5 percent of all arrests, including 32.7 percent of all arrests for the serious property offenses of burglary, larceny-theft, car theft, and arson (Bernard 1992, 23). At various times and places many conflicting policies have been urged in order to curb this epidemic: psychoanalysis, behavioral therapy, stiffer prison sentences, education, job training, supporting family values, and so on. But others have suggested that as long as we continue to implement our juvenile justice system as it has existed for about 150 years, the problem will not go away (Platt 1974).

Certainly some of the major Supreme Court decisions on juvenile justice have not loaded the dice on behalf of the young. In *McKiever v. Pennsylvania* (1971), the Court held that juveniles do not have a constitutional right to a trial by jury. In *Breed v. Jones* (1975) it was established that waiver proceedings do not constitute a violation of juveniles' protection against "double jeopardy." According to *Schall v. Martin* (1984) juveniles charged with delinquency may be detained before trial to prevent them from committing additional crimes. Finally, in 1989 the Court held that capital punishment for juveniles 16 years of age and older is constitutional (Berger 1991, 441). And all of these decisions were intended to "protect" the children.

In the administration of the law, conventional offenders are handled according to certain preconceived notions about their characteristics and behavior. Conventional offenders are among those offenders who usually do not reach the trial stage of the judicial process because their cases are settled by a plea of guilty. The prosecuting attorney and defense attorney often alter the charge through "bargaining" in order to avoid a trial. This process, in reality, has become the very mainstay of our criminal justice system today. Without it, the entire system would collapse. About 90 percent of all those arrested for felonies plead guilty, and if we include misdemeanors, the number goes up to 98 percent (Gaskins 1990). Since the penal code does not provide instructions for making decisions on complaint alterations, other guides must be devised by the attorneys. Nowhere are these guidelines written into the penal statutes. For example, district attorneys and others frequently place concrete cases into more general categories of criminal acts. Rather than referring to the statutory definition of burglary, reference is made to a nonstatutorily defined class of burglaries referred to as simply "normal burglaries." On the basis of a characterization of a normal or typical burglary, attorneys are able to agree upon an appropriate reduction from the original charge, such as reducing a "typical" burglary to petty theft (Sudnow 1965).

One criminologist lists six basic ways in which a plea bargain, which is so important to conventional offenders, can be arrived at by the defense and prosecuting attorneys:

1. The initial charges are reduced to those of a lesser offense. Thus, the sentence is automatically reduced. This takes place mainly in Class A felonies.

2. The charge is reduced from a felony to a misdemeanor. This exchange is often negotiated in conventional crimes such as burglary.

3. Where there is more than one charge, for example five charges of rape or five charges for five different crimes, only a single charge will be filed if the accused "cops a plea."

4. The prosecuting attorney may promise to recommend a lenient sentence in exchange for a plea. This exchange is more typical in misdemeanor cases.

5. When the charge carries with it a severe stigma (for example, child molestation), it can be changed to a lesser charge in exchange for a guilty plea.

6. Prosecutors may promise to get the defendant into some sort of treatment program in exchange for the plea. (Siegel 1992, 520-521)

The programs used in the treatment and prevention of conventional crime are generally based on conservative or liberal ideologies. The approaches to juvenile delinquency, for example, have usually consisted of custody, rehabilitation or redirection of individuals and families, neglecting the relation of offenders to more basic social conditions. Little or no effort is made to change basic social structures. The correctional policy takes the side of discipline, law and order, and rehabilitation, but not of progressive social change. In general, apart from weak policies that offer tax incentives to business investments in inner-city neighborhoods, little effort is made to change a local community by enlisting large-scale citizen participation and developing indigenous leadership and self-help to overcome norms, values, social conditions and structures that contribute to delinquency, violence, hopelessness and crime.

Stressing the priority of *social justice* over *criminal justice,* a number of alternative ways of dealing with conventional crime as well as other categories of offenses have been emerging from the humanist, feminist and critical peacemaking traditions (Pepinsky and Quinney 1991). Strategies of reparation, mediation, community-level conflict resolution and community service are being advanced. The thinking behind these strategies is that a just society's response to crime should restore what was lost to the victim and be rehabilitative (Quinney and Wildeman 1991; Walker 1989).

References

*Anderson, Elijah (1990). *Streetwise: Race and Class In An Urban Community.* Chicago: University of Chicago Press.

Berger, Ronald J., ed. (1991). *The Sociology of Juvenile Delinquency.* Chicago: Nelson-Hall.

*Bernard, Thomas J. (1992). *The Cycle of Juvenile Justice.* New York: Oxford University Press.

Block, Herbert A., and Arthur Niederhoffer (1948). *The Gang: A Study of Adolescent Behavior.* New York: Philosophical Library.

Blumstein, Alfred, Jacquline Cohen, Jeffrey Roth, and Christy Visher, eds. (1986). *Criminal Careers and "Career Criminals."* Vols. I & II, Washington, DC: National Academy Press.

Chilton, Roland (1991). "Urban Crime Trends and Criminological Theory." *Criminal Justice Research Bulletin* 6 (3). Huntsville, TX: Sam Houston State University Press.

Clinard, Marshall B. (1970). *Slums and Community Development: Experiments in Self-Help.* New York: Free Press.

*Clinard, Marshall B. (1978). *Cities with Little Crime: The Case of Switzerland.* Cambridge, England: Cambridge University Press.

Cloward, Richard A., and Lloyd E. Ohlin (1960). *Delinquency and Opportunity: A Theory of Delinquent Gangs.* New York: Free Press/Macmillan.

Cohen, Albert K. (1955). *Delinquent Boys: The Culture of the Gang.* New York: Free Press/Macmillan.

Cook, Philip J. (1986). "The Relationships between Victim Resistance and Injury in Noncommercial Robbery." *Journal of Legal Studies* 15 (2): 405-416.

Eitzen, Stanley D., and Maxine B. Zinn (1992). *In Conflict and Order: Understanding Society,* 6th ed. Boston: Allyn and Bacon.

Farrington, David, and R. Tarling (1985). "Criminology Prediction: An Introduction." In *Prediction in Criminology,* edited by David Farrington and R. Tarling. Albany, NY: State University of New York Press.

*Farrington, David, Lloyd Ohlin, and James Q. Wilson (1986). *Understanding and Controlling Crime: Toward A New Research Strategy.* New York: Springer-Verlag.

Freeman, Richard (1987). "The Relation of Criminal Activity to Black Youth Employment." *The Review of Black Political Economy* 16:99-107.

Freeman, Richard (1991). "Crime and the Economic Status of Disadvantaged Young Men." Paper presented at the Conference on Urban Labor Markets and Labor Mobility, Airlie House, Virginia.

Gaskins, Carla (1990). *Felony Case Processing in State Courts, 1986.* Washington, DC: Bureau of Justice Statistics.

*Gottfredson, Michael, and Travis Hirschi (1986). "The True Value of Lambda Would Appear to Be Zero: An Essay on Career Criminals, Criminal Careers, Selective Incapacitation, Cohort Studies and Related Topics." *Criminology* 24 (2): 213-234.

*Hagan, John (1991). "Destiny and Drift: Subcultural Preferences, Status Attainments and the Risks and Rewards of Youth." *American Sociological Review* 56 (5): 567-582.

Hagan, John (1992). "Juvenile Justice and Delinquency in the Life Course." *Criminal Justice Research Bulletin* 7 (1). Huntsville, TX: Sam Houston State University Press.

*Hagedorn, John M., and Perry Macon (1988). *People and Folks: Gangs, Crime and the Underclass in a Rustbelt City.* Chicago: Lake View Press.

Hirschi, Travis, and Michael Gottfredson (1983). "Age and the Explanation of Crime." *American Journal of Sociology* 89 (3): 552-584.

Hollingshead, August B. (1949). *Elmtown's Youth: The Impact of Social Classes on Adolescents.* New York: John Wiley.

*Jankowski, Martin Sanchez (1991). *Islands in the Street: Gangs and American Urban Society.* Berkeley, CA: University of California Press.

Jessor, Richard, John Donovan, and Frances Costa (1991). *Beyond Adolescence: Problem Behavior and Young Adult Development.* New York: Cambridge University Press.

*Kotlowitz, Alex (1991). *There Are No Children Here.* New York: Doubleday.

*MacLeod, Jay (1987). *Ain't No Makin' It: Leveled Aspirations in a Low-Income Neighborhood.* Boulder, CO: Westview Press.

Matza, David, and Gresham M. Sykes (1961). "Juvenile Delinquency and Subterranean Values." *American Sociological Review* 26 (5): 712-719.

Matza, David (1964). *Delinquency and Drift.* New York: John Wiley.

Miller, Walter B. (1958). "Lower Class Culture as a Generating Milieu of Gang Delinquency." *Journal of Social Issues* 14 (3): 5-19.

New York Times (1992). "On Stolen Wheels, Youths Defy Newark." August 10, A1.

New York Times (1992). "For Young Joy Riders in Newark, Idle Days Filled with Danger." August 11, A1.

*Pepinsky, Harold E., and Richard Quinney, eds. (1991). *Criminology as Peacemaking.* Bloomington, IN: Indiana University Press.

Petersilia, Joan, Peter Greenwood, and Marvin Lavin (1978). *Criminal Careers of Habitual Felons.* Washington, DC: U.S. Government Printing Office.

Platt, Anthony (1974). "The Triumph of Benevolence: The Origins of the Juvenile Justice System in the United States." In *Criminal Justice in America,* edited by Richard Quinney. Boston: Little, Brown.

President's Commission on Law Enforcement and the Administration of Justice (1967). *The Challenge of Crime in a Free Society.* Washington, DC: U.S. Government Printing Office.

Quinney, Richard (1970). *The Social Reality of Crime.* Boston, MA.: Little, Brown.

Quinney, Richard (1977). *Class, State, and Crime: On the Theory and Practice of Criminal Justice.* New York: David McKay.

Quinney, Richard, and John Wildeman (1991). *The Problem of Crime: A Peace and Social Justice Perspective.* Mountain View, CA: Mayfield.

Reiman, Jeffrey H. (1990). *The Rich Get Richer and the Poor Get Prison: Ideology, Class, and Criminal Justice,* 3rd ed. New York: Macmillan.

Roebuck, Julian B., and Mervyn L. Cadwallader (1961). "The Negro Armed Robber as a Criminal Type: The Construction and Application of a Typology." *Pacific Sociological Review* 4:251-262.

Sampson, Robert J., and W. Byron Groves (1989). "Community Structure and Crime: Testing Social-Disorganization Theory." *American Journal of Sociology* 94 (4): 774-802.

Shaw, Clifford R., and Henry D. McKay (1931). "Social Factors in Juvenile Delinquency." *The Causes of Crime.* National Commission on Law Observance and Enforcement. Report 13, Volume 2. Washington, DC: U.S. Government Printing Office.

*Shaw, Clifford R., and Henry D. McKay (1942). *Juvenile Delinquency and Urban Areas.* Chicago: University of Chicago Press.

Short, James F. (1965). "Social Structure and Group Processes in Gang Delinquency." In *Problems of Youth: Transition to Adulthood in a Changing World,* edited by Muzafer Sherif and Carolyn W. Sherif. Chicago: Aldine.

Short, James F. (1976). *Delinquency, Crime and Society.* Chicago: University of Chicago Press.

*Short, James F. (1990a). *Delinquency and Society.* Englewood Cliffs, NJ: Prentice-Hall.

Short, James F. (1990b). "Review Essays: Cities, Gangs, and Delinquency." *Sociological Forum* 5 (4): 657-668.

Siegel, Larry J. (1992). *Criminology.* New York: West.

Sourcebook of Criminal Justice Statistics (1990). Timothy J. Flanagan and Kathleen Maguire, eds. U.S. Department of Justice. NCJ-130580. Washington, DC: U.S. Government Printing Office.

Strasburg, Paul (1984). *Violent Juvenile Offenders: An Anthology.* San Francisco: National Council on Crime and Delinquency

Sudnow, David (1965). "Normal Crimes: Sociological Features of the Penal Code in a Public Defender Office." *Social Problems* 12:255-276.

Suttles, Gerald D. (1968). *The Social Order of the Slum: Ethnicity and Territory in the Inner City.* Chicago: University of Chicago Press.

Sykes, Gresham M., and David Matza (1957). "Techniques of Neutralization: A Theory of Delinquency." *American Sociological Review* 22 (6): 664-670.

Teeters, Negley K., and David Matza (1964). "The Extent of Delinquency in the United States." In *Readings in Juvenile Delinquency,* edited by Ruth Cavan, 2-15. Philadelphia: Lippincott.

Thornberry, Terence, and R.L. Christenson (1984). "Unemployment and Criminal Involvement: An Investigation of Reciprocal Causal Structures." *American Sociological Review* 49 (3): 398-411.

*Thrasher, Frederick M. (1927). *The Gang*. Chicago: University of Chicago Press.

U.S. Department of Justice, Federal Bureau of Investigation (1990). *Crime in the United States, 1989*. Washington, DC: U.S. Government Printing Office.

Walker, Samuel (1989). *Sense and Nonsense about Crime: A Policy Guide*. 2nd ed. Pacific Grove, CA: Brooks/Cole.

Werthman, Carl (1967). "The Function of Social Definitions in the Development of a Delinquency Career." *Task Force Report: Juvenile Delinquency and Youth*. Washington, DC: U.S. Government Printing Office.

Wildeman, John (1985). "Computer Crime: Breakthrough or Break-in? The Emergence of a Whole New Crime." Paper presented at the 37th meeting of The American Society of Criminology, San Diego, CA.

Chapter 6

Political Criminal Behavior

Up to the latter part of this century, crimes *by* government had not received much attention from criminologists. On the other hand, crimes *against* the state—treason, sabotage, violations of military draft laws and similar subversive actions—had been grist for criminology's mill. In this chapter we look at crimes against the government and crimes by the government along the lines of our typology: legal aspects, criminal careers, group support, correspondence between criminal and legitimate behavior and societal reaction/legal processing. Each of these types—crimes by and crimes against government—involves different offenses, different career patterns and different social and legal reactions.

Crime against the state is recognized in illegal attempts to protest against government decisions or to express beliefs about, or alter in some way (violent or nonviolent) the existing sociopolitical structure. Since nation states must strive to maintain absolute hegemony of power distribution within their borders, these crimes are taken seriously and are punished accordingly. These crimes—whether in violation of laws created for the suppression of such behavior or for other purposes (such as fostering what is considered an "alien" ideology or parading without a permit)—are regarded by political authorities as a threat to the state as it exists. Political crimes against the state include a wide range of classic crimes: treason, sedition, assassination, violation of military draft regulations, rioting or inciting to riot, civil rights violations, protest violations and violations of law in the course of advancing "radical" ideas and actions. Some have gone so far as to press for laws that would make it a crime to burn the American flag in the course of protesting governmental policy (the courts have found, however, that such laws would be in violation of the First Amendment). Failure to conform to certain laws because of religious convictions also can be a crime against the state. An example of this last threat to the state is seen in the refusal of certain religious communities, such as the Pennsylvania Amish, to send their children to public schools.

On the other hand, crime by government is constituted by unlawful government action against citizens. It consists of the criminal violations by governments themselves, or more particularly, by the agents of the government, whether police officers or presidents. Governmental crime can be further divided into:

1. *Violations of the civil liberties and rights of the citizens, or failure to safeguard these liberties and rights.* An example would be the violation of constitutional guarantees and civil rights legislation by various government officials, as in governmental violations of its own equal oppportunities statutes or governmental violations of privacy laws;

2. *Criminal acts committed in the course of enforcing the laws of the state,* as in the example of assault and murder by police and prison guards. The much-publicized Rodney King beating that led to the Los Angeles riots in the early 1990s is an example of this;

3. *Violations of international laws of warfare or national sovereignty.* Examples of this abound: Nazi genocide, the United States mining of Nicaraguan harbors, the seizure of Kuwait by the Iraqui government (although this text is concerned principally with violations of United States federal and state laws, we nonetheless include some limited discussion of such violations because many consider them political crimes);

4. *Violations of the federal law by high-ranking officials, such as giving false testimony to Congress or violating Congressional policy laws.* Examples include the Iran-Contra arms-for-hostages trade and "Watergate," the Nixon administration's raid of Democratic party headquarters and subsequent coverup. These crimes sometimes are the result of the contradiction between maintaining secret intelligence services in what is officially an open and democratic society.

An illustration of how crimes *against* the government can be provoked by crimes *by* the government is the above-mentioned Los Angeles/Rodney King case, which instigated some of the worst rioting this country has ever experienced.

> It was no surprise that the police in Los Angeles clubbed Rodney King into submission or that they exchanged nigger jokes over their high-tech communications systems, or that they had received the best training in the fine art of less-than-lethal cruelties. . . . Yet what they did, what they thought, and what they justified is not the aberrational madness of bad apples. (Platt 1992)

In attempting to preserve a particular social and political order, governments and their officials violate laws that exist to protect the citizen from the abuses of government in a democratic society. Often it is procedural law that is violated rather than substantive law. The fact that governments do not usually choose to prosecute themselves when these laws are broken does not make the violations any less criminal. It simply makes the violators harder to prosecute. Political crimes—crimes *by* or *against* the government—are particularly difficult to view objectively, for they always involve moral and ideological positions.

Any discussion of political crime is bound to be complicated by what are often conflicting views of a situation. For example, during the Vietnam era those opposed to the conflict on the grounds that it was unconstitutional vigorously opposed the government's prosecution of those who resisted conscription. For these people, not only was the government breaking the law by waging the war in the first place, but it was making an intolerable situation worse by punishing those who resisted. For others, those who resisted the war and the draft were the ones guilty of crimes against the government. Where one side saw crime by the government, the other side saw crimes against the government. The "war on drugs," declared by President Ronald Reagan and pursued by President George Bush, posed a similar dilemma. Some saw this "war" as involving heinous crimes by the federal government against the civil rights of the people of the United States and against the lives and safety of the citizens of drug-exporting countries like Peru and Colombia. Others saw it as an all-out attack by the government on those who would undermine the basic values of this country, hence crimes against the government and against public order. Consider the following facts:

> The international trade in illegal drugs is estimated to be worth up to $300 billion per year, with $50 to $100 billion generated by the United States alone. (Friends Committee 1990)

> The total money value is greater than that of the oil trade, second only to the arms trade. (Friends Committee 1990)

> In one area in one city—South Central Los Angeles—rock cocaine is a $5 million-plus-per-week business. Law enforcement officials seized more than $100 million in cash from drug dealers in 1988. (DeGeneste and Sullivan 1992)

These facts are open to interpretation, either as evidence of gross government malfeasance or of the crimes of the "illegal drug industry" and those who would bring the country down by producing, importing, and distributing controlled substances. Of course, there are many other considerations of great importance in this particular issue, but the point is that any discussion of political crime can turn out to be a two-edged sword. The same dilemmas arise when the state interferes with constitutional rights to free speech. Before the courts settled the issue, flag burning was thought by some to be a crime against the state while others felt that the state, by punishing flag-burning protesters, was itself in violation of the law.

A wide variety of crimes against the government are crimes of *omission*, crimes such as evasion of income tax laws, violations of customs regulations or operating or acting without a license when one is required. Income tax evasion is a world unto itself, and it covers a great deal of ground (as any CPA can testify). Some evasions are merely unethical and legally questionable, while others are outright crimes. Similarly, evasion or violation of customs laws boil down to avoiding the payment of taxes on items brought into or taken out of the country. Violations of licensing laws amount to the same thing in that the goal is usually to avoid paying for the license or to obtain a false license for one reason or another. We do not discuss these particular crimes at length in this chapter, since they are more fittingly dealt with as white-collar crimes, corporate crimes or actions of organized crime.

Legal Aspects of Selected Offenses

Crimes against Government

All freedom, including political freedom, is qualified. The history of the United States is replete with laws that have been enacted and enforced in order to contain real or perceived threats to the status quo and/or the government. Freedom of speech was severely abridged, for example, by the Sedition Act of 1798, which provided for the punishment of anyone who uttered or published statements against the government, and by the strengthening of the Espionage Act in 1917. The 1917 laws, sweeping and vaguely worded, constituted the most brutal attack on free speech in America since the Sedition Act 120 years earlier (O'Toole 1991). It empowered the federal government to carry out wholesale censorship of all communications, whether they be by mail, newpaper, telephone, telegraph or radio. Legal controls relating to security as well as economic matters have been established during war emergencies (Troy 1981). Concern (and what often amounted to a national paranoia) over native communism occurred during post-World War II instability and unrest (Murray 1955).

The federal statutes are filled with other antisubversive provisions enacted during periods of national crisis. To name only a few, the Voorhis Act of 1940 restricted the registration of persons and organizations who acted as agents of foreign powers; the Smith Act of 1940 forbade the advocacy of the overthrow of the government; the Internal Security Act of 1950 (McCarran Act) required the registration of Communist and the Communist-front organizations as well as strengthened other legislation on subversion; the Immigration and Nationality Act of 1952 (McCarran-Walter Act) provided for the deportation of resident aliens because of "disloyal" beliefs and associations; and the Communist Control Act of 1954 required the registration of Communist party members with the Attorney General. In addition to such legislation, loyalty and security programs have been initiated and blacklist procedures established (Brown 1958). In addition there was the internment of tens of thousands of loyal Japanese-Americans in prison camps during World War II (Baker 1981; Collins 1985; Daniels 1986).

The more political freedom there is in a particular nation at a particular time, the greater the struggle necessary to preserve and enhance it. This is the case with established democratic regimes. It is equally true that the less political freedom, the more difficult is the struggle to realize it in order to create a just and representative government. The peaceful prodemocracy student revolt at Peking's Tiananmen Square in 1989, which was put down in blood by the Chinese Communist Party leadership, is an example of this. But the existence of political freedom does not automatically eliminate intolerance on the part of those segments of society opposed to proposals for change. There may be laws guaranteeing civil rights and social justice for minority groups, but these laws do not ensure that other laws will not be invoked to neutralize their effectiveness. For example, there are many examples of criminal laws and civil statutes formulated to handle and control the enforcement of minority rights and the rights of political dissenters. The United States in particular has had a history of struggle in this area. It is important to bear in mind that in the case of crimes against the government, the dominant sociopolitical forces are usually able to use existing or new legislation to suppress dissent and protest.

In the past, demonstrators for civil rights, social justice and other causes have been arrested on such charges as disorderly conduct, breach of peace, parading without a permit, trespassing, loitering and violation of fire ordinances. Other protesters have been legally harrassed on charges of refusal to pay income taxes used for military purposes, for picketing military bases and for refusing to register for the draft. More recently, criminal law has been used to arrest and prosecute those who have denied the civil rights of others by blocking access to health clinics that perform abortions. All of these behaviors share the common element that the offenders are pursuing values out of conscience and conviction, but values differing from those of the groups that formulate and administer the criminal law. The result is that some persons and organizations are defined as criminal. The real struggle is to establish whose interests and values are reflected in the law.

The criminal laws that have been established to control perceived and real threats to the state are of an obvious political nature. They make no attempt to cover up their direct political intent. Existing governmental policy is to be honored and protected from any internal or external dangers. Even when certain procedural guarantees are recognized, such as due process, equal protection and the right to civil disobedience, the law can be qualified at every point in order to maintain the *status quo*. This was the point that Martin Luther King, Jr. brought out in his *Letter from Birmingham Jail:* "Sometimes a law is just on its face and unjust in its application. For instance, I have been arrested on a charge of parading without a permit. Now, there is nothing wrong in having an ordinance which requires a permit for a parade. But such an ordinance becomes unjust when it is used to maintain segregation and to deny citizens the First Amendment privilege of peaceful assembly and protest" (King 1963).

One effective tactic used by all governments against its citizens—usually those advocating political and social change—is the refusal to publicly and legally recognize the concept of political crime. In the case of the United States, the Anglo-American doctrine of legalism seems to justify this: obedience to existing law is a moral absolute.

> The situation in English and American society is often viewed as if all members of these societies had agreed to disagree on matters of morals and politics (we may doubt, however, how deep this disagreement has ever been), but agreed that all would respect the law because the law protected the right of each to his own separate opinion and a certain freedom in the expression of it. It is on a spirit of compromise and limited struggle within the legal rules of the game that the stability of English and American political institutions depends, and it is commonly felt that there would be anarchy without it. (Ingraham and Tokoro 1969)

Since opposition to the government could not be legally *and* morally recognized, political crime as a concept could not be incorporated into the law. Political offenders normally have been dealt with under "nonpolitical" laws. The political offender has been officially labeled and handled in the same way as the conventional offender. To admit the concept of political crime into domestic jurisprudence would be to recognize the limitations of liberal democracy. This doctrine is called "democratic elitism," wherein those in power, according to our present legal system, can effectively use the law to their own advantage. This point was made some time ago by a British historian who observed, "The function of State coercion is to overcome individual coercion, and, of course, coercion exercised by any association of individuals within the State" (Hobhouse 1911).

Crimes by Government

Criminologists, like most people, have been reluctant to face the possibility that government can act criminally (Schafer 1974). Following the classic image of government formulated by political philosophers such as Jeremy Bentham and John Stuart Mill, Americans have tended to regard governments as being above the law. Since governments supposedly have sovereignty over the people, governments are to control the citizenry—not regulate themselves. The classic idea is that governments need not regulate themselves, since they are simply expressions of the will of the people. Only in the more critical tradition is govern-ment regarded as an artificial institution created by the people to serve their needs. But as long as the classic tradition is followed—with government having complete sovereignty—the immunity of government from the law is tacitly accepted.

However, as a result of events that have taken place over the past 30 years, there has been an increasing recognition that the government is subject to its own laws as well as to international law. No longer is government naively accepted as above the law or incapable of violating the law. Government (the state) is no longer seen as in sole possession of complete and total sovereignty to the extent of being immune from law. The classic notion that governments need not regulate themselves according to law since they are absolute expressions of the will of the people is no longer uncritically accepted. Consequently, we have come to understand that the state itself is capable of crime—to the social harm and suffering of vast multitudes both at home and abroad (Barak 1991).

When a critical/progressive conception of democracy is held, however, it becomes apparent that governments as the principal makers and enforcers of law can themselves be lawbreakers. If the law is to some extent an institution of the people themselves (the citizenry), then that same law can be used to protect the people from harms committed against them by those who act in the name of the government. It need not be paradoxical that those who make and enforce the law are themselves lawbreakers. What we have tended to accept in the past, then, is a sort of double standard toward crime. The major emphasis has been on crimes against the government or crimes "against society," to the virtual neglect of crimes committed by the government against the people who create it and to whom it is responsible. One standard of legality and appropriate conduct has been maintained for one order of events while another standard has been used for the other. While individual violence (e.g., homicide) or collective violence (e.g., vigi-lantism) have been viewed as criminal, similar actions by the government have not been defined as acts of violence, or have been regarded as acts of "legitimate violence." However, the violence employed by law enforcement officers in quelling a civil protest can easily pass over the line into police brutality. Or the violence of the military in maintaining world hegemony and control over valued resources can become problematic with regard to lawful behavior.

Criminologists and others have begun to take note of this (Chambliss 1988, Chapter 13). Governmental crime is difficult to analyze and define, for if a state definition of crime is the only definition used, then we are left with only one definition of crime: crime is what the state says it is, and governments are not inclined to prosecute themselves. This is the case with totalitarian regimes: legally speaking, the state and its authorities can do no wrong. However, if the definition of state-organized crime proposed by most criminologists is accepted, then crime by the government "consists of acts committed by state or govern-ment officials in the pursuit of their job as representatives of the government" (Chambliss 1988, 327).

During the 1970s, violations by the President (Nixon) and his associates resulted in the imprisonment of 25 high-ranking officials, including the Attorney General and two top presidential aids. The President himself was spared from possible criminal action by a presidential pardon. The violations of law by these men included obstruction of justice, conspiracy to obstruct justice, perjury, accepting contributions or bribes from corporations, bribing persons to prevent testimony, illegal tactics or "dirty tricks" in conducting election campaigns, and the misuse for personal purposes of the FBI, the CIA and the IRS. In the 1980s another President (Reagan) authorized sending arms illegally to Iran in exchange for the political hostages they held. Some high-ranking officials in the administration were involved in two operations, one that would exchange arms for the hostages, another that would funnel the profits from the arms sale to aid political guerrillas in Nicaragua. Although no hostages were ever actually returned in exchange for arms, the sending of money to the "Contras" (as the Nicaraguan rebels were called) had been expressly forbidden by the United States Congress.

The problem of the homeless in the United States is relatively new, at least in its contemporary dimensions. Yet, the government insists on treating the homeless as criminals in many cases. A segment of our fellow citizens who have been driven from their homes, frequently by government neglect, is now being treated as criminal by agents of the state.

> The homeless are being treated across the U.S.A. as lepers and criminals. For example, they have been harassed and beaten by police in Phoenix and Tucson. To keep them from sleeping in Tompkins Square Park, despite an acute budgetary crisis New York city is spending millions reassigning police from nearby communities to the park. Similar assignments are being made in Seattle, where people have been cleared out of 13 downtown parks between 11:00 P.M. and 6:00 A.M. Seattle homeless have been criminalized and lumped with dope dealers . . . (Schwendinger and Schwendinger 1992).

The treatment of imprisoned people in the United States and other countries has frequently been the object of criminologists' critiques of crime by the state and agents of the state (Agee 1990; Brown 1989; Finn 1990; Jose-Kampfner 1990; National Prison Project of the ACLU 1988; Platt 1987). Violations of civil rights—even those of convicted felons—physical violence, deprivation of vital services, psychological terrorism, brutality and harassment by prison guards have all been cited by the courts as examples of crimes by agents of the state employed in guarding those sentenced to prison.

Attention recently has been given to the rise of what has come to be called "contract policing," the privatization of law enforcement in the United States and a situation of governmental crime by omission. The government's crime in this case is its failure to protect citizens against abuses and violations of their civil rights by private police personnel (Hougan 1978; Marx 1986, 1988; O'Toole 1978; Shearing and Stenning 1981; South 1989; Spitzer and Scull 1977; Wildeman 1991). What these crimes by the state essentially amount to is that "the exponential growth of contract policing has been accompanied by a diminution of civil liberties and rights such as privacy, confidentiality, and due process as well as by a vast and largely unrecognized increase in the power of the capitalist state" (Wildeman 1991, 230). It is claimed that the CIA has employed many spies and others to assassinate or attempt to assassinate national leaders perceived as being antithetical to American interests abroad, people such as President Ngo Dinh Diem of Vietnam, Patrice Lumumba of the Congo, President Trujillo Molina of the Dominican Republic, President Salvador Allende Gossens of Chile, Fidel Castro of Cuba, Muammar Qaddafi of Libya and many others (Chambliss 1988; Dinges and Landau 1980; Hinckle and Turner 1981; Hougan 1978).

A major problem in this area of criminal activity is that it is very difficult to gather any reliable data and cite empirical studies regarding crimes by the government. Still, in the case of war crimes, as with all governmental crimes, acts in violation of the law may be observed and studied as criminal offenses. And there are those instances where the legal apparatus sooner or later rises above the more narrow interests of particular states and governments and even political parties. The crimes of government are being recorded into legal and social history.

Criminal Career of the Offender

Crimes against Government

Political crime against the government is endemic and pervasive in American history, from Margaret Douglas, who was sentenced to prison "for teaching colored children to read" in 1853, through Emma Goldman in the early decades of this century, through Sacco and Vanzetti in the late 1920s, through Spiro Agnew in the 1970s. The names of political criminals leap from the pages of our history: Benedict Arnold, Nat Turner, John Brown, John Wilkes Booth, Eugene Debs, Alexander Berkman, Susan B. Anthony, Julius and Ethel Rosenberg, Lee Harvey Oswald, Cesar Chavez, the Berrigan brothers, Abbie Hoffman, H. Rap Brown (Kittrie and Wedlock 1986). They make strange bedfellows, but they do have in common their opposition to the existing social order. A list of the clients of the famous civil rights advocate William Kuntzler from the 1960s through the 1990s is a veritable dictionary of those accused or convicted of political crimes.

Political offenders share certain common characteristics. First, they usually do not see themselves as criminals and lawbreakers and do not identify with a life of crime. Second, for such people the objective is not to violate the law for personal gain, but to change social conditions or governmental policies that cause pain and suffering. Violation of the law is only incidental and necessary to make their case or be heard. Normally law-abiding citizens, they violate the law only when doing so makes a political point or has the potential of bringing about a desired change. In these instances, violation of the law can actually be a political tactic. (In the case of looting, the offenders often are disadvantaged people simply taking advantage of a chaotic situation.)

In this same context, many crimes against the government involve protests and expressions of beliefs that aim to change some existing social, political or legal structure. Those who protest may be sincerely expressing their commitment to a value or they may be paid agents of a foreign government or domestic organization or institution. Many of these crimes—treason, civil rights violations, and so forth—arise out of a perceived conflict between religious beliefs and state laws. Most such acts are prompted by a desire to improve the world or the existing political system. Political motivation is considered by some to be one of the main definitional criteria of political criminals (Minor 1975).

Finally, citizens arrested for crimes against the state (e.g., riots, disorderly conduct, looting, blocking access, protesting a war, and so forth) do not have personal gain in mind. They seek to effect change in the larger social context. Their actions are usually directed toward public gain rather than private gain. The typical political offender regards his or her behavior as important for a larger, higher purpose. Martin Luther King, Jr. did not have himself arrested in order to further his own career, but rather to change racist laws and practices in America. The same may be said for some union members who, during a strike, break windows of vehicles operated by strike-breaking scabs. The purpose is larger than a single individual's gain and the arrested protester does not usually consider himself or herself to be an outlaw or a criminal. In fact, it is the government and its law and policy that is seen as criminal.

Political protest that turns easily into violence, disorder, looting or mayhem undergoes what some social scientists have termed a "flashpoint." Normally law-abiding citizens who have no criminal career seem to go suddenly berserk due to forces beyond their control. They lose control over their own actions. Unless they have a history of this behavior, and most do not, they have no criminal career nor do they see themselves as felons and radicals. A study of civil disorders arising from demonstrations and protests found that "The policing of demonstrations is invariably a political matter, involving as it does the right to protest against authority. When the police become partisan in deed or word, disorder will result" (Waddington, Jones and Critcher 1989, 69). This same study found that "Disorder is not a random occurence. . . . What converts an incident into a flashpoint is not so much its inherent characteristics as the way the incident is interpreted at the time" (Waddington, Jones and Critcher 157). The conversion from peaceful protest to riot is triggered by a variety of structural and cultural factors. The point is that the vast majority of the participants do not consider themselves to be criminals. Theirs is a higher cause and they have suddenly been caught up in a vortex of forces beyond their control, forces often caused by the actions of agents of the state itself.

There has been only a limited attempt to describe the more specific personal and demographic characteristics of those who engage in political behavior that may eventually come to be defined as criminal. However, we know that at any historical period such characteristics as age, sex, ethnicity and social class do not differentiate political offenders as a group from the general population (Lemert 1951). In our pre-Civil War period of the nineteenth century, antislavery protests that sometimes became violent included citizens from all segments of society. Political offenders differ more from one another according to the type of political crime or "cause" than they do from the noncriminal population. For example, in regard to social class, people in the IWW (Industrial Workers of the World), many of whom were defined by the United States government as criminal, were of the working class, while the members of many other radical political organizations have been from the middle stratum of American society. Likewise, with respect to ethnic background, politically oriented movements have differed greatly from one another in their ethnic composition. It would seem that the crucial factors in the career of the political offender are not personal and social characteristics in and of themselves, but rather the values of the offender and the value systems that the offender is actively espousing.

For example, during the turbulent period of the war in Vietnam, those who resisted the war and the draft (compulsory military conscription) differed considerably from one another in personal and social characteristics. During those years, one social analyst observed that:

> Violation of Selective Service law, then, does not seem to be a criminally defined behavior that is typical of any one particular segment of our society with the notable exception of age and sex structures. Resistance to the arbitrary domination of power on the part of those held in subjection to that power is as ubiquitous and extensive as is that power itself. As the power of the government reaches across the void deeply into the lives of all the people, holding them in subjection to its criminal war policies, so too resistance and opposition to this incredible domination is found in every segment of the social structure. (Wildeman 1971)

Political criminals are committed to some form of social order. Even the anarchists are committed to a social order, though it does not include the existence of a state or governmental apparatus. The social order that political criminals have in mind, however, differs in some manner from the existing order. It is because of their commitment to something beyond themselves and conventional society that they are willing to engage in criminal behavior. Persons who occasionally engage in political crime are interested in their society, but at times find it lacking in critical ways. In short, they want to create a better world by their actions. Consequently, they may sever their commitment to the existing social order in place of a more just and desirable (according to their values) social order that could replace it. The society to which they are committed may be a modification of the one that exists or may be an entirely new one, as in the case of authentic social revolutions. The French Revolution at the end of the eighteenth century and the Chinese Revolution following World War II swept away old orders that defined the actions of the triumphant revolutionaries as criminal. In every case, whether it be total or partial change that is sought, the existing society and its policies, social structures and values always serve as a reference point for political offenders.

The traitor and the spy provide the classic examples of the political offender who is committed to another social order. The traitor is guilty of treason in giving aid to another government making war against his or her own government, or adhering to enemies of the state. Some argue that the infamous Rosenberg case of the 1950s is an example of this, while others vigorously deny it. The spy, on the other hand, is more often a citizen of another country and in the course of espionage obtains secret information, often of a valuable military nature, for a foreign power. Spying is deeply embedded in the American psyche. It is part of our folklore, literature and traditions. A classic example is James Fenimore Cooper's 1821 novel *The Spy*. The spy is committed to his or her own country but is definitely not attached to the country from which he or she secures the information, the country in which the spy is regarded as a dangerous political criminal. The entire career of such an offender may be devoted to spying, as, for example, some Central Intelligence Agency (CIA) operatives. For both the traitor and the spy, there is a commitment to a larger social order beyond their own self-interest.

The nature of the self-conceptions, morality and rationality of political offenders is obvious in the many accounts of those who resisted the long, drawn-out Vietnam War in the 1960s and 1970s and the brief Persian Gulf War in the early 1990s. One war resister, in prison, gives us an accurate picture of his reasoning:

> I believe in brotherhood and loving people. I suppose that on an individual basis it's a natural thing for a man to protect himself as a matter of self-defense, but it becomes a different thing, even for self-defense, when it's institutionalized. I think that military institutions have disunited and separated men, and that is contrary to a basic belief of mine. I couldn't take a life just for that. That other man might be my brother. I don't think any war is ever justified. While I do believe that I'm against war in general, this one particularly, just doesn't have anything to do with anything I believe in. I think all war is an expression of the sickness of mankind, part of that sickness which he should try to overcome. I just don't look at it as being a natural thing—like some people do. I just

don't understand people who can think of war as a part of the way of life. I feel this is not me, and I can't participate in something like a war which seems crazy merely because some agency says I should. Basically, I'm just not a violent person. (Gaylin 1970)

It seems clear that an understanding of political offenders calls for a conception of human beings that differs radically from the one that was frequently employed by criminologists in the past. The view that the criminal is to a large extent a product of impersonal forces beyond the individual's control has proven inadequate for the study of the political offender. Human introspection and critical thinking is obvious in the career of political offenders of every cut. The human animal alone is capable of considering alternative actions and of breaking from the established order. Those convicted of crimes against the state more often than not do have a moral system that they truly believe in, from flag-burners, to abortion clinic picketers and war resisters to police assassins and governmental officals who perjure themselves in courts of law. Behavior that can be labeled criminal may seem to the person to be the only possibility for bringing about social change. To that person the traditional channels of the political process are insufficient or insensitive to needed change. We approach now the slim border between crimes against the government and crimes by the government.

Crimes by Government

As in the case of crimes against the government, crimes *by* the government (and employees and representatives of the government) are multifold and complex. Often it is difficult to even speak of the criminal careers of individual offenders in this case, for the crimes frequently result from bureaucratic and impersonal state institutions wherein individuals become invisible. As such, the perpetrators, and even the crimes themselves, become difficult to nail down.

Crimes by government include illegal violations of congressional laws and policies by personnel in the executive branch, illegal concealment of information to congressional committees, and accepting bribes. They also encompass violations of the law by members of the Congress and Senate, such as bilking the government for personal expenses like travel, violating franking privileges or accepting bribes. To this list may be added crimes by the police, who are traditionally the most obvious and visible governmental offenders. Police brutality, and other forms of misconduct, such as corruption and fraud, are chronic and endemic in American history and have been documented throughout the history of policing in America. Police brutality is the unauthorized, unwarranted and criminal use of force and violence in taking a citizen into custody; in police language it is called "unauthorized use of deadly force." Forms of misconduct include actions like entrapment, shaking down traffic violators, accepting pay-offs to alter sworn testimony, stealing from burglarized establishments, being "on the take," planting weapons or controlled substances on suspects, and sell-ing confiscated controlled substances and weapons (Punch 1985). One criminol-ogist has formulated this definition of police corruption; "A public official is corrupt if he accepts money or money's worth for doing something that he is under a duty to do anyway, that he is under a duty not to do, or to exercise a legitimate discretion for improper reasons" (Sherman 1974). A dictionary of criminal justice terms defines police corruption simply as "behavior by a police official that is unethical, dishonest, or criminal" (Rush 1991).

While we cannot argue that police officers as a category have a criminal career—the vast majority of them do not—it nevertheless has been documented that a substantial minority has been seduced into corruption by situations in which the job of policing places them. The crimes must be seen within the con-text of their careers as peace officers. The young police recruit, during the train-ing period, adopts a particular outlook on the work and develops a justification for using certain procedures in the line of "duty" that are, to put it simply, defined in the subculture of policing as "expedient." In other words, officers learn an ideology that later affects their work. Because of the nature of police work, a rationale exists among the police for the use of harsh and oftentimes illegal methods. It is the fate of policework that a certain amount of criminality can easily be built into the career of the police officer. Just as any other employ-ee placed at risk of committing crime because of the nature of the job, the police officer begins to develop a criminal career with the first illegal act, whether it be an act of brutality or other misconduct. From that point on, resistance to tempta-tion begins to erode and exposure to others who are willing to break the law tends to snowball into a career in crime. In the case of policing, we then speak of the "bad apples." Because the very nature of policing easily lends itself to the produc-tion of the "bad apples," police work calls for men and women of strong moral character (and all too often efforts are not made to recruit such people).

Governmental crimes are also committed by those involved in goverment policy-making and the execution of policies; these are elected or appointed fed-eral, state or local officials and their subordinates, as well as those involved in military structures, from admirals and generals on down the line to persons like Oliver North, whose felony convictions related to the Iran-Contra affair were overturned on a technicality. Here again, the evolution of a criminal career is difficult to document, for guilt itself is often difficult to determine. More often than not, it is difficult to establish that a crime has in fact been committed. After five years of intense investigative work by a large staff, the independent counsel in the Iran-Contra case failed to produce sufficient evidence for an indictment of some of the leading suspects, including top-level CIA and White House Adminis-tration figures. The few that were indicted or convicted were subsequently pardoned by then President George Bush: "In pardoning Caspar W. Weinberger and five other Iran-Contra figures last week, President Bush pronounced his own caustic verdict on the process that had convicted four of the men and indicted the two others. 'The criminalization of policy differences,' the President called it." (*New York Times,* December 28, 1992, "Iran-Contra Figure Points to Wider Role for Bush").

The criminal careers of people involved in governmental crime are often inseparable from their own personal ideologies, drives and ambitions as well as the "structural conditions that inhere in nation-states." One student of these activities gives us a hint of this:

> Why would the CIA, the National Security Council, the Defense Department, and the State Department become involved in smuggling arms and narcotics, money laundering, and other criminal activities? The answer lies in the structural conditions that inhere in nation-states . . . . [P]rograms underway are sometimes undermined by a lack of funding and even by laws that prohibit their continuation (such as the Congress' passage of laws prohibiting support for the Contras). Officials of government agencies adversely affected by political changes are thus placed squarely in a dilemma: if they comply with the new limitations on their activities, they sacrifice their mission." (Chambliss 1990, 375)

In the last analysis, anyone who engages in criminal acts constructs rationalizations to justify their actions and to provide appropriate self-conceptions. Governmental criminals do the very same thing. The police officer is just "doing what is necessary to get the job done," or doing what is "expected" of him or her. The war criminal is usually able to convince himself or herself that it is in the protection of national interests that these things are done: Oliver North, for example, presented himself to the nation as the ultimate patriot.

Group Support of Criminal Behavior

Crimes against Government

Clearly, the extent and nature of group support for political crimes against the state varies. Some political criminals receive less group support than others. Also, the groups to which political offenders may belong differ greatly in their ideologies, loyalties and motives. In addition, the social organization of groups supporting political crime varies with the size of the group, cohesiveness of the group, formality of the organization, duration of the group, geographical distribution of the members, and patterns of leadership. Finally, groups differ in the techniques and tactics used by members in the course of committing offenses.

Techniques and tactics include such diverse forms as oratory, face-to-face persuasion, writing and propaganda, nonviolent coercion, passive resistance, inciting to riot, demonstrations, marches, strikes, suicide, street fighting, guerrilla warfare, and the passing of information to the enemy of the state. The activities of war resisters, dissident and outlawed political movements, and outright traitors all illustrate this.

In some cases there is a relatively high degree of group support for crimes against the state. Except for the isolated zealot or demented person, most of these actions are not carried out alone. In the case of war resisters, for example, although the act of refusal itself is that of the individual and is prompted by an individual decision, there is a usually a large reference group of like-minded people who support the decision (as well as a network of counselors and advisors). These people share the individual's position that the government is acting in an illegal and immoral way. During World War II as well as during the Vietnam war (and to a lesser extent the Persian Gulf war), many religious groups formed in support of war resisters (the Society of Friends stands out in particular). Those who objected and refused on philosophical grounds to serve were supported by organizations such as the Pacifist Research Bureau, the War Resisters League and the National Council Against Conscription.

In the course of political socialization and life experience, individuals and groups develop a conception regarding the relative legitmacy of existing political institutions and actions. A political system—the state and its policies—is regarded as legitimate when the authority of those in control is respected and the procedures in the political process are believed to be appropriate. Groups generally regard a political system and its actions as legitimate or illegitimate according to the way in which the values of the system correspond to their own. The acceptance of particular societal values tends to maximize the legitimacy of the existing system. Groups that do not share these values are more likely to question the legitimacy of the system and are likely to engage in oppositional political behaviors (usually referred to in the mainstream media as "extremist politics") that may be defined as criminal. For these citizens, to do otherwise is to be completely alienated from contemporary life and to withdraw from the realm of the social as an agent of change (in other words, to turn inward). Such a withdrawn populace is controlled without a great deal of effort on the part of political leaders. (It was indeed unfortunate for the King of England, George III, that the colonists of the American Revolution were not such passive people.)

Traitors, in their own eyes, are loyal to some value, social structure or ideal that they and the network that supports them value as more worthy of allegiance than the existing structure. Such citizens are conscientiously following a set of norms and values that differ from those of the individuals, organizations and classes that possess the power to define what being a good and loyal citizen means.

A consideration of some of the cases of treason during World War II sheds light on the degree of group support for these actions: *Haupt v. United States* (1947), *Chandler v. United States* (1948), and *Kawakida v. United States* (1942). Haupt was a naturalized citizen of German birth living in this country. His son, landed secretly by submarine, was sent by the Nazis to infiltrate and spy in this country. The father gave him shelter and obtained a job for him in a war materials plant. Haupt and his son were supported by a network of persons sympathetic to the German cause as well as outright agents of the Nazi government. The treason was impossible without this network of support. Chandler was an American citizen living in Europe when the war broke out. He volunteered his services to the Nazis, and was put to work in a German government corporation involved in broadcasting wartime radio propaganda. Chandler participated in both writing the propaganda and broadcasting it. His treasonous actions also would have been impossible without a strong network of group support. Kawakida was born in the United States of Japanese nationals, and hence was an American citizen. He was a student in Japan at the time the war began, and he acted as an interpreter for the Japanese government while employed in a private Japanese factory in Kobe. He inflicted brutalities on American prisoners of war employed in the factory in order to increase their productivity. Here again we see the obvious fact of intense group support for his actions—support both from his government, his employers and his fellow Japanese workers. "All of these defendants—Haupt, Chandler and Kawakida—were ruled to have been guilty of overt acts which aided an enemy of the United States, with intent to adhere to the enemy's cause" (Hurst 1971, 238).

Conspiracy means the support and cooperation of others in an act: "a combination or agreement between two or more persons to do an unlawful act, whether that act be the final object of the combination, or only a means to the final end, and whether that act be a crime, or an act hurtful to the public, a class of persons, or an individual" (Rush 1991, 65).

Commenting on the heroism/idealism and the societal support of treason and traitors, one historian observes:

> This heroic aspect of treason, so important a feature of the great figures of the American Revolution and the fight for independence (Washington, Jefferson, Hamilton, and many others), is closely linked to the problem of functionality. . . .
> For when a traitor appears as a hero, he does so as the pathfinder to a new order for which the destruction of the old one is an essential precondition; the traitor himself has this function of aiding in the destruction of a system which is presumed to be outworn and even noxious. When Patrick Henry declaimed in the Virginia House of Representatives that "Caesar had his Brutus, Charles the First his Cromwell, and George the Third ("Treason!" cried the Speaker) may profit by their example." His was the vision of the new order to come, and he filled the function which the traitor has in such a situation." (Friedrich 1972, 109)

Inner-city uprisings and riots may be included in the category of crimes against the government. Nevertheless, the riots were a group activity—an activity carried out independently of any single citizen or small group of citizens. Most were simply sympathetic to the suffering of their community and got caught up in the "spirit of the moment." They all shared the experience of living it. The match was put to the fuse and grievances were articulated in violent community action. What became defined as violence against the state is for most participants a means of achieving just demands and basic, fundamental human and civil rights (Fogelson 1970).

Crimes by Government

In crimes by the government, individual governmental offenders are often supported by their fellow workers. A major reason for this is that the illegal activity that the law-violator engages in is usually an integral part of governing and maintaining social control. For example, every so often police officers are convicted of extorting large sums of money from drug dealers. Here we have simple blackmail and extortion. However, the officer who breaks the law by using unnecessary force in making an arrest, or who shoots a citizen, may be following the norms of his or her group. Likewise, when the police are involved in political encounters in which their interests are at stake, they are disposed to act in ways that are in violation of the law. Police who riot and illegally block city streets and bridges in protest over political decisions to establish civilian review boards certainly enjoy peer group support (Cooper 1980; Ross 1976; Sherman 1974, 1980; Stark 1972). However, police who strike illegally, or who call in "sick" as a group, represent efforts to accomplish objectives in violation of the law. In the higher levels of government, those who formulate and execute criminal war policies work jointly to accomplish their objectives. However criminal their policies may be, support can be expected from their colleagues.

More often than not police officers backed by group effort need give little consideration to the legality of their actions in the course of enforcing other laws. The law that exists to protect the citizen from the abuses of government authorities is often seen by the police officer as an obstacle to law enforcement. "For him, due process of law is, therefore, not merely a set of constitutional guarantees for the defendant, but also a set of working conditions which, under increasingly liberal opinions by the courts, are likewise becoming increasingly arduous" (Skolnick 1966). From the viewpoint of the police, the civil liberties of the citizen are often an impediment to the performance of the job. In such a context of group support, laws—usually procedural laws—may be broken by those charged with enforcement of the law. Often when the arrest reaches the courts and is "thrown out" because the officer violated procedural law, the police response is that the courts "coddle the criminal."

When the state attempts to silence political dissent and dissenters by interfering with freedom of assembly or speech, whether by violent or nonviolent means, it frequently breaks laws. The democratic process itself is violated, and the interests of those in power are protected under the guise of democracy. The lawlessness of the FBI, as revealed by the Watergate scandal, led to tighter congressional scrutiny and more control over the agency. None of the law-violating behavior of the FBI at that time would have been possible without a definite "bureaucratic conspiracy" to protect the interests of the government itself (Poveda 1990). This situation has been described as:

> . . . . state agents systematically using their power and resources to subvert the democratic process by targeting generally law-abiding citizens for surveillance, "dirty tricks," or violence. It is hardly a secret that local, state, and federal agencies have engaged in extreme covert surveillance and disruption of groups of individuals of whom they disapprove. (Donner 1990; *see also* Thomas 1991, 89)

In 1992 an independent prosecutor ended a five-year, $31 million investigation of the Iran-Contra political scandal involving sale of arms to Iran in exchange for the release of American hostages held in Beirut, and the illegal diversion of the funds to support the "Contras" in their war against the Nicaraguan government (which support had been prohibited by Congress). Eleven completed prosecutions resulted in eight convictions or guilty pleas by middle-to-high federal officials, including national security adviser John Poindexter and National Security Council aide Oliver North (later overturned on appeal). It is important to note that none of these actions would have been possible without the knowledge and cooperation of a close network of like-minded government employees, elected officials, agents and appointed officials—a very tight group-support network of individuals sharing the same zeal, the same commitment and the same ideology.

Correspondence between Criminal and Legitimate Behavior

Crimes against Government

The behavior associated with crimes against government in the United States is normally consistent with the democratic principle of the right of expression and the right to dissent. The right of petition and association is guaranteed in the First Amendment of the United States Constitution, which states that Congress shall make no law abridging "the right of the people peaceably to assemble, and to petition the Government for a redress of grievances." Aside from terrorist crimes against government, most are in conformity with what is commonly regarded as legitimate behavior. It is true that one cannot parade without a license, one cannot block traffic or stone scabs in a union protest, one cannot block access to a health clinic, and one cannot incite others to violence and riot. But even these actions, while usually in violation of local ordinances and laws, are commonly regarded as minor violations that do not depart radically from legitimate behavior.

In actual fact there are limits to the freedom of expression. Although the behaviors included in political crime may correspond in principle to the democratic values of American society, the actual commission of the acts is restricted to what is generally regarded as politically legitimate. However, during times of intense civil unrest and dissatisfaction with state policy, the climate changes radically.

The boundaries and definitions of political freedom are by no means consistent within any political democracy. The latitude of dissent that is regarded as legitimate varies from one time period to another. During some periods a considerable amount and degree of dissent may be tolerated because it does not seriously threaten the stability of the government. During other periods, dissent may be suppressed with overwhelming police force or the use of the courts to exhaust the scant resources of dissident political or social movements. The point is that political legitimacy and the limits of governmental tolerance of dissent are concepts that are manipulated and defined by those in control of the state. When serious threats to state legitimacy are exerted by those outside the power structure, then the boundaries of political legitimacy may be severely restricted and the dissenting behavior is defined as being well outside legitimate and acceptable limits.

Abstract freedoms may flourish with ease. Under the First Amendment we are free to say what we wish to accomplish, but acting to accomplish it may be a political crime. When protests and actions become effective, civil liberties can be withdrawn. Not only may civil liberties be abridged, but repressive laws may be used to suppress potentially effective action. It is with these realizations that many individuals and groups in American society engage periodically in actions that threaten existing social and political arrangements. Many feel that human rights are not being fulfilled and that they have the right to create a society that promotes these basic human rights. Thus we are aware that many actions are political, and in so being are often illegal. What is defined as criminal may actually be the fulfillment of basic human rights. Crime against government in such times expresses these rights.

Crimes by Government

The correspondence between the crimes of government and legitimate behavior patterns is fairly simple and direct: They tend to be the same, in that those who legislate and enforce the law (thus determining what is to be regarded as legitimate) are in the position of violating the laws themselves without being criminally defined. True, there may be behavior patterns beyond the law that stipulate the illegitimacy of certain governmental actions, but in regard to the official interpretation of the law, what government does is legal. It is when the law on occasion is invoked against government authorities that the incongruity between their criminality and a higher morality is made clear.

The civil rights movement may illustrate the conflict between patterns of criminal and legitimate behavior. Although the United States Supreme Court defined various forms of discrimination as being criminal, local communities, supported by their elected or appointed officials, held that the traditional patterns of discrimination were legitimate. Thus, Mouledoux has argued that Southern history has been characterized by governmental crime (Mouledoux 1967). The politically criminal nature of Southern political power denied political identity to the black population and violated basic constitutional presuppositions of political community, that is, the right of all to live under law and to participate in making and executing that law. By developing this pattern of "exclusive" politics, the South created a police state rather than a political community. African-Americans were forced to accept subservient social status by techniques of extralegal violence supported by police power. Government authorities, as well as community members, responded to the civil rights movement by committing various criminal offenses. African-Americans who attempted to vote in primaries were assaulted and beaten, homes were bombed, and people were murdered.

As has been discussed, basic government agencies and their functions are legitimate and approved in a democratic process. However, such governmental functions are often marred by illegal behavior in their application. Examples include the crimes of officials who guard and "correct" those who have been convicted of felonies and sentenced to state and federal prisons. Ordinary criminals are to serve time, be punished and/or be treated for their transgressions, yet the personnel who perform these functions on the part of the state may violate criminal laws in the course of their duties. Their crimes are in close correspondence to the objectives of security and punishment. Prison guards, in particular, are expected to do whatever is necessary to maintain security and order in the prison. The result is sometimes governmental crime by these correctional guards. Inhumanity, racism, injustice and brutality are far too frequent in America's federal and state prisons as well as in city and county jails, from New York State's Attica in 1971 down to the present; "hopelessness has become institutionalized" in our prisons, not hope and rehabilitation (Takagi and Platt 1988).

Most incidences of crimes committed by corrections workers become known to the public following the prison riots that occur across the country periodically. In these riots the inmates respond to the harsh conditions in the prisons and jails, as well as the disparate sentences and overcrowding.

Another example of the correspondence between the crimes of government and the activities the government regards as legitimate can be seen in surveillance of citizens by the government. The act of governmental surveillance, according to a long series of Supreme Court rulings, is illegal in most situations. Such techniques as unreasonable search and seizure, interrogation, wiretapping and various forms of electronic surveillance have been declared unconstitutional except in a very few cases. Nevertheless, government agents continue to engage in these forms of surveillance.

Societal Reaction and Legal Processing

Crimes against Government

Political criminals frequently present a serious threat to the existing social, political and economic order. They are dealt with according to the officially defined seriousness of the threat. The more serious the threat, the harsher the punishment. In famous cases, anarchists Nicola Sacco and Bartolomeo Vanzetti were executed, as was union activist Joe Hill. The crimes of these offenders were defined by the courts as serious threats to the state. Joe Hill was convicted and sentenced to death by a Utah jury on what many have subsequently come to see as a trumped-up charge of murder, but his real crimes may have been his labor organizing activities, which posed an intolerable threat to the business interests of the copper mining moguls of Utah. In the 1920s the state of Massachusetts executed Sacco and Vanzetti for a crime that many believe they did not commit—not only because they were poor Italian immigrants but mainly because they were anarchists. Other crimes against the government, such as parading without a license, inciting to riot and blocking access to medical clinics, receive more lenient penalties. The degree of threat posed by the crime to the existing social order, the status quo or the existing power structure becomes the barometer by which the punishment is calculated.

Public reaction to activity regarded as threatening to political authority has taken many diverse forms in the United States. Social disorders of various kinds can be interpreted by the public as legitimate protests. It is far easier to regard a public demonstration or a disturbance as a crime or rebellion than to search for the motives and the grievances behind the actions. The labels thus tend to be simplistic and derogatory. Also, it must be remembered that public reaction to any particular act against the state or the legal system is by no means monolith-ic. If a person opposes abortion, for example, that person is not going to be very upset at the actions of those who break laws by blocking access to abortion clin-ics. Similarly, if a person opposes a foreign military involvement, such as Viet-nam or the Persian Gulf, that person is likely to sympathize with those arrested for breaking laws in the course of protesting that involvement.

During the domestic agony and crisis of the Vietnam War, public concep-tion of antiwar activities tended to be negative, largely as a result of the images of the protesters that were projected by political leaders and conveyed by the media. War protesters were defined in a very negative and unpatriotic light, and even their peaceful, law-abiding activities often did not receive police protection.

> Insults are common: at one march in New York City, onlookers yelled "trai-tors" and "kill a commie for Christ!" At a demonstration in Chicago the jeers were "chicken . . . scum . . . commie . . . cowards . . . sissies . . . punks . . . weirdos." Some spectators have grabbed signs and banners from marchers opposing the war. In Madison, Wisconsin, a local paper reported that police "stood by without interfering when counter-pickets kicked in the paper coffin" being carried by the opponents of the war. Eggs, beer cans, rocks, and red paint are now regularly thrown at demonstrators who march in large cities. At a march in Boston, the protesters were harassed by leather-jacketed motorcy-clists who zigzagged their cycles through the line of march. Some witnessing antiwar events have attempted to beat those who participated; some have suc-ceeded. For example, during a march in Berkeley, California in 1965, sixteen members of the Hell's Angels motorcycle club ran through a police line and attempted to seize the lead banner; according to the *San Francisco Chronicle,* a "melee" followed. In Boston, a group of pacifists held a demonstration on the steps of a courthouse, and four burned draft cards. Twenty-five high school students then attacked, kicked and pummelled the demonstrators, knocking at least seven of them to the ground. In perhaps the most extreme case, forty New York city patrolmen were required to rescue one opponent of the war who had been knocked to the ground, kicked, and stripped of his clothing. Several of the attackers were shouting "kill him" and "string him up." (Finman and Macaulay 1966)

That is how it was then and how it was even earlier, following World War I. Political leaders and public officials then, as now, defined the framework for public reaction to political offenders. Following that war, when some persons and groups were calling for the release of radicals and pacifists from prison, then Senator Warren Harding declared:

> No true American will argue that our laws should not be enforced. I refer to laws, no matter what nature, whether they be those which deal with ordinary crimes and misdemeanors, or those which deal with acts of treason to the Unit-ed States, threatening the Constitution and the fabric of social organization.

I wish no one to misunderstand me, and therefore, I will say as plainly as I can that for my part I can see no essential difference between ordinary crimes on the one hand and political crimes and political prisoners on the other hand. If there is a distinction, surely it is not a distinction which favors political crimes or political prisoners. The thief, or ordinary criminal, is surely less of a menace to those things which we hold dear than the man or woman who conspires to destroy our American institutions. (Ingraham and Tokoro 1969, 162-163)

Citizen opposition to governmental policies is used by government officials as a political tool, and a powerful one at that. They shape the image and define the parameters and are in a position to shape the public's conception of the political offender. An official reality is created. This is illustrated in the following analysis of war resisters:

We may conclude this discussion of the manner in which others react to the criminally defined resister with a reference to the intense struggle to create a stereotype[d] image of him in the mind of the general public. The arena in which this battle takes place is the mass media and the contenders are political leaders and others among the power elite who command access to the media. The prize is the satisfaction and security on the part of the rulers in government that they have successfully instilled their particular values and ideologies in the minds of the masses. It is in reality a power struggle, the result of which is the creation of a specific social reality of the resister. The ritual of much publicized exchanges takes place between political officials who, perhaps sincerely responding to their constituencies, perhaps seeking political exposure, praise these young men as heroes and true Americans. The majority, however, attack them viciously as cowards, criminals, and outcasts. The stereotype of the resister in the mind of the public, whether it be as criminal or hero, is a social creation, the result of the ongoing struggle between the powerful segments of society for control over the definition of reality in the minds of the people. (Wildeman 1971, 42-43)

Judicial proceedings have served to define and limit a variety of crimes against the state. The courts have been used by governments on behalf of political goals. Witness, for example, what the Chinese Communist leaders did to student leaders in the June 1989 Tiananmen Square democracy protest. Also relevant are the various court actions of the British government to suppress those working for the independence of Northern Ireland. In the United States, the use of the courts to eradicate the Black Panther party in the 1960s illustrates the power of the courts to eliminate dissent. Kirchheimer, in an analysis of the court's role in the control of opposing political viewpoints and actions, has noted that three types of political trials have been used to accomplish the goals of the political authority:

A.   The trial involving a common crime committed for political purposes and conducted with a view to the political benefits which might ultimately accrue from successful prosecution.

B.   The classic political trial: a regime's attempt to incriminate its foe's public behavior with a view to evicting him from the political scene.

C.   The derivative political trial, where the weapons of defamation, perjury, and contempt are manipulated in an effort to bring disrepute upon a political foe. (Kirchheimer 1961)

The United States has a rich history of political trials. While there have only been a few dramatic state trials for treason, the courts have been used by the government on numerous occasions for political purposes. "In the furious game of politics, the legal system offers a tempting opportunity for those in power to damage enemies, tarnish their image, and isolate them from potential allies by casting them as criminals" (Friedman 1970). In political trials, often the goal of the state is not to actually secure a conviction, but rather simply to harrass the dissident party, group or organization, drain its energies (and more importantly its finances) to the point of collapse. As long as governments regard certain persons and groups as threats to their functioning and to their very existence and stability, the criminal law will be used for political purposes. And as long as people have the will and courage to oppose oppressive governments or their policies, there will be behaviors that the courts define as criminal.

Crimes by Government

Instances of possible crimes by government or governmental agencies or officials are typically shrouded in deceit, cover-up and counter-accusation for years after the fact. Questions and doubts are planted, but the truth is elusive and allegations are rarely resolved. It is for this reason that public reaction to governmental crime is dulled and rendered impotent. Another factor in the flacidity of public reaction to governmental crime is that the public has been led to believe that the government can do no wrong, and often the media takes the lead in creating and fostering this impression. Government and law are one and the same, so therefore the government is, by definition, always right. What is forgotten is that government, in its true sense, is a process of rule *by* the people, not a process or entity *beyond* the people. We have come to *reify* the state, that is, we have given an autonomous existence to something we ourselves have created and by virtue of this we feel we owe it service, obedience and unquestioned loyalty. Regarding the first point, that of ambiguity and deceit, examples from recent years are abundant. President Richard Nixon actually was never tried for crimes in the Watergate affair, being protected by a presidential pardon from his successor, Gerald Ford. However, many of his top White House officials served prison time for felonies. One criminologist has observed:

> It is pointless to speculate on the prevalence of corrupt practices among those in government. There is simply no way of knowing how extensive political corruption is, and one is unlikely ever to find out with any certainty. . . . One reason is the insider-outsider barrier that politicians erect in their dealings with others who are not part of the political establishment. Another is the cronyism characterizing relations among politicians and their friends in business and government. This leads to a kind of "mutual aid society" and encourages a "politics is politics" attitude among insiders, who would rather look the other way than make public trouble for a colleague. . . . A third reason for the difficulty of learning about political corruption is that the agencies responsible for policing the politicians are themselves run by politicians. (Barlow 1990, 301-302)

It is precisely for these reasons that public reaction to governmental crime is normally not strong and effective. Not only do most people find it difficult to believe that their government engages in criminal behavior, but it is difficult for the public to form intelligent opinions about governmental crime when accusations and charges are made public. The problem is twofold. First, the news that the public gets is either heavily censored, as in the case of what the military did in the Persian Gulf War, or there is a particular conception of reality presented in the mass media. The second problem in reference to public opinion about governmental crime is the way in which the government imposes its consensus on the public. The public is inclined to believe its leaders, and the rulers are able to manipulate the conceptions that are presented to the public. The ultimate irony is that those who rule continue their policies even when public opinion rises against them. The popular phrase for this is "stonewalling it."

When governmental crimes are detected, legal processing is typically weak, drawn out and evasive. The results are usually predictable: the charges are dropped, the defendants are cleared, or, at most, an official may be dismissed from his or her former responsibilities. It often happens that misdemeanor and felony convictions are reversed on appeal, or they are pardoned, as was the case when President Bush pardoned a number of high officials in connection with the Iran-Contra affair. Legal processing of crimes by the state (and the accompanying public reaction to those crimes) tends to be weak unless the truth comes out quickly and the case is vigorously prosecuted. This, however, is rarely the case.

References

Agee, Philip (1990). "Torture as an Instrument of National Policy: France 1954-1962." Review of *Torture: The Role of Ideology in the French-Algerian War*, New York: Praeger, 1989, by Rita Maran. *Social Justice: A Journal of Crime, Conflict, and World Order* 17 (4): 131-138.

Baker, Lillian (1981). *The Concentration Camp Conspiracy*. Lawndale, CA: AFHA Publications.

*Barak, Gregg, ed. (1991). *Crimes by the Capitalist State: An Introduction to State Criminality*. Albany, NY: State University of New York Press.

*Barak, Gregg (1992). *Gimme Shelter: A Social History of Homelessness in Contemporary America*. New York: Praeger.

Barlow, Hugh D. (1989). *Introduction to Criminology*. Glenview, IL: Scott, Foresman/Little, Brown Higher Education.

Brown, David (1989). "Returning to Sight: Contemporary Australian Penality." *Social Justice: A Journal of Crime, Conflict, and World Order* 16 (3): 141-157.

Brown, Ralph S. (1958). *Loyalty and Security*. New Haven, CT: Yale University Press.

Chambliss, William J. (1988). *Exploring Criminology*. New York: Macmillan.

Chambliss, William J. (1990). "The State and Organizing Crime." In *Criminal Behavior: Text and Readings in Criminology*, edited by Delos Kelly. New York: St. Martin's Press.

Cohen, Stanley (1988). "Book Review: Rebellion and Political Crime in America." Review of *The Liberty Tree*, by Nicholas N. Kittrie and Eldon Wedlock, Jr. *Social Justice: A Journal of Crime, Conflict, and World Order* 15 (3-4): 197-203.

Collins, Donald E. (1985). *Native American Aliens*. Westport, CT: Greenwood Press.

*Cooper, John L. (1980). *The Police and the Ghetto*. Port Washington, NY: Kennikat Press.

Daniels, Roger (1986). *Japanese Americans: From Relocation to Redress*. Salt Lake City, UT: University of Utah Press.

DeGeneste, Henry, and John P. Sullivan (1992). "Policing Transportation Facilities: Illegal Drugs in Transit Pose Special Problems." *CJ: The Americas* 5 (4): 13-16.

Dinges, John, and Saul Landau (1980). *Assassination on Embassy Row*. New York: McGraw-Hill.

*Donner, Frank (1990). *Protectors of Privilege: Red Squads and Police Repression in America*. Berkeley, CA: University of California Press.

Finman, Ted, and Stewart Macaulay (1966). "Freedom to Dissent: The Vietnam Protests and the Words of Public Officials." *Wisconsin Law Review* (Summer): 41-42.

*Finn, John E. (1990). *Political Violence and the Rule of Law*. New York: Oxford University Press.

Fogelson, Robert M. (1970). "Violence and Grievances: Reflections on the 1960s Riots." *Journal of Social Issues* 26:160.

Friedman, Leon (1970). "Political Power and Legal Legitimacy: A Short History of Political Trials." *The Antioch Review* 30:157.

Friedrich, Carl J. (1972). *The Pathology of Politics.* New York: Harper & Row.

Friends Committee (1990). "The Challenge of the Drug Crisis: To Heal a Wounded Nation." *Washington Newsletter* (February).

*Gaylin, Willard (1970). *In the Service of Their Country: War Resisters in Prison.* New York: Grosset & Dunlap.

*Henderson, Joel H., and David R. Simon (1994). *Crimes of the Criminal Justice System.* Cincinnati: Anderson.

Hinkle, Warren, and William Turner (1981). *The Fish Is Red: The Story of the Secret War Against Castro.* New York: McGraw-Hill.

Hobhouse, L.T. (1911). *Liberalism.* London: Oxford University Press.

*Hougan, Jim (1978). *Spooks: The Haunting of America—The Private Use of Secret Agents.* New York: William Morrow.

Hurst, James Willard (1971). *The Law of Treason in the United States: Collected Essays.* Westport, CT: Greenwood.

Ingraham, B.L., and Kazuhiko Tokoro (1969). "Political Crime in the United States and Japan: A Comparative Study." *Issues in Criminology* 4:145-170.

Jose-Kampfner, Christina (1990). "Coming to Terms with Existential Death: An Analysis of Women's Adaptation to Life in Prison." *Social Justice: A Journal of Crime, Conflict, and World Order* 17 (2): 110-125.

*Kellner, Douglas (1992). *The Persian Gulf TV War.* Boulder, CO: Westview Press.

King, Desmond S. (1990). Review of *Flashpoints: Studies in Disorder,* edited by Waddington et al. *American Journal of Sociology* 96 (2): 475-477.

*King, Martin Luther, Jr. (1991). "Letter from Birmingham Jail." In *Philosophy: An Introduction to the Labor of Reason,* edited by Gary Percesepe. New York: Macmillan.

*Kirchheimer, Otto (1961). *Political Justice: The Use of Legal Procedure for Political Ends.* Princeton, NJ: Princeton University Press.

*Kittrie, Nicholas N., and Eldon Wedlock, Jr. (1986). *The Tree of Liberty: A Documentary History of Rebellion and Political Crime in America.* Baltimore: Johns Hopkins University Press.

Kozol, Jonathan (1967). *Death at an Early Age.* New York: Houghton Mifflin.

*Kozol, Jonathan (1991). *Savage Inequalities: Children in America's Schools.* New York: Crown.

Lemert, Edwin M. (1951). *Social Pathology*. New York: McGraw-Hill.

Marullo, Sam (1992). "Political, Institutional, and Bureaucratic Fuel for the Arms Race." *Sociological Forum* 7 (1): 29-54.

Marx, Gary (1986). "The Iron Fist in the Velvet Glove: Totalitarian Potentials Within Democratic Structures." In *The Social Fabric*, edited by James Short. Beverly Hills, CA: Sage.

*Marx, Gary (1988). *Undercover: Police Surveillance in America*. Berkeley, CA: University of California Press.

Minor, William J. (1975). "Political Crime, Political Justice and Political Prisoners." *Criminology* 12:385-398.

Mouledoux, Joseph C. (1986). "Political Crime and the Negro Revolution." In *Criminal Behavior Systems: A Typology*, edited by Marshall B. Clinard and Richard Quinney. New York: Holt, Rinehart & Winston.

Murray, Robert K. (1955). *A Study in National Hysteria, 1919-1920*. Minneapolis: University of Minneapolis Press.

National Commission on Law Observance and Enforcement (1931). *Report on the Police*. Washington, DC: U.S. Government Printing Office.

National Prison Project of the ACLU Foundation (1988). "Report on the High Security Unit for Women, Federal Correctional Institution, Lexington, Kentucky." *Social Justice: A Journal of Crime, Conflict, and World Order* 15 (1): 1-19.

New York Times (1992). "C.I.A. Is Planning to Unlock Many Long-Secret Nazi Files." September 10, A9.

New York Times (1992). "Counsel Is Ending Arms-Sale Inquiry." September 18, A1.

New York Times (1992). "Senior Navy Officers Suppressed Sex Investigation, Pentagon Says." September 24, A1.

New York Times (1992). "Ex-Official Cites Doubt on P.O.W.'s." September 25, A8.

New York Times (1992). "Iran-Contra Figure Points to Wider Role for Bush." September 25, A12.

New York Times (1992). "Justice Dept. Criminal Unit Is Investigating F.B.I. Chief." October 14, A23.

O'Toole, George J. (1978). *The Private Sector: Rent-a-Cops, Private Spies and the Police-Industrial Complex*. New York: Norton Press.

*O'Toole, George J. (1991). *Honorable Treachery: A History of U.S. Intelligence, Espionage, and Covert Action from the American Revolution to the C.I.A.* New York: Atlantic Monthly Press.

*Platt, Tony (1987). "U.S. Criminal Justice in the Reagan Era: An Assessment." *Crime and Social Justice* 29:58-69.

*Platt, Tony (1992). Editorial, "The Fire This Time." *Social Justice: A Journal of Crime, Conflict, and World Order* 19 (1): i-iii.

*Poveda, Tony (1990). *Lawlessness and Reform: The FBI in Transition.* Pacific Grove, CA: Brooks/Cole.

Punch, Maurice (1985). *Conduct Unbecoming.* London: Travistock.

Purdue, William D. (1989). *Terrorism and the State: A Critique of Domination Through Fear.* New York: Praeger.

Ross, Nicholas (1976). *The Policeman's Bible: The Art of Taking a Bribe.* Chicago: Regnery Press.

Rush, George E. (1991). *The Dictionary of Criminal Justice.* New York: Dushkin Publishing Group.

Schafer, Steven (1974). *The Political Criminal: The Problem of Morality and Crime.* New York: Free Press.

Schurmann, Franz (1974). *The Logic of World Power: An Inquiry into the Origins, Currents, and Contradictions of World Politics.* New York: Random House.

Schwendinger, Herman, and Julia Schwendinger (1992). "Book Review: Greg Barak, Gimme Shelter." *Social Justice: A Journal of Crime, Conflict, and World Order* 19 (1): 144-149.

Shank, Gregory (1987). "Contragate and Counterterrorism: An Overview." *Crime and Social Justice* 27-28:i-xxvii.

Shearing, C., and P. Stenning (1981). "Modern Private Security: Its Growth and Implications." In *Crime and Justice—An Annual Review of Research,* Vol. 3, edited by M. Tonry and N. Morris. Chicago: University of Chicago Press.

Sherman, Lawrence W., ed. (1974). *Police Corruption.* Garden City, NY: Doubleday, Anchor Books.

*Sherman, Lawrence W., ed. (1980). *The Police and Violence.* Philadelphia: American Adademy of Political and Social Science.

*Skolnick, Jerome H. (1966). *Justice without Trial: Law Enforcement in Democratic Society.* New York: John Wiley.

*South, Nigel (1989). *Policing for Profit: The Private Security Sector.* Newbury Park, CA: Sage.

Spitzer, Steven, and A. T. Scull (1977). "Privatization and Capitalist Development: The Case of the Private Police." *Social Problems* 25 (1): 18-29.

Stark, Rodney (1972). *Police Riots.* Belmont, CA: Wadsworth.

Takagi, Paul, and Tony Platt (1988). " Editorial Overview." *Social Justice: A Journal of Crime, Conflict, and World Order* 15 (11): ii-iii.

Thomas, Jim (1992). Review of *Protectors of Privilege*, edited by Frank Donner. In *Contemporary Sociology: A Journal of Reviews* 21 (1): 88-89.

*Troy, Thomas F. (1981). *Donovan and the C.I.A.: A History of the Establishment of the Central Intelligence Agency.* Frederick, MD: University Publications of America.

*Waddington, David, Karen Jones, and Chas Critcher (1989). *Flashpoints: Studies in Disorder.* London: Routledge.

Wildeman, John (1971). *War Resistance and the Governmental Process.* Manuscript, Department of Sociology, Hofstra University.

Wildeman, John (1991). "When the State Fails: A Critical Assessment of Contract Policing in the United States." In *Crimes by the Capitalist State: An Introduction to State Criminality,* edited by Gregg Barak. Albany, NY: State University of New York Press.

Chapter 7

Occupational Criminal Behavior

Edwin Sutherland, the "dean" of American criminology, first formulated the concept of white-collar crime in 1939 and introduced it in his presidential address to the American Sociological Society that year. It was akin to an earthquake in American criminology, for up to that time criminologists had been focusing almost entirely on what is today called "street crime"—murder, robbery, larceny, assault and rape—crimes of violent aggression and theft. Sutherland published a printed version of his 1939 address in the *American Sociological Review* in 1940 (Sutherland 1940). His opening sentence was, "This paper is concerned with crime in its relation to business." Then in 1949 he published *White Collar Crime* (Sutherland 1949). In the introduction he wrote,

> The thesis of this book, stated positively, is that persons of the upper socio-economic class engage in much criminal behavior; that this criminal behavior differs from the criminal behavior of the lower socio-economic class principally in the administrative procedures which are used in dealing with the offenders; and that variations in administrative procedures are not significant from the point of view of causation of crime . . . . White collar crime may be defined approximately as a crime committed by a person of respectability and high social status in the course of his occupation." (Sutherland 1949, 9)

Of particular note here is that in his original formulation of white-collar crime, Sutherland uses the term "person" rather than "business" or "corporation."

Between the publication of his original article and his later book, a debate continued through the decade of the 1940s, principally between Sutherland and another leading criminologist, Paul Tappan. Tappan, with the dual credentials of a Ph.D. in sociology and a law degree, argued that only persons convicted of crime in criminal court ought to be called "criminals" (Tappan 1947). The dispute continues to this day. In any case, Sutherland's book on white-collar crime was considered the publishing highlight in criminology of the 1940s. A 1978 survey of 100 of the most frequently cited criminologists found that *White Collar Crime* was the most important and influential contribution to criminology in the decade (Sutherland 1983, xxviii; Wolfgang, Figlio and Thornberry 1978).

The realization that middle- and upper-class persons commit their own forms of crime was by no means limited to Sutherland (Geis 1968). Some earlier sociologists had criticized unscrupulous behaviors by individuals in business that occurred in the course of achieving the "American dream." E.A. Ross, in particular, directed his attention to what he labeled "criminaloids," a term that predated white-collar crime by over 30 years. During the 1930s, criminologist Albert Morris called attention to "criminals of the upperworld." But it was with Sutherland's work that such crime began to be taken seriously as an object of study by criminologists.

Sutherland's concept of white-collar crime turned the attention of criminologists to a consideration of the relation of crime to the pursual of one's legitimate occupation. Gradually the concept was expanded to include the violations that occur in all occupations, irrespective of social class. In his critique of white collar crime, Newman, for example, suggested that "farmers, repairmen, and others in essentially nonwhite collar occupations, could through such illegalities as watering milk for public consumption, making unnecessary 'repairs' on TV sets, and so forth, be classified as white collar violators" (Newman 1958). In his research on wartime black market violations, Clinard included gasoline station operators and those of any other occupations, regardless of their social status (Clinard 1952). Quinney suggested that an expansion of the concept of white-collar crime to include all violations that occur in the course of occupational activity—regardless of the social status of the offender—would increase the utility of the concept (Quinney 1964). Thus, occupational crime can be defined as violation of the criminal law in the course of activity in a legitimate occupation.

There is, however, a need for yet further refinement and reformulation, because the concept of white-collar crime is multidimensional and calls for more detailed specification. Even if Sutherland's original concept is expanded by considering all occupations, there remain the questions of the larger context of the violation, the structural context within which the violation takes place, and the nature and motivation of the violator. Sutherland added considerable ambiguity to the concept by referring to occupational activity but then engaging in research on the violations that take place in the context of large corporations. Furthermore, rather than regarding the corporations per se as the violators, he studied the policy-making officials of corporations. In this typology we take the position that corporations themselves are violators and should be set apart from individual occupational criminals.

The problem seems to resolve itself into a fundamental question: "Who is the criminal: the individual or the organization?" There are two levels of analysis here: the psychological and the sociological. Of course, each criminal act is committed by an individual person, but "for the good of whom?" Is it for the sake of the corporation itself or solely out of self-interest? Social structures powerfully nourish or retard individual malfeasance. Furthermore, the social structures into which people are locked can foster law violation for individual advantage alone or primarily for the advantage of the organization, with individual advantage as a secondary by-product, e.g., career advancement. It seems that people act illegally for one of two reasons: (1) in order to foster the goals of the organization, whether it be a corporation or a basketball team, in this case it is the official or unofficial *policy* of the organization to encourage this kind of illegal behavior, or (2) in order to advance and foster their own careeer by law-violating acts that are in direct opposition to official policy. The former is an example of corporate crime; the latter is an example of occupational crime.

Consequently, for the purpose of this typology of criminal behavior systems, we are dividing white-collar crime into these two distinct types: occupational crime and corporate crime. *Occupational crime* consists of offenses committed by individuals for themselves in the course of their occupations. *Corporate crime* consists of the offenses committed by corporate officials on behalf of their corporations and the offenses of the corporations themselves. The general public or the consumer may be exploited in the course of both occupational and corporate crime. When consumer fraud is committed by the individual businessperson or the professional, such crime will be included in occupational crime; when consumer fraud is committed by corporations or corporate officials, it will be included in corporate crime. The discussion in this chapter will be limited to occupational crime. Corporate crime will be discussed in the following chapter.

Another criminologist has introduced a subtypology in which white-collar, or occupational crime, is itself subdivided into four categories: (1) ad-hoc violations (welfare fraud, tax evasion); (2) abuse of trust (embezzlement, bribery); (3) collateral business crimes (antitrust violations, environmental crimes); and (4) con games (sale of false securities, fraud in land sales) (Edelhertz 1970). Yet another criminologist has created a typology of organizational crime that is divided into seven categories that range "from an individual using a business enterprise to commit theft-related crimes, to an individual using his or her place within a business enterprise for illegal gain, to business enterprises themselves collectively engaging in illegitimate activity (Moore 1980; Siegel 1992, 355). It is important to note that in each of these typologies, reference is to the individual, not the corporation, as a legal entity.

Legal Aspects of Selected Offenses

Lawbreaking is often divided into two categories: *traditional* or *conventional crimes,* such as larceny, burglary and robbery, which are usually punished under the criminal law; and *white-collar crimes,* which consist of *occupational crimes* and *corporate crimes,* those violations of law that are not usually punished through the use of the criminal law but rather through civil law and administrative law. Punishment by the government through the civil law includes injunctions, treble damage suits and license suspension suits. Administrative actions include license suspensions, seizure of illegal commodities, monetary payments, and so on.

The study and analysis of white-collar crime raises two problems at the outset: problems of definition and problems of the availability of data. There are a variety of legal responses to occupational crime: responses from the perspective of criminal law, administrative law, consumer law and government regulation. In the course of detecting and uncovering occupational crimes, many different actors may be involved: Internal Revenue Service investigation and review, independent accountants' audit reviews, or federal agency analyses of (for example) payments to Medicaid providers. Then there is the additional question of whether the illegal action is to be dealt with in terms of the status of the suspected offender (e.g., physician, accountant, business executive, bank executive/employee), the characteristics of the behavior itself, or the harm and injury that is inflicted on the victim.

Research on occupational crime has concentrated on offenses committed by businesspersons, politicians and government employees, labor union officials, doctors and pharmacists, and lawyers. Crime is extensive among persons in many occupations and in business. Repairpersons, for example, who service automobiles, television sets and other appliances make many fraudulent repairs (Vaughan and Carlo 1975). Auto mechanics may fail to replace parts, yet charge customers for them. Occupational crime may include, among other illegal transactions, income tax violations, illegal financial manipulations (e.g., embezzlement and various types of fraud), misrepresentation in advertising, expense account misuse, and bribery of public officials. In the investment business, brokers sell fraudulent securities, misrepresent asset statements and illegally use customer assets. Stockbrokers may themselves engage in "insider trading," where they gain illegal profits based on information about possible mergers or corporate takeovers that they obtain before the public has information about them. A series of insider trading scandals took place in the late 1980s, and several prominent brokers and investment bankers were convicted and incarcerated as a result. In each instance, the offender had used a position of trust to commit the crime (Shapiro 1990).

In prosecuting much occupational crime there are problems on every level: first, the detection of the suspected crime; second, its investigation; third, regulation aimed at preventing future malfeasance; and finally, how to go about prosecuting the criminal. There is a tremendously wide variety of behaviors involved in occupational crime, ranging from fraud and the misuse of entrusted funds to what has come to be called "computer crime," that is, illegal electronic transfers of money, stock and bonds, or the violation of copyright law (Edelhertz and Overcast 1982).

It is often difficult or impossible to establish the actual cost in dollars resulting from occupational crime. The extent of injury to the victim is usually vague and tenuous, subject to a variety of definitions. Then there are the difficult questions of who is the perpetrator and who is the victim. Occupational offenders are rarely charged with violations of penal statutes (U.S. House of Representatives, Subcommittee on Crime 1979). In addition there is the question of the role of deterrence if the offender does not make a career out of this illegal behavior.

With increasing frequency the medical profession is coming under fire for what one extensive study calls *Prescription for Profit: How Doctors Defraud Medicaid* (Jesilow, Pontell and Geis 1993). The development of Medicare and Medicaid has created new kinds of questionable medical practices. Practices such as submitting bills for X-rays taken without film, ordering needless and expensive procedures, submitting bills for various samples that were never actually analyzed and billing for treatments that are different and more costly than those actually performed. "The extent of crimes perpetrated by physicians against Medicaid is unknown. Estimates range from 10 percent to 25 percent of the total program cost—which in 1989 was $61 billion—but we have not found any evidence to support either figure" (Jesilow, Pontell and Geis 1993, 12). As with much of occupational crime, however, the actions of those physicians actually arrested, charged and convicted of crimes probably represent only the proverbial "tip of the iceberg."

The generic term "computer crime" encompasses illegal transfer of funds as well as copyright violations and theft of data. This is a relatively recent development in the area of occupational crime, and it usually involves offenses connected with businesses. Because more and more businesses and individuals depend on computers in business, banking and everyday life, we have only recently become aware of a number of ethical and legal issues surrounding their use (Ermann, Williams and Gutierrez 1990). It is now clear that computers can be "weapons" with which to commit crime as well as being the objects of criminal acts. They have been used either unethically or illegally for transfers of huge sums of money, to obtain unauthorized information, to steal copyrights, to alter or steal competitors' data and even to change university grades in the registrar's office. Attempts to prevent these types of crimes include highly sophisticated new code systems to prevent unauthorized access to computer files. Some states have passed legislation to deal with such crimes in the criminal justice system. However, traditional police methods are not adequate to deal with these crimes, and other expertise is needed. Embezzlement is a common form of occupational crime committed by businesspersons of various types, especially bankers and insurance executives, and increasingly computers are used in the commission of these crimes. In developing countries violations by businesspersons of income tax laws, import and export regulations, and currency control measures are common.

Politicians and government employees commit various occupational offenses, including direct misappropriation of public funds or the illegal acquisition of these funds through padded payrolls, illegal placement of relatives on the payroll, or monetary payment from appointees. Their illegal activities are usually more subtle, however. Politicians and government employees may gain financially by furnishing favors to business firms, such as illegal commissions on public contracts (crimes committed by Nixon's vice president, Spiro Agnew, while governor of Maryland), issuance of fraudulent licenses or certificates, and tax exemptions or lower tax evaluations. Labor union officials may engage in such criminal activities as misappropriating or misapplying union funds, defying the government by failure to enforce laws affecting their unions, entering into collusion with employers to the disadvantage of their own union members or using fraudulent means to maintain control over the union. Doctors may illegally prescribe narcotics, make fraudulent reports or give false testimony in accident cases, and split fees. Fee splitting, wherein a doctor gives part of his or her fee to the doctor referring the case, is illegal in many places in the United States because of the danger that such referrals might be based on the fee rather than on the practitioner's ability. Doctors may bill Medicaid or Medicare for office visits never made or for treatments never rendered, or they may prescribe expensive treatments that are not warranted by sound medical or psychiatric practice. Lawyers engage in such illegal activities as misappropriating funds in receiverships, securing perjured testimony from witnesses and participating in "ambulance chasing" in various forms, usually to collect fraudulent damage claims arising from an accident. Members of other occupations may also violate the law in various ways.

The legal regulation of occupations has a long and varied history. The beginnings are to be found in the development of licensure practices among the medieval guilds toward the end of the feudal period in Europe. These practices sought to protect the economic interests of the guild members and to protect the community from harmful economic and trade activities. By the beginning of the nineteenth century, the tradition of professional and occupational licensing was well-established in America, especially in the case of law and medicine. Later in the century the laws were greatly modified, and in many instances repealed, following the laissez-faire philosophy propagated by developing capitalism. But with the eventual founding of national and state occupational associations, regulations were once again established. The founding of these associations was largely for the purpose of promoting the interests of the particular occupations (Akers 1968).

By 1900 all the established professions had laws, due to pressure from their respective associations. Hence, occupational associations in many areas such as medicine and law (not the general public or the legal system) have been responsible for many of the laws that regulate occupations or professions. To this day, the statutes and administrative codes that regulate occupations and professions are largely influenced by the occupations and professions themselves, which represent their own parochial interests (Freidson 1986). This is known as professional self-discipline, and while it is a desirable policy, it is open to widespread abuse.

Criminal Career of the Offender

A major characteristic of occupational crime is the way the offender conceives of himself or herself. The lack of a conception of self as a "criminal" can be as significant as the presense of such a self-concept. Since these offenses take place in connection with a legitimate occupation or profession and the offender generally treasures a concept of self as a "decent, respectable citizen," he or she does not regard himself or herself as a criminal. At most, the self is defined as perhaps a lawbreaker, or one who "skirts the edge" of the law (but with ample justification). The attitude of such an offender is similar to that of those convicted of such crimes as nonsupport of dependents or drunken driving. Because the occupational offender is a member of a legitimate occupation or profession, it is difficult for the general public to conceive of that person as being a "real criminal," even though the offending behavior itself may be condemned. This social definition of others is reflected in the offender's self-image. In fact, many people may secretly admire offenders who are sent to prison for crimes like insider trading, who may make millions or even billions of dollars out of the swindle. A large crowd of admirers stood outside the court house and applauded Michael Milken, a prominent figure in the investment business, and a notorious inside trader in the 1980s, after he was convicted of and sent to prison for white-collar felonies that netted hundreds of millions of dollars. It is the dark side of the ideology of laissez-faire capitalism that may produce this sort of admiration of the criminal.

In his study of white-collar embezzlers, Cressey argued that the maintenance of a noncriminal self-concept by the offender is one of the essential elements in the process leading to occupational crime. In his study of 133 persons imprisoned for violations of trust, Cressey found that three interrelated steps were present in all the cases: (1) a "non-sharable" financial problem, (2) knowledge of how to violate, and an awareness that the problem could be secretly resolved by violating their position of trust, and (3) rationalizations about the violations (Cressey 1953). Typical occupational criminals are able to reconcile their concept of themselves as trusted, decent persons with their concept of themselves as illegal users of entrusted funds or property. Potential trust violators normally define the situation through rationalizations that enable them to regard their criminal behavior as essentially noncriminal. Cressey found that the

behavior of his sample was rationalized either as merely "borrowing," as justi-
fied, as part of the "general irresponsibility" for which the offenders were not
completely accountable, or as due to unusual circumstances.

Frequently occupational offenders regard the law they are breaking as unfair
and unjust in the first place and thus deserving of violation. Occupational
offenders are thus able to rationalize their law-violating behavior. Similar rationalizations are found among blue-collar occupational offenders. One study
found that workers in an electronics assembly plant would on occasion remove
company property from the plant for their own use (Horning 1970). The workers
who stole the plant property shunned a definition of their actions as theft.
Rather, the spin they put on their offenses was "the company expects this to happen from time to time" or "the company doesn't mind." A further rationalization
might be "for what they pay me, I deserve this." These rationalizations are particularly clear in the case of physicians:

> In the course of our research we interviewed forty-two physicians apprehended
> for Medicaid scams. To hear them tell it, they were innocent sacrificial lambs
> led to the slaughter because of perfidy, stupid laws, bureaucratic nonsense, and
> incompetent bookkeepers. At worst, they had been a bit careless in their record
> keeping; but mostly they had been more interested in the welfare of their
> patients than in deciphering the arcane requirements of benefit programs. . . .
> [W]e were surprised by the number of rationalizations that these doctors
> offered, by the intensity of their defenses of their misconduct, and by their con-
> summate skill in identifying the villains who, out of malevolence or ineptitude,
> had caused their downfall. In these doctors' system of moral accounting, their
> humanitarian deeds far outweighed their petty trespasses against Medicaid.
> (Jesilow, Pontell and Geis 1993, 148)

A 1990 study of occupational criminals that was based on an earlier sample
of offenders convicted of eight federal crimes of antitrust offenses, securities
and exchange fraud, postal and wire fraud, false claims and statements, credit
and lending institution fraud, bank embezzlement, IRS fraud, and bribery, found
that, contrary to common assumptions, white-collar criminals are often repeat
offenders. The data also suggested that these offenders normally begin their
criminal careers in occupational crime when they are well into their legitimate
careers, but that they offend less frequently than do criminals convicted of
"street crimes" (Weisburd, Chayet and Waring 1990; Wheeler, Weisburd and
Bode 1982). The "slippery slope" metaphor applies here. The occupational
offender begins transgressing the law well into his or her professional or occupational career, and once the first step is taken, it is relatively easy to move further
down the "slope" and commit more offenses without actually defining oneself as
a "real criminal." In addition, because white-collar crimes are committed for
utilitarian purposes rather than for purposes of emotional expression (as are

crimes of violence), the threat of punishment has a powerful deterrent effect on occupational criminals (Chambliss 1984).

Embarrassment and shame typically accompany the public degradation that follows upon conviction of occupational crime (Denzin 1983; Mann, Wheeler and Sarat 1980). Such emotional reactions, however, are often matched by anger and rage, which tends to render the justice system counterproductive. One study of 30 convicted white-collar offenders convicted for occupational crimes ranging from embezzlement, securities and exchange violations, and antitrust violations, to postal and wire fraud, and income tax evasion, found that the degradation ceremonies of conviction fuel anger and techniques of neutralization such as condemning the condemners. "When offenders feel anger toward a society that stigmatizes them, they also may feel less respect for the legitimacy of law. This feeling in turn may strengthen the cohesion of subcultures of noncompliance in the business world" (Benson 1990, 526; Braithwaite 1989).

Further, the high social status and respect of most occupational offenders, compared to that of violent offenders and other conventional criminals, makes it very difficult for the general public to conceive of occupational offenders as being involved in "real" criminality; this in turn also influences the noncriminal self-conception of occupational criminals (Coleman 1989). Another factor at work is the social good the occupational criminal may be doing. For example, researchers in the pharmaceutical industry who deliberately falsify research findings on the side effects of drugs are also likely to be convinced that they are not criminals because they are involved in the manufacture of other medicines and drugs that clearly save lives and help people (Braithwaite 1984).

It seems clear that the life organization of the occupational offender is not built around a criminal role. Such a person plays a variety of roles, the most prominent one being that of "respected, decent citizen." The reputations of such offenders have been observed in several studies, and the conclusion seems to be that in terms of career lifestyle, the occupational offender can hardly be distinguished from the occupational nonoffender. Some studies have found that medical doctors convicted of malpractice have enjoyed an *increased* practice following their conviction. It seems that their fellow doctors take pity on them and increase their referrals to the convicted physician. This, however, is in the case of a malpractice finding in civil court, not a conviction in criminal court. This observation leads us on to the next variable in our typology: group support of criminal behavior.

Group Support of Criminal Behavior

What is called occupational crime appears to have greatly increased in recent years. It has expanded along with (a) the expansion of techniques of doing business, (b) the social structure of the economy, and (c) the contraction of governmental control and regulation on the federal and state levels that took place during the 1980s. No longer is occupational crime "nickel and dime" behavior; it has expanded into the billions of dollars. To the concept of group support—meaning the support of one's fellows and the support of a network of people facilitating and approving of the offense—must be added the concept of organizational structure and the changing nature of production itself. As our economy has shifted from a manufacturing/productive form of capitalism to a service/finance form, so the nature of group support of this type of offense has changed apace.

Since the time that Sutherland introduced the concept of white-collar crime, most studies of occupational crime through the 1960s to the early 1970s viewed the behavior in terms of the group attachments and associations of the offender. Occupational crimes were generally explained according to the principle of differential association, whereby criminal behavior is learned from others who define the behavior favorably and in isolation from those who do not. While this remains true today, the nature of occupational crime, and thus the nature of group support for it, has changed perceptibly. The issue of group support is not as important as is the issue of organizational structure, external regulation and control and—most important of all—the shift from manufacturing to finance capitalism that took place in the 1980s.

Nevertheless it remains true that in some occupations members may learn specific techniques by which the law can be violated, and build up such rationalizations as "business is business" or "good business demands it." This diffusion of illegal practices is spread from a person already in the occupation to persons new to it, and from one business establishment, political machine or white-collar group to another. Although many forms of occupational crime can be satisfactorily explained by a theory of differential association (it would seem obvious where there has been continuous and intimate association with unethical and illegal norms and isolation from other norms), this theory has several limitations as an explanation for *all* cases of occupational crimes. Many individuals do not engage in these practices, even though they are familiar with the techniques and rationalizations of violation and frequently associate with persons similarly familiar. A business or professional person could hardly remain in a business or profession for any length of time without acquiring a rather complete knowledge of the illegalities involved. This is true in some occupations and professions more than in others. For example an accountant is quite likely to be well-acquainted with the illegal practices of some of his or her professional colleagues. Persons appear to accept or reject opportunities for occupational crime according to their orientations toward their roles and their attitudes toward general social values like honesty and integrity. Some of the other factors leading to law-violating or law-abiding behavior are attitudes toward other persons in general, the relative importance attached to the status symbol of money, the importance of law observance in general and the relative importance attached to personal, family or business reputations.

Each occupational or work situation contains its own set of group norms concerning the possibility of illegal behavior. This has been borne out in the study of theft in the electronics assembly plant. It was found that the work group subculture contains a set of norms that prescribes the kinds of property that may be pilfered, the conditions under which pilfering may occur and the situations in which the workers can expect the support of their fellow workers. The work group provides two broad guidelines for the pilferer:

> The first sets the limit by indicating that pilfering should be confined to the "valueless" property of uncertain ownership. The second indicates that pilfering should be limited to that which is needed for personal use. To exceed these limits was viewed as a threat to the entire system. Those who exceeded the limits were no longer granted the tacit support of the work group, which includes the right to neutralize one's guilt feelings and deny oneself the definition of one's acts as theft. (Horning 1970, 62)

In a study of prescription violations by pharmacists it was found that violations occur more frequently among business pharmacists and least often among professional pharmacists, with professional-business pharmacists and indifferent pharmacists (those not oriented to either role) being intermediate in frequency of violations. It was concluded that prescription violation is related to the structure of the occupation and the "differential orientation" of retail pharmacists to the roles within the occupation (Quinney 1963). Each occupation contains its own supports both for and against the violation of occupational laws.

Some researchers in the area of law and society have introduced the concept they call "collective embezzlement," which is the siphoning off of corporate funds for personal use by top management. This criminal activity, an occupational crime, is distinct from corporate crime in that it is carried out by individuals within an economic structure that is increasingly centered on the management and manipulation of money itself. Drawing on data from government documents, congressional hearings and news media accounts, researchers were able to "isolate the forces facilitating crime and fraud in these industries, and to link those forces to their base in the industries' structure" (Calavita and Pontell 1991, 95). Here the group support comes not from other individuals but from the very structure of the savings and loan, banking and insurance industries. "Different from the traditional embezzlers described by Sutherland and Cressey, the perpetrators of collective embezzlement are not lone lower-level employees but institutions' owners and operators, acting within networks of co-conspirators inside or outside the institutions" (Calavita and Pontell, 91).

This finding ties in with that of other criminologists studying occupational crime:

> To oversimplify only slightly, the social background characteristics do a lot to put persons in positions that allow the conduct of organizationally complex crimes. But it is being in such a position directly in an organization or with access to it, rather than status or background itself, that is the primary mechanism enabling the commission of the offense of greatest victimization. (Weisburd et al. 173)

Group support for occupational crime increasingly comes from the very structure of the organization of financial institutions as well as from other socializing agents. The same holds true for group support of what is called "insider trading," or violation of securities laws by individuals (Kornbluth 1992). Likewise, group support for occupational crimes such as fraudulent billing of Medicaid and Medicare in the medical health industry comes as much from the structure of payment bureaucracies as it does from other professionals in the industry who support such criminal actions with the "everyone does it" argument.

Correspondence between Criminal and Legitimate Behavior

Occupational crime cannot be fully understood without reference to the structure and values of the general society. The values involved in the regulation of commercial transactions may conflict with those of free enterprise, individualism, supply and demand, trickle-down economics or the "open market." An individual's attitude toward selective obedience to a "good" or "bad" law becomes the key to compliance. "The demand of law arises out of the conflicts in cultures, and because there is conflict in cultures, the law is not effective as a deterrent upon other groups that did not at first demand the law" (Cohen, Lindesmith and Schuessler 1956). The auto business, from the manufacturers down to the dealers, is saturated with rip-offs, rackets and law violations. One writer has referred to the business environment in the auto industry as a "criminogenic market structure," with sales methods that virtually force those in marketing to commit fraud and other unethical practices (Wright 1979). Auto manufacturers often set conditions that contribute to dealers' violations of ethical and legal standards. Imposed on the dealers is a pricing system that necessitates high volume and generally low unit profit. Such a policy results in high profits for the manufacturers and a profit "squeeze" on the dealers who must meet certain sales quotas. Manufacturers often award prizes to dealers who underspend their warranty repair budgets, thus emphasizing sales and not service. To keep ahead of the game, dealers may engage in fraudulent services such as charging for work not actually performed or repairs not made (Clinard 1990, 21).

One of the most important reasons for the high degree of correspondence between some forms of occupational crime and patterns of legitimate behavior is that many of the activities are only defined gradually over time as they surface and attract official attention. What happens as a result is that public opinion gradually comes to define them as criminal. In a highly and increasingly differentiated and segmented society the ambivalence of average citizens, businesspeople and lawyers reflects structured conflicts in social roles and the larger social system. Additional studies are continually giving us some idea of the conditions that lead to the definition of behavior as criminal and of the ways in which legal norms intersect and are integrated with the norms of other institutional structures. Values, norms and other aspects of middle- and upper-class cultures may help explain occupational crime in much the same way that knowledge of the culture of the lower class is necessary to understand conventional crimes.

Almost three decades ago, speaking of embezzlers, Cressey suggested that the extent of correspondence between some occupational crime and legitimate patterns is indicated in our everyday language. This language can easily provide the offender with appropriate verbalizations. Furthermore, these verbalizations may actually be "vocabularies of motive" for the offender. As in the case of embezzlers:

> Vocabularies of motive are not something invented by embezzlers (or anyone else) on the spur of the moment. Before they can be taken over by an individual, these verbalizations exist as group definitions in which the behavior in question, even crime, is in a sense *appropriate*. There are any number of popular ideologies that sanction crime in our culture: "Honesty is the best policy, but business is business"; "It is all right to steal a loaf of bread when you are starving"; "All people steal when they get in a tight spot." Once these verbalizations have been assimilated and internalized by individuals, they take a form such as: "I'm only going to use the money temporarily, so I am borrowing, not stealing," or "I have tried to live an honest life but I've had nothing but troubles, so to hell with it." (Cressey 1965)

Occupational crime is not far removed from the legitimate realm of American society. It is simply the reverse side of the coin, the darker side. It is not uncommon that individuals convicted of occupational crimes such as Medicaid fraud, junk bond fraud, insider trading or computer invasion are the objects of widespread popular admiration for their ingenuity. In discussing "our criminal society," Schur has described the relation between criminal behavior and certain values, drawing upon Taft's insightful notion of the "criminogenic" character of American society:

Of course, this undercurrent of values conducive to business crimes and related offenses is not surprising, given the extensive influence of the "business spirit" in our society. Indeed, certain of the values that help promote criminality in America are far from being subterranean in character. Thus, sociologist Donald Taft has cited the following "characteristics of American society" as having possible significance in the causation of crime: "its dynamic quality, complexity, materialism, growing impersonality, individualism, insistence upon the importance of status, restricted group loyalties, survivals of frontier traditions, race discrimination, lack of scientific orientation in the social field, tolerance of political corruption, general faith in law, disrespect for some law, and acceptance of quasi-criminal exploitation." . . . These are clearly dominant values or characteristics of American life, and they seem in some sense to have very real bearing on at least some types of criminality. (Schur 1969)

Perhaps there is no need to look for individual pathologies when parts of the "American dream" can help us understand crime.

Societal Reaction and Legal Processing

There are two factors that dominate the detection and legal processing of occupational crime: (1) how to detect it, and (2) what to do with it once it has been uncovered. Thus, the successful prosecution of occupational crime involves two distinct problems. One is the difficulty of gaining access to increasingly sophisticated information, and the second is arrive at a legal decision regarding how harshly to punish it once it has been detected. What sanctions are appropriate deterrents? The first problem is essentially a question of constitutional law: To what extent can the state demand that professionals, such as doctors and lawyers, and other workers reveal their private actions and affairs? The second problem is establishing suitable federal and state guidelines for punishment for occupational crimes. At issue are the dual issues of the protection of privacy versus the discovery of law violators, and the deterrent effectiveness of sanctions (Levi 1987; Schlegel 1990).

As a generalization we can say that occupational crime differs from other crime not only in its unique form of activity but in the toleration and support it receives from the public at large as well as from the courts, both on the federal and state level. Punishments given for occupational offenses normally differ in severity and harshness from the punishments given for offenses such as burglary, auto theft and, particularly, those (such as robbery) that involve the threat or actual use of violence in property crimes. The "saving grace" of occupational crime is that it usually does not involve any kind of violence. Among other reasons for the public's toleration of occupational crime is the fact that occupational crime is usually more complex, and diffused over a longer period of time, than ordinary crime, and this fact obscures the esssential criminality of the acts. The truism seems to be "steal a little from a great many over time rather than a lot from a few in a short time." In addition, the type of publicity given to occupational crime (that is, the role of the media) seldom creates much public resentment or fear, as contrasted to the depiction of more overt crimes like burglary or larceny.

Another study involved an inspection of the socioeconomic status of the occupational offender and the severity of sentence received. It concluded that, while the majority of occupational criminals come from the broad middle segment of the socioeconomic status range, judges normally tend to punish offenders of higher status much more harshly than their less socially and economically privileged fellow occupational offenders (Weisburd et al. 1991). In a related vein, a study of eight types of occupational offenders (perpetrators of bank embezzlement, postal fraud, credit fraud, false claims, tax fraud, bribery, antitrust violations and securities fraud) summarized the findings as follows:

> The results show that a minority of men but only a handful of women fit the image of a highly placed white collar offender. Most employed women are clerical workers, and most employed men were managers or administrators. Women were more likely to be nonwhite, less likely to have completed college, and owned less in economic assets. Men were more likely to work in crime groups and to use organizational resources in carrying out crimes, and their attempted economic gains were higher. Occupational marginality, not mobility, better explains the form of women's white collar crime. *The results raise questions about white collar arrest data and the nature of the crime and offenders in white collar sentencing samples.* They compel an investigation of the multiple influences of gender, class, and race relations in generating varieties of white collar crime and in being caught and prosecuted for white collar crime. (Daly 1989, 769; emphasis added)

In addition, other studies have concluded that the effect of current events in the larger society can have a powerful effect on sentencing policies and practices in the case of occupational offenses. A process of readjustment of sentences for this category of crime is set in motion by events elsewhere in the social structure, for example, by political crime and the traumatic social effects of political crime. In the case of the study cited below, the Watergate affair of the mid-1970s was somewhat of a watershed in sentencing policies for judges in cases of occupational crime:

> It is shown with data from one of America's most prominent federal district courts that changes did occur in sentences imposed before (1973) and after (1975) Watergate, but with off-setting results: after Watergate, persons convicted of white collar crimes were more likely to be sentenced to prison, but for shorter periods of time, than less-educated persons convicted of common crimes. (Hagan and Palloni 1986, 603)

A number of studies have pointed to and highlighted the symbolic nature of the criminalization of and punishment for occupational crime. One study, for example, on the basis of reviews of state and federal efforts to criminalize various forms of computer abuse, strongly suggested that the criminalization and punishment of computer abuse can be understood and interpreted as a symbolic gesture. Thus understood, it constitutes an attempt to educate and socialize the younger generations of computer users by extending traditional definitions of property and privacy to cover computer-stored data and information (Hollinger and Lanza-Kaduce 1988; Wildeman 1985). A similar conclusion was arrived at on the basis of another study of violations of the Immigration Reform and Control Act of 1986 by employers who depend on immigrant labor. Using interviews with 103 such employers in three southern California counties, the study found that employer violations of the Act are numerous and that violators feel relatively safe from punishment (at least harsh punishment).

> The study shows how legislative and implementation processes produced a low-risk crime, indicating that the shape the law took from the beginning ensured that its effect would be primarily *symbolic* and that violations would be widespread. This pattern suggests . . . the *symbolic* nature of the law. (Calavita 1990, 1041; emphasis added)

The tide of immigrant farm workers from Mexico continued to swell in the years following the 1986 Immigration Reform and Control Act. This was principally the result of lax enforcement, widespread fraud in the form of counterfeit documents, and sanctions ranging from a $100 fine to six months in jail. Sanctions such as these are a mere "slap on the wrist" in comparison to the immense profit the growers reap from employing cheap, illegal immigrant-workers. Again, the lenient attitude of the criminal justice system toward this and other forms of occupational crime is a reflection of the generalized and pervasive weak societal reaction to occupational crime.

So it is that in the laws directed at the illegal behavior of offenders there has been a strong tendency to enact lenient statutes and to enforce them in a similar fashion, showing favoritism to offenders of high social status. Many of these laws provide no criminal sanctions, and where criminal sanctions are included, they have been used hesitantly. Thus, the laws outlawing occupational offenses differ from conventional laws of crime not only in their origin, but also in philosophy, in the determination of responsibility or intent, in enforcement and prosecution procedures and in the sanctions used to punish the violators.

The enforcement and administration of occupational laws depend largely on specially created agencies rather than on police and prosecutors. The administrative process of hearing cases, rather than undertaking criminal trial procedures, closely approximates juvenile court procedures. The actions are often remedial in nature, as in the use of cease-and-desist orders, rather than consisting of direct punishment of the offender through imprisonment or stiff fines. This becomes apparent when one considers that an apprehended burglar or robber is punished by a jail or prison sentence, a fine or probation, whereas a doctor may be punished by a government warning or injunction, the levying of civil damages or the suspension of his or her license to practice medicine.

Regulation of the medical profession gives us an excellent example of the manner in which occupational laws are enforced and administered. A special administrative agency exists in most states for regulating medical practice laws. In New York, for example, a board of examiners is appointed by the Regents of the state. Moreover, the board is composed of medical practitioners, appointed by the governor with the consent of the state senate. The board issues licenses and has the responsibility of disciplining members, which may consist of revoking licenses after a hearing. Only as a last resort are cases turned over to the state's attorney general for criminal prosecution. It is a case of the profession policing itself, one not dissimilar from the police passing administrative judgements on other police in cases involving charges of brutality, harrassment or unauthorized use of force.

The physician, thus, is virtually a free agent. Once licensed, he or she has a lifetime certificate to practice largely at his or her own discretion. When violations of medical practice laws are detected, the state board is rarely quick to act. Thus, self-discipline among medical practitioners may be more illusory than real.

> Within the profession itself the disciplining of colleagues has little support; physicians do not like to police their fellows, and this reluctance is reflected at every level of organized medicine. At that, the strongest penalty a medical society or hospital staff can levy is expulsion. But removal from a society or hospital has no bearing on the doctor's license; though unacceptable to his peers, the offender retains his legal privilege to treat patients. Moreover, just as the profession is slow to prosecute violators within its ranks, so also it is loath to pursue the cause of more effective laws. As a result, the inadequate statutes currently on the books are likely to remain unamended for the foreseeable future. (Lewis and Lewis 1970)

In sum, a number of factors can be isolated to account for and explain the lenient treatment of occupational offenders by the legal system: (1) the absence of interpersonal violence, (2) the latitude of the general public, (3) the social status of the offender, and (4) the protection afforded by a professional organization.

References

Akers, Ronald L. (1968). "The Professional Association and the Legal Regulation of Practice." *Law and Society Review* 2:465.

*Benson, Michael L. (1990). "Emotions and Adjudication: Status Degradation among White Collar Criminals." *Justice Quarterly* 7 (3): 515-528.

*Braithwaite, John (1984). *Corporate Crime in the Pharmaceutical Industry.* London: Routledge and Kegan Paul.

Braithwaite, John (1989). *Crime, Shame and Reintegration.* Sydney: Cambridge University Press.

Calavita, Kitty (1990). "Employer Sanctions Violations: Toward A Dialectical Model of White Collar Crime." *Law and Society Review* 24 (4): 1041-1069.

*Calavita, Kitty, and Henry N. Pontell (1991). "'Other People's Money' Revisited: Collective Embezzlement in the Savings and Loan and Insurance Industries." *Social Problems* 38 (1): 94-112.

Chambliss, William J. (1984). "Types of Deviance and the Effectiveness of Legal Sanctions." In *Criminal Law in Action.* 2nd ed., edited by William Chambliss, 398-407. New York: Wiley.

Clinard, Marshall B. (1952). *The Black Market: A Study of White Collar Crime.* New York: Holt, Rinehart & Winston.

*Clinard, Marshall B. (1990). *Corporate Corruption: The Abuse of Power.* New York: Praeger.

Cohen, Albert K., Alfred Lindesmith, and Karl Schuessler, eds. (1956). *The Sutherland Papers.* Bloomington, IN: Indiana University Press.

*Coleman, James W. (1989). *The Criminal Elite: The Sociology of White Collar Crime.* New York: St. Martin's Press.

*Cressey, Donald R. (1953). *Other People's Money.* New York: Free Press.

Cressey, Donald R. (1965). "The Respectable Criminal." *Transaction* 3.

Daly, Kathleen (1989). "Gender and Varieties of White Collar Crime." *Criminology* 27 (4): 769-794.

Denzin, Norman K. (1983). "A Note of Emotionality, Self, and Interaction," *American Journal of Sociology* 89:402-409.

Edelhertz, Herbert (1970). *The Nature, Impact and Prosecution of White Collar Crime.* Washington, DC: U.S. Government Printing Office.

Edelhertz, Herbert, and Thomas D. Overcast, eds. (1982). *White Collar Crime: An Agenda for Research.* Lexington, MA: Lexington Books.

*Ermann, M. David, Mary B. Williams, and Claudio Gutierrez, eds. (1990). *Computers, Ethics, and Society.* New York: Oxford University Press.

Freidson, Eliot (1986). *Professional Powers: A Study of the Institutionalization of Formal Knowledge.* Chicago: University of Chicago Press.

Geis, Gilbert, ed. (1968). *White Collar Criminal: The Offender in Business and the Professions.* New York: Atherton Press, 1-19.

*Geis, Gilbert, and Paul Jesilow, eds. (1993). *White Collar Crime.* Newbury Park, CA: The Annals, Sage.

*Hagan, John, and Alberto Palloni (1986). "'Club Fed' and the Sentencing of White Collar Offenders before and after Watergate." *Criminology* 24 (4): 603-621.

*Hirschi, Travis, and Michael Gottfredson (1987). "Causes of White Collar Crime." *Criminology* 25 (4): 949-974.

Hollinger, Richard C., and Lonn Lanza-Kaduce (1988). "The Process of Criminalization: The Case of Computer Crime Laws." *Criminology* 26 (1): 101-126.

Horning, Donald N.M. (1970). "Blue-Collar Theft: Conceptions of Property, Attitudes toward Pilfering, and Work Group Norms in a Modern Industrial Plant." In *Crimes Against Bureaucracy,* edited by Erwin Orson Smigel and H. Laurence Ross, 46-64. New York: Van Nostrand Reinhold.

*Jesilow, Paul, Henry N. Pontell, and Gilbert Geis (1993). *Prescription for Profit: How Doctors Defraud Medicaid.* Berkely, CA: University of California Press.

Kornbluth, Jesse (1992). *The Crime and Punishment of Michael Milken.* New York: William Morrow.

*Levi, Michael (1987). *Regulating Fraud: White Collar Crime and the Criminal Process.* London: Tavistock.

Lewis, Howard R., and Martha E. Lewis (1970). *The Medical Offenders.* New York: Simon & Schuster.

Mann, Kenneth, Stanton Wheeler, and Austin Sarat (1980). "Sentencing the White Collar Offender." *American Criminal Law Review* 17:479-500.

Moore, Mark (1980). "Notes Toward a National Strategy to Deal with White Collar Crime." In *A National Strategy for Containing White Collar Crime,* edited by Herbert Edelhertz and Charles Rogovin, 32-44. Lexington, MA: Lexington Books.

New York Times (1992). "Computer Savvy, With an Attitude." Thursday, July 23, B1.

Newman, Donald J. (1958). "White Collar Crime." *Law and Contemporary Problems* 23:737.

Quinney, Richard (1963). "Occupational Structure and Criminal Behavior: Prescription Violation by Retail Pharmacists." *Social Problems* 11:179-185.

Quinney, Richard (1964). "The Study of White Collar Crime: Toward a Reorientation in Theory and Research." *Journal of Criminal Law, Criminology and Police Science* 55:208-214.

*Quinney, Richard, and John Wildeman (1991). *The Problem of Crime: A Peace and Social Justice Perspective.* Mountain View, CA: Mayfield.

Schlegel, Kip (1990). *Just Deserts for Corporate Criminals.* Boston: Northeastern University Press.

Schur, Edwin M. (1969). *Our Criminal Society: The Social and Legal Sources of Crime in America.* Englewood Cliffs, NJ: Prentice-Hall.

Shapiro, Susan P. (1990). "Collaring the Crime, Not the Criminal: Reconsidering the Concept of White Collar Crime." *American Sociological Review* 55 (3): 346-365.

Siegel, Larry J. (1992). *Criminology.* New York: West.

Sutherland, Edwin H. (1940). "White Collar Criminality." *American Sociological Review* 5 (1): 1-12.

*Sutherland, Edwin H. (1949). *White Collar Crime.* New York: Dryden Press.

Sutherland, Edwin H. (1983). *White Collar Crime: The Uncut Version.* New Haven, CT: Yale University Press.

Tappan, Paul W. (1947). "Who is the Criminal?" *American Sociological Review* 12:96-102.

U.S. House of Representatives, Subcommittee on Crime, Committee on the Judiciary (95th Congress, 2nd Session) (1979). *Hearings on White Collar Crime* 31-2. Washington, DC: U.S. Government Printing Office.

Vaughan, Diane, and Giovanna Carlo (1975). "A Study of Victim-Responsivenes." *Journal of Research in Crime and Delinquency* 12:153-161.

*Weisburd, David, Ellen F. Chayet, and Elin Waring (1990). "White Collar Crime and Criminal Careers: Some Preliminary Findings." *Crime and Delinquency* 36 (3): 342-355.

Weisburd, David, Stanton Wheeler, Elin Waring, and Nancy Bode (1991). *Crimes of the Middle Classes: White Collar Offenders in the Federal Courts.* New Haven, CT: Yale University Press.

Wheeler, Stanton, David Weisburd, and Nancy Bode (1982). "Sentencing the White Collar Offender: Rhetoric and Reality." *American Sociological Review* 47:641-659.

Wildeman, John (1985). "Computer Crime: Breakthrough or Break In?" Paper presented at the 37th Annual Meeting of the American Society of Criminology. San Diego, CA.

Wolfgang, Marvin E., Robert M. Figlio, and Terence P. Thornberry (1978). *Evaluating Criminology.* New York: Elsevier.

Wright, J. Patrick (1979). *On a Clear Day You Can See GM.* Detroit: Wright Enterprises.

Chapter 8

Corporate Criminal Behavior

The term "corporate crime" refers to the illegal activities of large corporations, generally the larger industrial corporations (the Fortune 500 or 1,000) and the executives acting on their behalf. It involves violations of laws, statutes and regulatory standards affecting corporations for corporate profit and not for the sake of personal gain by an individual (or groups of individuals) working for the corporation. Little research has been done on large corporations in banking, investment, insurance and transportation. Corporate crime is white-collar crime that consists of two different types: occupational and organizational. Occupational crime is committed by individuals in the course of their occupations, such as those by businesspersons, lawyers, doctors and accountants. Organizational crime involves large units that coordinate efforts in the attainment of collective goals by a corporation, industry or labor union. Such crimes can only be understood by examining the social system and social structure, and determining how they relate to the attainment of goals by lawful or unlawful means. As organizations, large corporations vary in the way in which their social structure generates unlawful organizational behavior.

Today's corporations are huge economic conglomerates with assets that total billions of dollars. In 1988 the annual combined sales of the largest United States corporations, the Fortune 500, totaled nearly $2 trillion, with profits of $115 billion. General Motor's sales of $121 billion made it the world's largest corporation. Although all of these giant conglomerates have one or more leading lines of business, most have acquired a variety of other product lines. Consequently they have amassed power, both political and economic, that extends well beyond that of the traditional large corporation operating in a single product line. Although they may well have other goals (such as lobbying clout or increased corporate power and prestige) along with their corporate growth and stability, their paramount objectives remain the maximization of corporate profits and the general financial success of the corporation, whether through sales, market shares or increased assets.

Along with the greatly increased productive power of the large corporations, an equally significant potential for social harm and a lack of social responsibility have evolved (Bradshaw and Vogel 1981). There have been many extensive violations of the law, as revealed by government investigative committees, both state and federal, that have looked into banking institutions, railroads, and the oil, food, drug and defense industries, among others. Widespread corporation payoffs, domestic and foreign, and illegal political contributions also have been exposed by investigations.

In spite of the limited number of government investigative and prosecutory staffs available, nearly two-thirds of the Fortune 500 corporations were charged with violations of corporate law over a two-year period (1975-1976); one-half of these were charged with serious or moderately serious violations (Clinard and Yeager 1980). At least one sanction was imposed on 321 of the corporations. One study found, using imposed court sanctions, that 11 percent of the Fortune 500 were involved in a major law violation betweeen 1970 and 1979 (Ross 1980). A more recent study found that 115 corporations of the Fortune 500 had been convicted of at least one major crime between 1970 and 1980 or had paid civil penalties for serious illegal behavior. The largest of these corporations have been found to the the chief violators (Clinard and Yeager 1980). They also have received a widely disproportionate share of the sanctions for serious and moderate violations (Clinard 1983).

The estimated annual costs of corporate crime range as high as $200 billion, as compared to the estimated annual losses from street crime of $3 to $4 billion. A single incident of corporate crime may cost millions or even billions of dollars, as in the case of Exxon's $2 billion illegal gasoline overcharges during the 1970s when price controls were imposed because of the Arab oil embargo. Law violations in the defense industry, including fraud, have cost taxpayers billions of dollars, while the loss incurred in an average burglary in 1991 was $1,246, an average robbery $817 per incident, and an average theft $478 per incident (*Uniform Crime Reports* 1992).

A considerable number of Fortune 500 corporations, however, have long been able to compete successfully while demonstrating a relatively high degree of social responsibility and compliance with the law. They belie any stereotype that all large corporations are lawbreakers or that they exhibit little concern for ethical behavior and social responsibility. Some have long-standing reputations for working closely with consumers to clarify product advertising and to improve the quality and safety of products.

The achievement of corporate goals is accomplished within the complex hierarchical context of expectations and social relationships. The social structure in large companies consists of those with much power—the board of directors, top executives like chairs of the board, presidents, chief executive officers and vice-presidents, and those with less—the middle managers, the supervisors and the workers. Because aspirations and pressures within this hierarchy differ, they can be conducive to unethical or illegal conduct at a number of levels. In the same way, the extended relationships between the parent corporation and its subsidiaries may be crime-generating as a result of the immense pressure to show profits.

Corporate law violations include illegal restraint of trade (such as price-fixing), false advertising, violations of laws protecting consumers, fraud in government contracts, illegal kickbacks, domestic and foreign bribery (prohibited by law), income tax evasion, unsafe working conditions, unfair labor practices and violations of laws protecting the environment. Corporate crime can result in both economic and physical harm. While people cringe at the increasing possibility of murder or assault, they seldom realize that the business practices of large corporations kill or injure far more persons than do individuals. The production and distribution of defective products, as in the case of unsafe vehicles and prescription drugs, kill and injure countless consumers; every year many workers are killed, maimed and injured by unsafe working conditions and illegal exposure to chemicals; and thousands of citizens are injured each year by corporate pollution of the air, water and earth, as well as the illegal disposal of waste products. Investigators have found that, in some cases, chief executives have knowingly concealed the fact that certain unsafe products and hazardous environments have brought injury, sickness and death to many people.

Concrete examples of corporate crime abound: abuse of the consumer can amount to reckless homicide, as in the case of the Ford Pinto (Cullen, Maakestad and Cavender 1987); crimes against public safety and health, as in the case of the Dalkon Shield intrauterine device (Frank 1985; Hills 1988); crimes against the democratic process itself through corporate bribes of political figures (Jackson 1988); abuse of workers and local communities, as in violations of laws requiring prior notification of plant closings (McKenzie 1972); criminal abuse of the environment (Yeager 1991); and criminal abuse of the Third World, as in Union Carbide's 1984 Bhopal disaster (Everest 1986; Kalelkar 1988).

Two public opinion surveys, in 1978 and 1982, revealed that the public considers many corporate offenses equal to or even more serious than many ordinary offenses such as burglary and robbery (Wolfgang 1980; Cullen, Link and Polanzi 1982). The 1982 study found particularly strong public reaction toward corporate offenses that resulted in death or injury (from, for example, defective vehicles) and toward corporate price-fixing. Corporate crimes that result in physical injury or death were viewed as much more serious than those ordinary offenses involving property loss or damage (Meier and Short 1982).

A close inspection of major corporations often turns up an avalanche of data that contradicts their claims of integrity. General Electric (GE) has long maintained that it is an exemplary corporation interested in the public good and devoted to the excellence of its products. However, this company actually has a long history of unethical and illegal practices, according to an in-depth study done by one investigator (Woodmansee 1975). In 1988 the *Multinational Moni-*

tor named GE one of the 10 worst corporations because of its practices. During the past 70 years the government has charged GE with price-fixing and other monopolistic practices in producing light bulbs, turbines, generators, transformers, motors, relays, radio tubes and heavy metals. The Department of Justice has brought at least 67 suits against General Electric, and the corporation has been convicted several times of price-fixing, bribery and procurement fraud. It also made huge illegal contributions to the 1972 Nixon presidential campaign and engaged in extensive bribery of foreign officials. In 1974 the courts charged the company with widespread illegal discrimination against women and minorities in its hiring policies, and General Electric agreed to a $32 million settlement.

Unethical and illegal practices continued into the 1980s (Clinard 1990, 15-17). In 1981 the government convicted GE and two former high executives in connection with a $1.25 million bribe paid to a Puerto Rican official to obtain a $93 million power plant contract. In addition, in 1985 the corporation became the first contractor to be indicted and found guilty of charges of defrauding the government for overcharging on defense contracts. The corporation had tried to minimize cost overruns on defense contracts by illegally transferring charges from one contract to another. It had also falsified time cards that defrauded the government on defense contracts. In 1988 GE paid $3.5 million to settle four lawsuits brought by the federal government and four whistle-blowers under the False Claims Act for fraud in military contract work. Moreover, General Electric is one of the nation's prime environmental polluters. It has been involved in many cases of toxic waste dumping, some of a serious nature. Of the 195 toxic waste sites targeted for Superfund money by the EPA, GE was found to be responsible for 22, the largest number of any major corporation (Clinard 1990).

Sutherland pointed out in 1949 that while corporate law violations are extensive, they are largely "administratively segregated" from ordinary crime, not because of what they do but because their offenses are generally dealt with by government agencies employing administrative or civil law. He found that among the 70 largest industrial and mercantile corporations in the United States, courts and commissions had made 547 adverse decisions against them. An average of 7.8 decisions had been taken against each corporation, with each corporation having at least one adverse decision. In addition to antitrust, the laws that the corporations violated were those that penalized false advertising, certain labor relations and infringement of patents and trademarks. Sutherland argued that all of these violations were actually crimes since they were socially injurious and penalties were provided in the laws.

It is clear in retrospect that Sutherland himself had some difficulty distinguishing clearly between behavior of corporations and behavior of officials of corporations. It was some time later that Geis was to provide clarification and state the problem in a precise manner:

The major difficulty in *White Collar Crime* as criminological research lies in Sutherland's striking inability to differentiate between the corporations themselves and their executive and management personnel. Corporations are, of course, legal entities which can be and are subjected to criminal processes. There is today little restriction on the range of crimes for which a corporation may be held responsible, though it cannot, for obvious reasons, be imprisoned. For the purpose of criminological analysis, however, corporations cannot be considered persons, except by recourse to the same type of extrapolatory fiction that once brought about the punishment of inanimate objects. Sutherland attempted to resolve this obvious dilemma by maintaining, not without some acerbity, that the crimes of corporations are precisely the crimes of their executives and managers. (Geis 1962)

Sutherland's pioneer work on corporate crime was a highly significant contribution to criminology, and it aroused great interest.

Legal Aspects of Selected Offenses

The economic and political power of the corporate world has been successful in seeing that most illegal behavior is largely punished by sanctions other than criminal. The growth of regulatory agencies has enabled varied sanctions to be used to deal with violations, even when the law provides criminal sanctions. Because corporate violations rarely result in criminal prosecutions, the public perceives that many such violations are of a "noncriminal" type, and therefore not serious in nature. This attitude tends to protect violators from the "criminal" label that invariably stigmatizes persons who are prosecuted under the criminal law. In the event of a law violation, a wide range of administrative and civil penalties are available as an alternative to criminal prosecution, including warnings, injunctions, consent orders and noncriminal monetary payments.

Even when a criminal penalty is available, it is rarely applied because of the greater amount of investigative and prosecutorial effort and time its use entails. As a result, the gravity of a corporate violation is not necessarily related to the type of penalty invoked. A wide-scale study of sanctions imposed for corporate law violations determined that administrative penalties were employed in two-thirds of serious corporate law violations (Clinard and Yeager 1980). Slightly more than two-fifths of the sanctions imposed for serious or moderately serious violations consisted simply of a warning to the corporation not to commit the offense again. Consequently, the only genuine definition of corporate crime must include any corporate violations punished under either administrative, civil or criminal law. Many see this as the only way to bring corporate law violations into the same perspective as ordinary criminal offenders.

Today, the law defines as illegal many acts of modern capitalist corporations, multinational as well as national, that were not illegal in the past. A series of historical developments led to many corporate activities falling into the category of illegal acts. A partial list of these developments includes: (1) the evolution of technology; (2) the development of capitalist production techniques and methods; (3) rapid changes in marketing and advertising of corporate products; and (4) a growing public awareness of dangers posed to the environment and the human element in the environment by corporations. It was not until the beginning of the nineteenth century that certain corporate business practices and activities were made illegal in the United States and in other advanced capitalist countries. Gradually such activities as the following were defined as illegal and punished in one form or another by the state: restraint of trade, false advertising, insolvency of banks due to fraud or negligence of officials, sale of fraudulent securities, theft or misuse of trademarks, manufacture of unsafe foods, drugs and other health products, and the pollution of the environment (Clinard and Yeager 1980; Michalowski and Kramer 1987).

Before the dawn of the twentieth century, an uncritical and innocent philosophy of *laissez-faire* (hands off) and *caveat emptor* (let the buyer beware) dominated general social, political and economic thinking in the capitalist world, prohibiting the development of certain legal restrictions on corporate business activities. New legislation grew out of industrialization, the replacement of the entrepreneur by the corporation and the development of large-scale labor unions. In short, these new laws were largely the result of the evolution of industrial capitalism into corporate capitalism. Laws emerged that were directed chiefly at the new forms of economic enterprise of corporate capitalism.

Toward the end of the nineteenth century, an antimonopoly movement emerged in response to these new economic forces. This movement was accompanied by the belief that the problem of monopoly could be solved only through government intervention. The result was the creation of a new kind of criminal law, which not only protected private property but also assisted in maintaining a particular kind of national economy. American corporate capitalism was thus secured, rather than threatened, by the new legal restrictions on corporate activities. Antitrust law was soon enacted in the Sherman Antitrust Act of 1890. To combine in restraint of trade and to monopolize became public offenses and the federal government was empowered for the first time in its history to proceed against serious violations of the criminal law by powerful and influential corporations. Sutherland pointed out, however, that the corporate world had it both ways: they wanted to eliminate unfair competition on the part of their corporations, but they often violated the law to their own advantage.

Many other factors, largely starting in the 1970s, helped to arouse society's interest and condemnation of corporate misbehavior, particularly the growth of the consumer movement, increased concern with the environment, and the extensive involvement of corporations in the illegalities of the Nixon reelection campaign. Federal and state intervention has become essential to protect both the public and law-abiding corporations. The Sherman Act was enacted in order to discourage excessive industrial concentration that might lead to monopolistic control and excessive prices. By 1906 Congress passed limited legislation to protect the public from impure and unsafe foods, drugs and cosmetics. The Federal Trade Commission (FTC), established by Congress in 1914, was designed to help prevent unfair competition such as price-fixing and to deal with unethical and deceptive trade practices such as false and misleading advertising.

In the 1960s and 1970s, as citizens became more aware that corporate conduct was endangering people's civil rights, safety and even their physical environment, they began to demand even greater corporate regulation. As a result, the federal government created several new types of agencies. The purpose of the Equal Opportunity Commission (EOC), created in 1965, was to enforce previously enacted laws that sought to prevent discrimination on the basis of race, sex, religion or national origin. With the creation of the National Highway Traffic Safety Administration (NHTSA) in 1966, it became possible for the government to intervene in auto safety problems that that resulted in thousands of needless deaths and hundreds of thousands of injuries—problems the automobile industry had ignored. The Occupational Safety and Health Administration (OSHA) came into being in 1970 to regulate the safety of the workplace and to protect the work force from harmful chemicals and other substances. The Environmental Protection Agency (EPA), also created in 1970, was designed to protect the nation's environment, including the control of air and water pollutants. In 1972, Congress passed further legislation to prohibit corporations from giving direct contributions to political candidates in federal elections (contributions that often constituted little more than bribes made to influence favorable votes). After studies revealed massive injuries to consumers from their use of unsafe corporate products, the government created the Consumer Product Safety Commission (CPSC) in 1972 to ban the sale of hazardous and defective products. The purpose of the Foreign Corrupt Practices Act, passed in 1977, was to prevent wide-scale corporate bribery of foreign officials by American corporations. In addition to these federal efforts, most states have created agencies of their own to regulate such harmful corporate behavior as consumer fraud and price conspiracies.

Among its many responsibilites the FTC is charged with: promoting free and fair competition; protecting the public from false and deceptive advertising; preventing unlawful price discrimination; prohibiting interlocking directorates; requiring accurate labels on textiles; regulating the packaging and labeling of consumer products; prohibiting credit discrimination on the basis of sex, race, etc.; prohibiting the sending of unordered merchandise to consumers; and prohibiting debt collection agencies from harassing consumers. Today, many of these activities have become accepted business practices without any FTC inter-ference whatsoever. During the decade of the 1980s, the Reagan-Bush years, many business and corporate organizations that had long chafed under FTC restrictions—minimalist as they were—saw the opportunity to press for congres-sional action to rein in the commission still further. They were largely successful in their efforts. The resulting dwindling budgets of the Commission saw a diminution of workyears (roughly equivalent to numbers of employees in key administrative and supervisory positions) from 1,677 in 1981 to 970 by 1991.

In 1970 the EPA became an independent agency in the executive branch of the government. Among the multiple responsibilities of the EPA are: to establish United States air quality levels; to set limits on the level of air pollutants emitted from factories and chemical plants; to establish emission standards for cars; to set allowable levels of toxics in gasoline; to develop criteria that enable states to set water quality standards; to regulate the disposal of waste material, including sludge and radioactive discards; to set national drinking water standards; to inventory existing hazardous waste dump sites; to track more than 500 haz-ardous compounds from point of origin to final disposal sites; to provide for emergency cleanup of hazardous dumps, whether of nuclear or chemical waste; to regulate existing chemicals considered seriously dangerous to human life—including fluorocarbons, asbestos and polychlorinated biphenyls (PCBs); to reg-ulate the manufacture of pesticides, insecticides and herbicides; to monitor and regulate levels of radiation in water and air; and to set acceptable noise levels for construction and transportation equipment (Barnett 1994; Yeager 1991).

Often the corporate entities that break the law are the very same ones that are influencing the passage of legislation favorable to the corporate structures of the country. This "circulation of elites" means that some leaders in the private field of corporate executives are recruited into top governmental regulatory posi-tions, positions from which they are then able to influence law and policy that favor the corporate sector.

> Furthermore, corporate lawbreakers double as corporate lawmakers. Corporate America has saturated the legal or non-criminal world in a way that by any common standard of justice would be considered illegal and criminal, and it has obstructed legislation that would outlaw the violent activity. For example, the tobacco and automobile industries have, over the years, blocked attempts to ban or curb the marketing of tobacco, and to require that automobiles be manufac-tured with life-saving passive restraints . . . The result is a legal system biased in favor of the corporate violator and against its victims. (Mokhiber 1988, 5)

In the EPA, as with the FTC and most of the other major federal regulatory agencies, top executives from the corporate world are often recruited by the fed-eral government to "do public service" as top administrators in these agencies (Yeager 1991). The situation is one in which a key inner circle of technocrats and bureaucrats from the public and private sectors may make official regulatory policy with regard to their own industries and corporations. Oftentimes the result has been not only lax enforcement but in many cases actual deregulation of many federal controls.

A further example is the Nuclear Regulatory Commission (NRC), which began operations in January of 1975. The existence of nuclear dumps of both high-level and low-level radiation waste across the country in the 1990s testifies to the failure of this commission to adequately protect the public from some of the most toxic substances yet produced by the human race.

> The problem behind this threat to our lives is that those governmental agencies that we trust to protect our vital interests are betraying that trust. Government and industry are so closely and intimately interlinked in the nuclear industry that any separating line between them is virtually indistinguishable. The term "regulatory" agency becomes a mock. Normally many of the top executives and policy makers in regulatory agencies such as the NRC are recruited from the nuclear industry itself and from corporations with extensive investments in nuclear energy. This amounts to nothing less than industry self-regulation under the veneer of state legitimacy. . . . It is a closed circle of professional experts, a circle from which the underclass has been completely and totally alienated. Furthermore, the irresistible lobbying efforts have subverted the democratic process by compromising the public interest in favor of the accumulation of ever more profit. (Caldicott 1978; Wildeman 1983, 166)

Criminal Career of the Offender

In this section we concern ourselves with the criminal careers of those who formulate the policies of the legal entity, that is, the corporation. Although corporations are indeed legal entities, individual decision-makers within corporations make policy for them. These individual persons may or may not be subjected to criminal prosecution, although the corporation itself may be. For example, the policies of corporate entities such as General Motors, General Electric, RCA, Atlantic Richfield, Exxon, DuPont, and so on—while resulting from decisions made by individuals or groups of individuals—are recognized by the legal system as policies of the corporate entity itself, and thus it is the corporation that is held responsible.

As crimes against the environment have been taken more seriously by the American public (since the first "Earth Day" in 1969 and the establishment of the EPA), the character of the corporation as an offender has been understood with increased clarity. What has become obvious is that many of the nation's leading corporations are committing destructive acts against nature and against human beings. Moreover, these activities are being done systematically and repeatedly rather than randomly and occasionally. Corporate crimes against nature (e.g., the Exxon *Valdez* oil spill in Prince William Sound in Alaska) are committed as standard operating procedure (it is cheaper for Exxon to build a single-hull tanker than a double-hull one). In order to ensure profits at a minimum of expense, such corporations are willfully engaging in crime. The corporations themselves, as legal entities, as well as the corporate officials who make specific decisions, are increasingly being defined by the public as criminal. What is of note is that once these systematic activities become normal operating procedures, they are not then the responsibility of any one individual in the corporation. Rather, they are corporate crimes, in the sense that the corporation itself is the criminal. The offending individual becomes invisible, and individual accountability vanishes.

From an organizational point of view, unethical practices and law violations within a corporation can sometimes be attributed to the *internal* corporate structure rather than to such *external* factors as the unfair practices of competitors, or to a corporation's difficult financial position in the market. Moreover, in cases of unethical or illegal behavior, the complex structural relationships within large corporations often make it difficult to disentangle delegated authority, managerial discretion and the ultimate responsibility of top management. In one study, the general theme expressed by most middle management executives who were interviewed was that top management, in particular the chief executive officer (CEO), sets the corporate ethical tone (Clinard 1983). These views were not found to be due to antagonisms or to jealousy of top management as such; the respondents simply felt that top management dominated the overall ethical tone of their corporations. Over half of the interviewees went even further, believing top management to be directly responsible for the violation of government regulations. In fact, top management's influence took precedence, in their views, over the possibility of a pre-existing ethical (or nonethical) general corporate cultural pattern. One middle management executive described the prime role of top management succinctly when he said:

> Ethics comes and goes in a corporation according to who is in top management. I worked under four corporation presidents, and each differed—first was honest, next was a "wheeler-dealer," the third was somewhat better, and the last one was bad. According to their ethical views, pressures were put on middle management all the way down. (Clinard 1983, 138)

The decisive role of top management in setting the ethical standards of a corporation are in line with most of the literature in the field. One study of employee theft in large corporations, for example, found that when the integrity, fairness and ethical standards of a corporation and its top management were questioned by the workers, the likelihood of finding property theft and other deviance was greater (Clark and Hollinger 1982). After he had surveyed various data, Gross concluded that "most persons who will engage in crime on behalf of the organization will most likely be the officers of the organization, its top people" (Gross 1978, 71). In elaborating this conclusion, he states:

> In sum, then, the men at the top of organizations will tend to be ambitious, shrewd and possessed of a non-demanding moral code. Their ambition will not be merely personal, for they will have discovered that their own goals are best pursued through assisting the organization to attain its goals. While this is less true, or even untrue at the bottom of the organization, those at the top share directly in the benefits of organizational goal achievement, such as seeing their stock values go up, deferred compensation, and fringe benefits. (Gross 1978, 71)

CEOs, presidents or board chairpersons participate in key decisions not only about finances, but also about the ethical direction of a corporation in relation to workers, consumers, competitors and the government. A leading writer in the study of corporations concluded: "That top managers generally control large corporations is an established truth, which serves as a premise—not something to be proved—in most serious analyses in the field of industrial organization and policy" (Herman 1981, 14). Neither the board of dirctors nor the stockholders are actually in charge of running a corporation, although large holders like financial institutions and large family holdings may have some general influence on policy. The basis of top management control, or "managerism," lies in its strategic position and its decision-making.

Top corporate managers possess great autonomy—and, therefore, considerable power—in making decisions regarding production, investments, advertising, pricing and marketing. The driving force of the corporate executive is the "bottom line"; often it is corporate profits, not ethical standards, that provide the ultimate test of the effectiveness of top management. "If external forces drive the executive to meet the challenge of innovative competition, the internal forces push the executive towards learning how to use power to achieve the ends set by the external environment" (Madden 1977, 71). Their very rank generates identity, power and the many perks that go with it.

Top management's particular character and personality often influence the internal structure of the corporation. A major distinction is between the "financially oriented" executive and the more "technical" types. Some financially oriented executives, for example, are interested primarily in securing financial prestige and quick profits for the corporation, and increased compensation for themselves. Such top executives are likely to engage to a greater extent in unethical and illegal practices than are the more technical and professional types who have been trained in such specialized areas as engineering or computers. As one middle management executive said: "Our CEO was a technical man, an engineer, and not a financially oriented person interested in the fast buck" (Clinard 1983, 136).

One researcher on corporate crime found that the types of top corporate managers more likely to be involved in this type of crime are the financial type:

> Persons who actually act for the organization in the commission of such crimes will, by selective processes associated with upward mobility in organizations, be likely to be highly committed to the organization and be, for various reasons, willing and able to carry out crime, should it seem to be required in order to enable the organization to attain its goals, to prosper, or, minimally, to survive. (Gross 1978, 72)

A similar distinction has been made between "fiduciary" top managers and "entrepreneurial" managers (Evan 1976). Fiduciary managers have an ethical commitment of service to beneficiaries; they do not make self-serving decisions, and they try to promote the interests of the organization as a corporate entity. On the other hand, the entrepreneurial manager governs the corporate body entirely on behalf of the owners, and his or her behavior is directed exclusively toward the corporation's profit maximization. One middle management executive contrasted these types:

> My personal feeling is that those corporations that are unethical are managed by persons (CEOs) who are highly competitive, wanting to improve the corporation's profit margins and thinking that they will not get caught. Such CEOs are trying to improve their personal positions and that of their corporations. The only way to do it is often unethical. (Clinard 1983, 136)

Another factor that leads to violations is the nature of the ethical standards of top-management persons who tend to be mobile, moving from one corporation to another, and who are recruited into a corporation from the outside. These executives are more likely to be aggressive and interested in their own corporate achievements (and consequent publicity in financial journals); they have limited concern for the corporation's long-term reputation. One middle-management executive described this type of executive:

> The upper management structure, particularly the CEO, leads to unethical practices. They are the "Go-Go" type of managers. Such a CEO does not intend to stay for more than two years, and he cares little about the corporation's reputation. Like sharks, they gobble up other corporations. Such CEOs end up with lots of executive perks and their names are favorably mentioned as go-getters in the *Wall Street Journal* and *Fortune*. (Clinard 1983, 137)

In contrast to this type of executive are those top executives who have come up from the ranks as workers, supervisors or middle managers, particularly in production; they have had a long-term indoctrination into the corporate history and product quality, and they have pride in the corporation. They tend to occupy top management positions for lengthy periods of time, and they are less likely to tarnish the corporate name and reputation by permitting the corporation to engage in unethical or illegal behavior.

In studying the criminal careers of corporate executives, we are dealing with people whom the public generally perceives as "honorable" men and women, people who are not acting for their own private gain, but for the corporate entity that they represent and to which they owe their success. They work for their stockholders, for capital and for "the people." The public most often sees them as shrewd executives who are "part of the team." Whether looking at corporate crime as violence, theft, deception, simple corporate greed or any combination of the above, the public normally perceives the individual actors who make up the corporate entities as fundamentally virtuous individuals who, if they transgress, are only following the orders of those higher in the corporate hierarchy. Indeed, as Vold noted many years ago, there is a contradiction here, a dialectic at work:

> There is an obvious and basic incongruity involved in the proposition that a community's leaders and more responsible elements are also its criminals. Business leaders and corporation executives by and large play important roles in civic and community affairs. They more often than not constitute an important source of imaginative leadership for community enterprises of all kinds. (Vold 1958, 253)

Corporate officials and executives in general are typically drawn from the middle and upper segments of American society; and even if not, they are highly regarded in the community by virtue of their executive positions. Typically they are graduates of prestigious institutions of higher education, often have served in the armed forces, are generous contributors to charitable causes, are married with children, and are hardworking, solid citizens: persons without stigma. They frequently serve on boards of trustees of nonprofit organizations and give their time and money to altruistic causes. Rationalizations, neutralizations and self-justifications are present, for they make a distinction between what they define as simply "illegal" behavior and criminal behavior. When corporate officials violate the law, they often have the appropriate rationalizations to view their conduct. In the process, they maintain a noncriminal self conception. The testimony of a Westinghouse executive at the heavy electrical equipment congressional hearing on antitrust violations illustrates this point:

> *Committee Attorney:* Did you know that these meetings with competitors were illegal?

> *Witness:* Illegal? Yes, but not criminal. I didn't find that out until I read the indictment. . . . I assumed that criminal action meant damaging someone, and we did not do that. . . . I thought that we were more or less working on a survival basis in order to try to make enough to keep our plant and our employees. (Geis 1967, 144)

Geis considered the testimony of some top-level offenders in large corporations involved in the heavy electrical equipment antitrust conspiracy cases that resulted in the loss of tens of millions of dollars for consumers and taxpayers. In explaining the rational character of the offenders and their decision to violate the law, he wrote:

> For the conspirators there had necessarily to be a conjunction of factors before they could participate in the violations. First, of course, they had to perceive that there would be gains accruing from their behavior. Such gains might be personal and professional, in terms of corporate advancement toward prestige and power, and they might be vocational, in terms of a more expedient and secure method of carrying out assigned tasks. The offenders also apparently had to be able to neutralize or rationalize their behavior in a manner in keeping with their image of themselves as law-abiding, decent, and respectable persons. The ebb and flow of the price-fixing conspiracy also clearly indicates the relationship, often overlooked in explanations of criminal behavior, between extrinsic conditions and illegal acts. When the market behaved in a manner the executives thought satisfactory, or when enforcement agencies seemed particularly threatening, the conspiracy desisted. When market conditions deteriorated, while corporate pressures for achieving attractive profit-and-loss statements remained constant, and enforcement activity abated, the price-fixing agreements flourished. (Geis 1967, 150-151)

Group Support of Criminal Behavior

Acts by corporations or their officials on behalf of a corporation often receive considerable support from similar, even competing, individuals and businesses. In fact, it may be said that the very milieu of the corporate social organizational setting may often constitute group support for criminal behavior. Law-breaking can become a normative pattern within corporations, and such norms are often shared between corporations and their executives. Corporate officials learn the necessary values, motives, rationalizations and techniques favorable to particular kinds of offenses. Many businesspersons may be partially isolated from law-abiding definitions of business conduct. Further, businesspersons are often shielded from criticism and find a considerable degree of support for their activities in the media. In addition, business executives associate chiefly with other business executives, both at work and in their social activities, so the implications of corporate crime may be removed from personal scrutiny. Often the thinking is, "if we don't do this particular thing, we are at serious risk of losing a considerable share of the market," and where profit is the bottom line, there can be considerable group support to violate criminal codes and regulatory restrictions.

The very existence of crimes by corporations frequently implies a considerable degree of organization among the participants. The degree of organization may range from the comparatively simple reciprocal relationships involved in a business transaction to the more complex procedures involved in the illegal activities of several large corporations acting in collusion. In this latter case, the violations may not only include other corporations, but may extend to many corporations and subsidiaries. The organization of the illegal activity may be quite informal (as in false advertising); it may be organized very simply; or it may be complex, as in the case of antitrust violations. Considerable group support for violation was found in the antitrust conspiracies of the large electrical equipment corporations. There were even *plans* drawn up for violating antitrust laws.

> The offenders hid behind a camouflage of fictitious names and conspiratorial codes. The attendance roster for the meetings was known as the "Christmas card list" and the gatherings, interestingly enough, as "choir practice." The offenders used public telephones for much of their communication, and they met either at trade association conventions,where their relationship would appear reasonable, or at sites selected for their anonymity. It is quite noteworthy, in this respect, that while some of the men filed false travel claims, so as to mislead their superiors regarding the city they had visited, they never asked for expense money to places more distant than those they had actually gone to—on the theory, apparently, that whatever else was occurring it would not do to cheat the company. (Geis 1967, 143)

The corporate officials in this case would even draw lots to determine who would submit the pricing bids. Promotions within the corporation depended upon the willingness of officials to go along with these schemes. Price-fixing, in other words, had become an established way of corporate life. Part of the job assignment was to engage in price-fixing arrangements.

Two important factors play a significant role in a corporation's compliance with, or violation of, the law: the corporation's own cultural or ethical climate and the conduct of its top executives. A *New York Times* business section reported: "Too many companies are ignoring the issue of corporate morality, and thus fostering corporate cultures devoid of ethical values." Each corporation builds its own cultural history over the years: it becomes permeated with the firm's own particular attitudes about ethical standards and law obedience. Some critical factors in this development appear to be: the corporation's expectations of the ethical standards of top management; the emphasis on developing and maintaining a good corporate reputation; the degree of concern for employees, consumers and the environment; the firm's customary competitive practices; and its attitudes toward continued corporate expansion and power, even at the sacrifice of social responsibility.

Just as a general pattern of respect for law obedience permeates this corporate cultural history, law-breaking can also become a pattern, regardless of the economic environment, and with or without pressures for profits (Barnett 1994). Simply put, some corporations take pride in protecting their reputations more than do others. In an interview, one Fortune 500 board chair said that ethical and law violations must be "congenial to the climate of the corporation," while another said, "Some corporations, like those in politics, tolerate corruption" (Clinard and Yeager 1980, 60). A middle-management executive of another corporation expressed the same view: "A corporation's history often starts from the original founders and their ethical standards prevail from the beginning; corporate reputation means a lot to some, similar to that of a Japanese corporation." Another said, "Often corporations develop a way of doing business unethically and it takes a lot at the top to change it" (Clinard 1983, 66).

The other internal source of illegal corporate behavior is the role played by top management, particularly the chief executive officer (CEO). The prior corporate cultural situation in top management is important. If the founder or subsequent influential executives have established a long history of expected ethical practices, two results can be anticipated. New top executives will be recruited to fit this pattern, or top executives will tend to go along with the established corporate practices of doing business. As Vaughan has pointed out: "It is common knowledge that organizations selectively recruit new members who in many ways match those already there. . . . Because business firms depend on their members' skills to attain goals, they must ensure that members' motivations and values are consistent with the organization's needs" (Vaughan 1982, 1389).

Other researchers have not made such distinctions in the types of top managers. Instead, they have pointed broadly to the *personal* characteristics of many of those who have made it to the top of large corporations. Gross (1978) argues that all these people are characterized by excessive ambition and competitiveness. Others have expressed it this way: "The meek shall not inherit top management" (Lewis and Stewart 1961). Other prevailing characteristics include shrewdness and moral flexibility, the latter being the ability "to change his moral beliefs with little distress so that they match whatever is called for by the organization" (Gross 1978, 69). This sort of explanation recalls the "I was just doing my duty" defense.

Corporate wrongdoing sometimes reflects the normative structure of a particular industry. That is, criminal behavior by the corporation and its executives often is the result of the diffusion of illegal practices and policies within the industry. Frequently it is not the corporate organization itself that must be examined but the corporation's place in the industry as a whole. For example, Cressey (1976) found that generally corporations in the same industry have similar rates of recidivism.

The role of industry ethics in law violations is exemplified by a widespread price conspiracy that resulted in the indictment of 23 carton manufacturing corporations (many of them Fortune 500) and 50 of their executives in 1976 (*United States v. Alton Box Board Company et al.,* Defendants, Criminal Action No. 76 CR 199, U.S. District Court, Northern District of Illinois, Eastern Division. All references and quotations are from court documents. Also see Clinard and Yeager 1980, 61-62, 64-65, 72-73). Included were International Paper Company, Container Corporation of America, Packaging Corporation of America, Weyerhauser, Diamond International Corporation and Alton Box. American industry and individual consumers depend enormously on goods packaged in folding cartons, and in terms of corporate annual sales (over $1 billion), number of defendants, duration of the conspiracy (1960 to 1974) and number of transactions involved, this case represented one of the most flagrant violations of the Sherman Antitrust Act in the law's 86-year history. In the following indictment the conspirators were charged with the following crimes:

1. Disclosing to other members of the conspiracy the price being charged or to be charged for a particular folding carton to the buyer of that folding carton, with the understanding that the other members of the conspiracy would submit a noncompetitive bid, or no bid, on that folding carton to that buyer.

2. Agreeing with other members of the conspiracy who were supplying the same folding carton to a buyer on the price to be charged to that buyer.

3. Agreeing with other members of the conspiracy on increases in list prices of certain folding cartons.

One executive of a large corporation stated: "[T]he meetings and exchange of price information were well known to the senior management and in the industry as a whole." Another stated: "Meetings of competitors were a way of life in the folding carton industry." Shortly after being indicted, all but one of the corporate executives pleaded guilty; later some tried to change their pleas to *nolo contendere* (no contest), an effort that was vigorously opposed by the government. According to the government statement,

These defendants were not engaged in a short-term violation based on sudden market pressures; price-fixing was their way of doing business. The participants demonstrated a knowing, blatant disregard for anti-trust laws. One grand jury witness testified that during a six year period he personally engaged in thousands of price-fixing transactions with competitors which were illegal. (Illegal telephone calls between corporate executives were frequent. As one conspirator put it concerning price increases of cartons sold to the frozen food industry, "If there was a need for an increase he would call the others, see if [the] . . . percentage increase that he proposed was acceptable to them and if it was, then all the companies would move in the general area of the same percentage.") This illegal conduct was carried on in all parts of the country by all management levels in the billion dollar folding carton industry. The thousands upon thousands of exchanges of prices with competitors, the dozens of meetings with competitors were done with a single purpose and design—to eliminate price competition in this industry. (Government's Statement of Reasons and Authorities in Opposition to Defendants' Motions to Plead Nolo Contendere, *United States v. Alton Box Board Company,* Criminal Action No. 76, CR 199 (May 7, 1976) at 10-11.)

Widespread prevalence of unethical and illegal practices is particularly characteristic of the oil, automobile and pharmaceutical industries. A major study of corporate crime concluded that these industries have the highest rates of illegal behavior (Clinard and Yeager 1980, 119-123). That poor economic conditions do not generally cause corporate crime is shown by the fact that the oil and pharmaceutical industries characteristically have higher profits than most others, with the pharmaceutical industry having the highest. Until recently the automobile industry also had high profit margins.

The oil industry's long history of industry-wide violations of law includes price-fixing, illegal overcharges, theft of oil royalties, illegal political campaign contributions and environmental pollution. The oil refining industry was charged in one out of every five legal cases brought in 1975-1976, one out of every 10 cases involving both serious and moderate violations (Clinard and Yeager 1980). Corporations in this particular industry had nearly three-fifths of all serious and moderately serious financial violations, almost half of the total environmental violations, and more than one-third of the serious and moderately serious environmental violations. In the oil refining industry, 22 of the 28 companies violated the law at least once; 20 had one or more serious or moderately serious violations. The oil refining industry had a ratio of 3.2 times its share of total violations, 1.7 times for serious or moderately serious violations.*

For a long time the automobile industry has been tarnished by a general disregard for laws designed to protect consumer safety, reduce fraud and protect the environment. The motor vehicle industry was responsible for one out of every six cases of violations charged and one out of every five serious or moderately serious violations. For manufacturing violations, it was responsible for one-third of both the total and the serious or moderate infractions. Eighteen of the 19 firms in this industry had at least one violation; 17 had one or more serious or moderately serious violations. Four motor vehicle industry firms had 21 or more violations. The motor vehicle industry had 3.9 times its share of total violations, 5 times its share of serious or moderately serious violations (Clinard and Yeager 1980).

---

*Note: A ratio of 1.0 means that the industry violations were the same as the industry proportion in the total sample of corporations; a ratio over 1.0 means that the industry had more than the industry's share of total violations.

The pharmaceutical industry has frequently been involved in the production and distribution of unsafe drugs and medical equipment. Pharmaceutical corporations accounted for one out of every 10 cases of violation, and one of eight serious or moderately serious violations. These firms had one-fifth of both the total and the serious or moderately serious manufacturing cases, and one out of every seven of the total and the serious or moderately serious administrative violations. All 17 pharmaceutical corporations violated the law at least once in a two-year period; 15 (88.2 percent) committed at least one serious or moderately serious violation. Two corporations had 21 or more violations. The pharmaceutical industry had 2.5 times its share of total violations, 3.2 times for serious or moderately serious infractions (Clinard and Yeager 1980).

Correspondence between Criminal and Legitimate Behavior

In the past the "American ethic" has consisted of a firm belief that technology is the surest way to progress, that production and consumption can achieve unlimited proportions, and that the natural environment can be be exploited indiscriminately by humans. The overemphasis on technology, the "technological quick fix," production for its own sake, and unnecessary consumption has caused Americans to commit crimes against the environment. The increasing gross national product has been the index of the standard of American life.

Many of today's crimes—corporate crimes in particular—are related to this ethic. Indeed, a great deal of corporate crime corresponds closely to what are commonly and legally accepted as legitimate behavior patterns. Much environmental destruction around us is supported by one of America's basic traditions: the Judeo-Christian religious tradition. That tradition, enhanced by Western science and positivism, has been one of "humankind against nature." In Genesis we read that humans are to "have dominion over the fish of the sea and over the birds of the air and over every living thing that moves upon the earth." From this has followed practices that range from pollution of the air and waters to defoliation of vast areas of wilderness.

This correspondence between criminal behavior and legitimate patterns of pursuit of capital accumulation is by no means limited to corporate crimes against the environment. Basic to price-fixing is an attempt on the part of large corporations to attain a secure economic market situation. Attaining a secure economic market situation is one thing. Doing so through law-violating practices and regulation evasion is quite another. It is all too often passed off as simply expedient, rational action that is necessary to attain the goal of production for profit, not production for need satisfaction. Practices such as price-fixing are all too easily accepted as models of free market competition, whereas in reality they are just the opposite of a "free" market. Crime, from the standpoint of the corporation, may be a secondary consideration when the higher stakes involve secure economic arrangements and, of course, an ever-expanding market.

The public often views some of the practices that evade, skirt or break the law as not necessarily illegal behavior, and may accept them as good business practices. Such is the close resemblance between legitimate and criminal advertising practices. Fraudulent and deceptive advertising has been around for a long time, but only in recent years have consumer activist groups begun to pressure for laws on truth in advertising, particularly in the diet and health food category. Words such as "light," "fat-free," "cholesterol-free" and "healthy," often fraudulently used in advertising food and beverage products, have come under increasing fire. Consequently, new and stringent labeling rules were put into effect by the Food and Drug Administration in 1993. Among other violations singled out by consumer advocacy groups are distortions in a product's printed label of the claims for usefulness beyond what has been approved, and citations of studies (actually commissioned by the corporation) allegedly proving the safety or usefulness of the product.

Societal Reaction and Legal Processing

Corporations are so huge and the violations so diffused and complex that it is often extremely difficult for the general public to react to corporate criminality to the same degree as to ordinary or occupational crime. Yet the public is not indifferent to these crimes, for generally it condemns many of them. One reason for the lack of a strong negative reaction is that consumers often do not know that they have been victimized, as for example when a company illegally raises the price of its product. A price conspiracy between breakfast food manufacturers may produce a two-cent increase in the price of breakfast cereal, an increase that most consumers would not notice or would attribute to inflation, not crime, while the total cost to consumers could well be in the tens of millions of dollars. Similarly, the relative lack of past public awareness of (and reaction to) environmental pollution and consumer fraud was primarily the result of the public's lack of information about it. In recent years, however, this has changed greatly and will continue to change, partly as a result of activist organizations like the Sierra Club and others. No longer are government agencies easily able to evade their legal enforcement responsibilities and their accountability to the American consumer. Dangerous products, false advertising and large corporations' practices of polluting the environment are also increasingly coming under angry public scrutiny.

Ralph Nader, through his pioneering 1971 report *Water Wasteland,* was among the first to call public attention to corporate crimes that result in large scale pollution of the fresh water resources in this country (Zwick and Benstock

1971). A virtual eruption of consumer guidebooks came out during the 1980s and 1990s advising consumers how to avoid the hazards of food contamination, the dangers of the use of additives, antibiotics, polluted water and irradiated foods, to name a few (Isaac and Gold 1987). Much of this public awareness of corporate polluters of food and beverage products and their victims was again pioneered by Nader and his associates (Nader, Brownstein and Richard 1981). Some earlier classics had initially alerted Americans to the threat of pollution: Rachel Carson's *Silent Spring* (1963), Murray Bookchin's *Our Synthetic Environment* (1962), James Turner's *The Chemical Feast* (1970) and Barry Commoner's *The Closing Circle* (1971).

Public opinion polls have shown that large segments of the public have grave doubts about the honesty and integrity of major American corporations. Yet, as some criminologists have noted, it remains difficult to nail down this dishonesty, lack of integrity and outright law violation.

> Corporate theft is similar to other forms of theft—in the sense that property is taken from people—yet it is significantly different, primarily because it does not entail a face-to-face confrontation and it is not easily apparent that a crime has been committed. Three of the most costly and prevalent forms of corporate theft are deceptive advertising, financial fraud, and price fixing. (Beirne and Messerschmidt 1991, 191)

Corporate crimes such as the production of hazardous products, false advertising and environmental pollution are coming under increasing scrutiny. Studies reveal, however, that relatively few violations of the Fortune 500 corporations and subsequent enforcement actions have received much general publicity in the media. Rarely does the public have an opportunity to view a television news show about transgressions of large corporations and seldom do corporate crimes make the evening news. This may be because many of these huge corporations own and control the media. Even the Public Broadcasting System (PBS) tends to shy away from such a hot subject as it becomes increasingly dependent upon corporate contributions. The media often do not carry even prominent cases of corporate crime. Even when they do carry them they tend to appear in business or financial sections. A survey of the news coverage of 12 leading cases of corporate crime revealed that less than one-third to one-half of leading newspapers and news magazines carried stories of the cases, and they were usually brief news items on back pages. Corporate cases were downplayed, understated or omitted altogether.

A survey of the general newspaper coverage of the price-fixing conspiracy case in the folding carton industry concluded that "newspapers protect corporate reputations by failing to provide frequent, prominent, and criminally oriented coverage of common corporate crimes such as price-fixing" (Evans and Lundman 1983, 541). Only half of the 29 newspapers that the survey covered publicized the corporate pleas and the sentences the court handed down; only four named all 23 corporations (the rest named only a few); and only one newspaper used the word "crime" in its account of the case. None of the papers surveyed covered the sentencing of the corporations on the front page, and only 7 percent covered the sentences given to the corporate executives. In actuality, only the *Wall Street Journal* and some trade journals regularly report illegal corporate behavior, primarily because they are financial publications; such news is of special interest and may have significant financial repercussions. Injurious and harmful corporate actions often are not presented to the public as "criminal" either by the official spokespersons of the government or by the media, because "crime is viewed in the media as a threat to the American way of life, and the right of the state to intervene in controlling crime is presented as the only legitimate reality" (Quinney 1974, 156).

An increase in consumer use of product liability laws also helps to control corporate misbehavior and law violation. Most states have laws that enable victims to sue corporations to recover compensatory and punitive damages for product injuries they have sustained. Product liability suits on behalf of several named plaintiffs, repesenting a class action, offer even more effectual deterrence. Such a class action suit allows thousands of individuals to pool their legal resources against the far greater corporate resources. The United States Supreme Court, in a 7-0 decision in 1989, ruled that states may permit individuals or groups of individuals who suffer indirect financial losses, as a result of state antitrust price fixing violations, to sue the violators. Fifteen states have such laws.

Some criminologists have advocated self-regulation on the part of corporations as the most effective solution to their illegal behavior (Braithwaite 1982). However, other studies have concluded that, self-regulation aside, federal attempts to control hazardous water pollution from industrial wastes do not work even under favorable conditions for enforcement (Yeager 1991). It does not appear feasible to rely on corporate self-regulation (such as corporate or industry codes of ethical conduct) to control corporate misbehavior. Such codes have little or no possibility of being followed by any severe self-regulation measures. Larger and more effective government enforcement staffs are a prerequisite for the detection, investigation and prosecution of corporate offenses. One study that examined the recidivism patterns of a sample of 38 corporations between 1928 and 1981 concluded that strong enforcement does have an effect on future behavior: "Though not robust, there is some evidence that past guilty verdicts and charges in penalties for law-breaking from misdemeaners to felonies inhibit recidivism" (Simpson and Koper 1992, 347). Law-breaking corporations, however, rarely receive severe penalties. Of penalties imposed on 477 Fortune 500 corporations for law violations over a two-year period, nearly half were simply governmental warnings or product recalls (Clinard and Yeager 1980). Even in serious or moderately serious cases, slightly more than 40 percent of the penalties imposed were merely warnings not to repeat the violation.

The overwhelming number of cases of corporate illegal behavior do not involve the use of the criminal penalty. Instead they use civil injunctions, wherein the court enjoins the corporation from further law violations by a consent decree, which is a compromise settlement of the violations, or by a monetary penalty. Consent decrees usually state that the corporation "neither admits nor denies" the accusations. A corporate monetary fine—whether administrative, civil or criminal—is extremely small if measured in terms of billions in corporate assets and sales. Fines rarely equal the illegal profits; to some corporations they are just another cost of doing business.

Because the United States has an exclusively criminal legal system for individuals and largely an administrative or civil legal system for corporations, the effectiveness of the criminal justice system is undermined in dealing with corporate violators. An increase in statutory penalties (i.e., a corporate criminal prosecution) labels and stigmatizes a corporation, making it far more effective than an administrative or civil action. Obviously, the courts cannot imprison a criminally convicted corporation; the best they can do is levy a fine.

Normally, criminal actions are not brought even when the use of the product causes death or severe physical or psychological injury. Instead, civil or administrative actions predominate. For example, the General Motors Corporation (GM) was aware as early as 1983 that its popular pickup trucks with dual gasoline tanks mounted outside the frame (from 1973 through 1987) could be made "much less vulnerable" to collisions that could break open the tanks and cause a conflagration. Yet the company did not change the design of the trucks until 1988. In the meantime, an estimated 300 people were killed in fires that resulted from gas tanks that ruptured in collisions. In spite of these deaths, no criminal action was brought against GM, but the company became a defendant in over 100 lawsuits in connection with the defective design (*New York Times,* November 17, 1992). The only action threatened against the corporation by the government was the possibility of ordering a recall of the vehicles involved for relocation of the gasoline tanks inside the frame. At the time these defects were brought to light, GM argued that there was no danger to the driving public, as demonstrated by its statistics. Subsequently the corporation provided federal highway officials with new data. It appears that GM had originally given officials potentially misleading statistics in order to bolster its claims of the safety of millions of these trucks.

Because a corporation cannot be imprisoned (although it can be fined or placed on probation), the only alternative is to criminally prosecute top corporate officers. Top management either can lead the corporation into illegal activities or it can create a "corporate climate" favorable to law violators. While corporate executives may well be responsible for law violations within their company, the law rarely holds them personally accountable for the actions they direct. A study of over 1,500 proceedings against Fortune 500 corporations covering a two-year period revealed that corporate executives were convicted of failure to carry out their legal responsibility in only 1.5 percent of the total actions (Clinard and Yeager 1980). Corporate executives fear imprisonment far more than they fear a criminal conviction in which a fine is imposed. If convicted, executives rarely receive prison sentences, and if they do, the sentences are generally far below the maximum provided by the law (for example, a possible three years for a price-fixing conviction). Generally, they are given probation, fined or assigned some type of community service.

Since the impact of the law tends to be insignificant, corporations have a far greater fear of adverse publicity that tarnishes their corporate images and reputations. Media publicity can significantly affect corporations that have found themselves in legal trouble. In 17 case studies of corporations that had undergone serious and highly publicized ethical or legal difficulties, media publicity related to wrongdoing tended to flow over into other unrelated issues, such as reducing corporate earnings and decreasing executive morale (Fisse and Braithwaite 1983). Because corporate illegalities receive such limited press coverage, the compulsory use of publicity, in which a corporation buys media coverage to advertise its own guilt, becomes a necessary sanction in many corporate crime cases. If the courts force corporate defendants to publish certain information about their offenses and the measures being taken to correct them, public awareness of the offense is even better assured.

A study of investigations of all criminal prosecutions of collusive trade agreements filed by the Antitrust Division of the United States Department of Justice from 1946 through 1970 concluded that "public exposure of trade conspiracies serves as a deterrent despite weak penalties" (Scott 1989, 559). It is not the official deterrent that is most effectual; it is that the public exposure of malfeasance on the part of the corporation that places limits on corporate law violation. In this instance, fear of strong societal reaction is more effective than legal processing.

Regardless of size, all corporations operate under a government charter that subjects them to different measures of control. Corporations obtain these national and international business charters through individual states, which benefit from the substantial revenues brought in by incorporation fees and taxes. But state governments lack both the incentives and the resources to examine critically the vast scope of a large chartered corporation's operations throughout the United States and around the world. Perhaps a better system would be a federal corporate charter that would make the enforcement agent—namely, the federal government—a better match for the large corporations under its control. Specific penalties for corporate law violations could include obligatory management reorganization, the suspension of top executives or even a revocation of charter.

Innovative sanctions, along with greater use of criminal sanctions when appropriate, could go a long way toward controlling corporate criminality.

More than two decades ago, the President's Commission on Law Enforcement and Administration of Justice reported that corporate crimes seriously affect the moral climate of American society. A *Fortune* editor once wrote, "How much crime in the streets is connected with the widespread judgment that the business economy itself is a gigantic rip-off?" Derelictions by corporations and their top executives (whom the public generally regard as community leaders) set examples that erode the moral basis of the law. When corporations disregard the rules by which the free enterprise system is supposed to operate—particularly the basic tenets of free and open competition, they endanger the system itself. The economic drive for profit, power and productivity is not in itself criminal; it is likely to become so only when these objectives dominate all other considerations. Price-fixing offenses victimize consumers as well as law-abiding corporations. Income tax violations deprive the government and all those who depend on it for needed revenue. The criminal law alone will not assure adequate corporate compliance as long as those corporations that are controlled exercise political control and influence over regulatory agencies and courts. What is needed is increased political control over the corporations by the public. This highlights the importance of organized and well-financed consumer groups, the grass roots opposition to corporate crime.

References

*Akard, Patrick J. (1992). "Corporate Mobilization and Political Power: the Transformation of U.S. Economic Policy in the 1970s." *American Sociological Review* 57(5) 597-615.

Barnett, Harold C. (1994). *Toxic Debts and the Superfund Dilemma.* Chapel Hill, NC: University of North Carolina Press.

Baucus, Melissa S., and Janet P. Near (1992). "Can Illegal Corporate Behavior Be Predicted? An Event History Analysis." *Academy of Management Journal* 34:9-36.

Beirne, Piers, and James Messerschmidt (1991). *Criminology.* New York: Harcourt Brace Jovanovich.

*Boyle, Robert H., and the Environmental Defense Fund (1980). *Malignant Neglect.* New York: Vintage Books.

Bradshaw, T., and D. Vogel, eds. (1981). *Corporations and Their Critics.* New York: McGraw-Hill.

Braithwaite, John (1982). "Enforced Self-Regulation: A New Strategy for Corporate Crime Control." *Michigan Law Review* 82:1466-1507.

Braithwaite, John (1985). *To Punish or Persuade: Enforcement of Coal Mine Safety.* Albany: State University of New York Press.

Braithwaite, John (1987). "Toward a Theory of Organizational Crime." Paper presented at the 39th annual meeting of the American Society of Criminology, Montreal, Canada.

Cairns, John Jr., and Ruth Patrick eds. (1986). *Managing Water Resources.* New York: Praeger.

Caldicott, Helen, M.D. (1978). *Nuclear Madness.* Boston: Autumn Press.

Clark, J.P., and Richard C. Hollinger (1982). *Theft by Employees in Work Organizations.* Washington, DC: National Institute of Justice.

*Clinard, Marshall B. (1983). *Corporate Ethics and Crime.* Beverly Hills, CA: Sage.

*Clinard, Marshall B. (1990). *Corporate Corruption: The Abuse of Power.* New York: Praeger.

*Clinard, Marshall B., and P.C. Yeager (1980). *Corporate Crime.* New York: Free Press.

*Coleman, James (1989). *The Criminal Elite.* New York: St. Martin's Press.

Cressey, Donald R. (1976). "Restraint of Trade, Recidivism and Delinquent Neighborhoods." In *Delinquency, Crime, and Society,* edited by J.F. Short, Jr. Chicago: University of Chicago Press.

Cullen, Francis T., Bruce G. Link and Craig Polanzi (1982). "The Seriousness of Crime Revisited: Have Attitudes Toward White-Collar Crime Changed?" *Criminology* 20:83-101.

Cullen, Francis T., William J. Maakestad, and Gray Cavender (1987). *Corporate Crime under Attack: The Ford Pinto Case and Beyond.* Cincinnati: Anderson.

Evan, W. M. (1976). *Organizational Theory: Structure, Systems, and Environments.* New York: John Wiley.

Evans, Sandra S., and Richard Lundman (1983). "Newspaper Coverage of Corporate Price Fixing: A Replication," *Criminology* 21 (4): 529-541.

Everest, Larry (1986). *Behind the Poison Cloud: Union Carbide's Bhopal Massacre.* Chicago: Banner Press.

*Fisse, Brent, and John Braithwaite (1983). *The Impact of Publicity on Corporate Offenders.* New York: Oxford University Press.

Frank, Nancy (1985). *Crimes against Worker Health and Safety.* San Francisco: Sierra Club Books.

Geis, Gilbert (1962). "Toward a Delineation of White-Collar Offenses." *Sociological Inquiry* 32:160-171.

Geis, Gilbert (1967). "The Heavy Electrical Equipment Antitrust Cases of 1961." In *Criminal Behavior Systems: A Typology,* edited by Marshall B. Clinard and Richard Quinney. New York: Holt, Rinehart & Winston.

Gofman, John, M.D. (1976). "The Plutonium Controversy." *Journal of the American Medical Association* 236 July.

Gross, E. (1978). "Organizational Crime: A Theoretical Perspective." In *Studies in Symbolic Interaction,* edited by N. Denzin. Greenwood, CT.: JAI.

Herman, E.S. (1981). *Corporate Control: Corporate Power.* New York: Cambridge University Press.

*Hills, Stuart L. (1988). *Corporate Violence: Injury and Death for Profit.* Totowa, NJ: Rowman and Littlefield.

Isaac, Katherine, and Steven Gold, eds. (1987). *Eating Clean: Overcoming Food Hazards.* Washington, DC: Center for Study of Responsive Law.

Jackson, Brooks (1988). *Honest Graft: Big Money and the American Political Process.* New York: Knopf.

Kalelkar, Aashok (1988). *Investigation of Large-Magnitude Incidents: Bhopal as A Case Study.* London: Arthur D. Little Press.

Kramer, Ronald (1982). "Corporate Crime: An Organizational Perspective." In *White Collar and Economic Crime: A Multidisciplinary and Crossnational Perspective,* edited by Peter Wickman and Timothy Dailey. Lexington, MA: Lexington Books.

Lewis, R., and R. Stewart (1961). *The Managers: A New Examination of the English, German and American Executive.* New York: New American Library.

*Madden, C. (1977). "Forces which Influence Ethical Behavior." In *The Ethics of Corporate Conduct,* edited by C. Walton. Englewood Cliffs, NJ: Prentice-Hall.

McKenzie, Richard B., ed. (1972). *Plant Closings: Public or Private Choices?* Washington, DC: Cato Institute.

McKenzie, Richard B. (1984). *Fugitive Industry.* San Francisco: Pacific Institute of Public Policy Research.

Meier, Robert F., and James F. Short (1982). "The Consequences of White Collar Crime." In *White Collar Crime: An Agenda for Research,* edited by Herbert Delhertz and Thomas Overcast, 23-49. Lexington, MA: Lexington Books.

Michalowski, Raymond J., and Ronald C. Kramer (1987). "The Space between Laws: The Problem of Corporate Crime in a Transnational Context." *Social Problems* 34, 34-53.

*Mokhiber, Russell (1988). *Corporate Crime and Violence: Big Business Power and the Abuse of the Public Trust.* San Francisco: Sierra Club Books.

Nader, Ralph, Ronald Brownstein and John Richard, eds. (1981). *Who's Poisoning America?* San Francisco: Sierra Club Books.

New York Times (1992). "Falsifying Corporate Data Becomes Fraud of the 90s." September 21, A1.

New York Times (1992). "Data Show G.M. Knew for Years of Risk of Pickup Trucks' Design." November 17, A1.

New York Times (1992). "Grand Jury Seeks Inquiry on Weapons Plant Case." November 19, A10.

Quinney, Richard (1974). *Critique of Legal Order.* Boston, MA.: Little, Brown.

Ross, Irwin (1980). "How Lawless Are Big Companies?" *Fortune,* December 1, 57-64.

*Scott, Donald W. (1989). "Policing Corporate Collusion." *Criminology* 27 (3): 559-587.

*Simon, David, and Stanley Eitzen (1992). *Elite Deviance.* New York: Allyn and Bacon.

Simpson, Sally S., and Christopher S. Koper (1992). "Deterring Corporate Crime." *Criminology* 30 (3): 347-375.

Sutherland, Edwin H. (1949). *White Collar Crime.* New York: Holt, Rinehart and Winston.

Sutherland, Edwin H. (1956). "Crime of Corporations." In *The Sutherland Papers,* edited by Albert Cohen, Alfred Lindesmith and Karl Schuessler. Bloomington, IN: Indiana University Press.

*Szasz, Andrew (1986). "Corporations, Organized Crime, and the Disposal of Hazardous Waste: An Examination of the Making of a Criminogenic Regulatory Structure." *Criminology* 24 (1): 1-27.

Uniform Crime Reports (1992). Washington, DC, U.S. Department of Justice: U.S. Government Printing Office.

Vaughan, E. (1982). "Toward Understanding Unlawful Organizational Behavior." *Michigan Law Review* 80:1377-1402.

Vold, George (1958). *Theoretical Criminology.* New York: Oxford University Press.

Wildeman, John (1983). *Social Problem America: Alienation and Discontinuity.* New York: Irvington.

Wolfgang, Marvin (1980). "Crime and Punishment." *New York Times,* March 2, E21.

Woodmansee, John (1975). *The World of the Giant Corporation: A Report from the G.E. Project.* Seattle: North Country Press.

Yeager, Peter C. (1986). "Analyzing Corporate Offenses: Progress and Prospects." *Research in Corporate Performance and Policy* 8:93-120.

*Yeager, Peter C. (1991). *The Limits of the Law: the Public Regulation of Private Pollution.* New York: Cambridge University Press.

Zey-Ferrell, Mary, and O.C. Ferrell (1982). "Role-set Configuration and Opportunity as Predictors of Unethical Behavior in Organizations." *Human Relations* 35:587-604.

Zwick, David, and Marcy Benstock (1971). *Water Wasteland: Ralph Nader's Study Group Report on Water Pollution.* New York: Grossman.

Chapter 9

Organized Criminal Behavior

Although organized crime is one of those things that "everybody knows about," in reality, few understand its workings, structures, personnel or networks. Nor do people generally understand its extent or the degree of threat it poses to the social fabric and the major institutions of a society. It is variously perceived as sinister, secretive, terrifying, romantic, fascinating and necessary. Over the years it has provided the subject matter for popular entertainment. Not only in the United States and other industrialized countries but in developing countries as well, organized crime is mythologized as an exotic, simultaneously attractive and repellant phenomenon. It is found around the globe, from The People's Republic of China to the United States, Europe, South America, Africa, the former Soviet republics, and more.

As understood from a more disciplined perspective, organized crime refers to business enterprises organized for the rational purpose of generating economic gain—that is, profit—through illegal activities (Sellin 1963). Another definition is that "[o]rganized crime consists of a series of illegal transactions between multiple offenders, some of whom employ specialized skills, over a continuous period of time, for purposes of economic advantage, and political power when necessary to gain economic advantage" (Rhodes 1984, 4). It bears a remarkable resemblance to legitimate corporate structure, both in its organizational forms and in the potential harm it has for a large number of people as a result of its operations and activities. Just as in legitimate corporate organizations, organized crime provides (albeit illegally) needed—or at least desired—services: drugs, sexual services, loans, protection, etc. In fact, in the late 1960s a Presidential Commission defined it as involving "thousands of criminals, working within structures as complex as those of any large corporation, subject to laws more rigidly enforced than those of legitimate governments. Its actions are not impulsive but rather the results of intricate conspiracies, carried on over many years and aimed at gaining control over whole fields of activity in order to amass huge profits" (President's Commission, *The Challenge of Crime in a Free Society* 1967, 194). This quote could be applied with little modification to some legitimate corporate activities.

Legal Aspects of Selected Offenses

Currently, organized crime is one of the major forms of crime in American society, although numerically it does not involve a large proportion of criminal offenders. Large-scale organized crime did not exist in the United States prior to this century. During the frontier period in American history (a period officially declared ended in 1895 when the U.S. Census Bureau stopped using "frontier" on its official maps), a number of outlawed activities were carried out on a modest scale by roving criminal groups. In cities, various adult criminal groups gained control of illegal activities in their localities, such as gambling, prostitution, distribution of beer and liquor, and various rackets. These gangs prospered because they provided desired, although illegal, services for the public and because of their connections with local politics. In a general way, their activities resembled present-day organized crime.

After the turn of the century, organized crime expanded into a wider range of activities and extended over a larger geographical area. The event that brought about the greatest change in organized crime was Prohibition, which forbade by law the sale and distribution of alcoholic beverages. Because of the Eighteenth Amendment Prohibition Act ("The Great Social Experiment"), adopted in 1919, organized crime was able to provide the illegal services and commodities demanded by millions of citizens. Conflict between organized gangs and widespread use of violence were inevitable as rival groups competed to serve the public. A number of the strongest gangs finally dominated the scene. These organized groups, because of the large sums of money they amassed and the elaborate organization they achieved, continued in illegal activity after Prohibition was repealed in 1933 (Sinclair 1964). During this tumultuous period, national gangster syndicates held sway over huge empires of crime, ranging from corruption of city and state officials and administrations, through labor unions and industry. Names like Al Capone, "Dutch" Schultz, "Lucky" Luciano and Frank Costello entered the national vocabulary. The purpose of racketeering is to secure financial gains on a regularized basis. Racketeering is infinitely varied in terms of the methods of operation and the kinds of organizations victimized. For the most part in the United States, it has been concentrated in organizations engaged in the distribution of services and commodities, often hijacked or stolen by other means.

The modern era of organized crime is represented by the crime syndicate. Organized crime has been expanded to the point where leaders coordinate illegal activities over state and regional boundaries. This new era is also represented by the extension of organized crime into an increasing number of legitimate businesses and occupational activities. The characteristic features of modern organized crime can be summarized as follows:

1. Hierarchical structure involving a system of specifically defined relationships with mutual obligations and privileges.

2. Monopolistic control or establishment of spheres of influence among different organizations and over geographic areas.

3. Dependence upon the potential use of force and violence to maintain internal discipline and restrain competition.

4. Maintenance of permanent immunity from interference from law enforcement and other agencies of government.

5. Large financial gains secured through specialization in one or more combinations of enterprises.

Organized crime can be generally distinguished from other criminal behavior by the elements of "corruption" and "enforcement."

> There are at least two aspects of organized crime that characterize it as a unique form of criminal activity. The first is the element of corruption. The second is the element of enforcement, which is necessary for the maintenance of both internal discipline and the regularity of business transactions. In the hierarchy of organized crime there are positions for people fulfilling both of these functions. But neither is essential to the long-term operation of other types of criminal groups. . . . Organized-crime groups . . . are believed to contain one or more fixed positions for "enforcers," whose duty it is to maintain organizational integrity by arranging for the maiming and killing of recalcitrant members. And there is a position for a "corrupter," whose function is to establish relationships with those public officials and other influential persons whose assistance is necessary to achieve the organization's goals. By including these positions within its organization, each criminal cartel, or "family," becomes a government as well as a business. (President's Commission on Organized Crime 1967, 8)

A number of estimates have placed the potential income from what is referred to as the "hidden economy" at well over $100 billion, a figure that is constantly adjusted upward as a result of both inflation and increased business volume (Simon and Witte 1982). Illegal producers switched from "moonshine" to marijuana when the latter came into great demand in the 1960s. Organized crime itself actually consists of a number of different types of individual crimes. For the most part, seven specific areas predominate: (1) illegal gambling; (2) racketeering; (3) illegal drugs; (4) usury or loan sharking; (5) illicit sex; (6) sale of stolen or hijacked goods; and (7) control of legitimate business (Clinard and Meier 1992). However, the following general classification can be used to include most forms of organized crime: (1) control of illegal activities, (2) control of legitimate business, and (3) racketeering.

Control of Illegal Activities

Much organized crime traditionally has been found in areas of illicit behavior, such as gambling, loan sharking, prostitution, and more recently, the use and sale of controlled substances (e.g., marijuana, cocaine, heroin). Organized crime syndicates control all but a small part of illegal gambling in the United States and they are the principal importers and wholesalers of controlled substances. With regard to these areas, public sentiment is divided over the actual immorality of such behavior; thus, there is limited opposition from the public when the syndicates control them. Furthermore, organized crime provides a service for sections of the public when it assures access to these activities. Gambling was the largest source of revenue for organized crime in this country up until the 1960s, when two developments occurred: (1) the gradual legalization of various forms of gambling in several states, and (2) the relatively sudden appearance and popularity of what have come to be referred to as controlled substances, that is, illegal drugs. Organized crime groups have seen diminished revenues with the advent of state lotteries. Off-track horse betting also has declined a bit in popularity with organized crime because of state-controlled betting in many states (Off Track Betting, OTB, for example, in New York State). Also affecting organized crime is the fact that numbers games, large dice games and illegal casinos have been legalized in many states.

Gambling operations are highly complex and sophisticated, utilizing up-to-date modern technologies. Betting syndicates utilize bookies and wire services in extensively developed networks that in some cases reach across the country. There is organized betting on sporting events involving all of the major spectator sports in the entertainment industry, from football and baseball to hockey and boxing. Gambling devices ranging from cards to slot machines and roulette wheels, all "fixed" to favor the syndicate or the house taking the bets, exist alongside legal casinos and gambling houses in many states. Even lotteries still thrive in spite of the state-run lotteries. The practice of "running numbers" still brings in sizable sums to organized crime groups. The numbers games are more popular with the less affluent segments of the population because they are relatively simple and involve far less money than other forms of gambling (Pace 1991). Numbers games involve placing a bet on a sequence of three numbers, such as the last three digits of the daily U.S. Treasury balance (Light 1977). A complicated organization is required to secure the bets, record them and pay off the winners. Numbers runners (who record the bets and collect the money from betters) are usually small-time criminals who are part of the larger syndicate. Generally they receive between 15 and 25 percent of all bets they take in, from one-third to one-half of the losses of a new customer and a 10 percent tip from the customer who wins (Plate 1975).

There are few organized gambling operations in large cities that are not tied to such operations. Bets may vary from a dollar or two to very large sums; and the profits for organized crime are enormous, ranging into the hundreds of millions of dollars. Gambling operations are highly complex:

> Most large-city gambling is established or controlled by organized crime members through elaborate hierarchies. Money is filtered from the small operator who takes the customer's bet, through persons who pick up money and slips, to second-echelon figures in charge of particular districts, and then onto one of several main offices. The profits that eventually accrue to organization leaders move through channels so complex that even persons who work in the betting operation do not know or cannot prove the identity of the leader. Increasing use of the telephone for lottery and sports betting has facilitated systems in which the bookmaker may not know the identity of the second-echelon person to whom he calls in the day's bets. Organization not only creates greater efficiency and enlarges markets, it also provides a systematized method for corrupting the law enforcement process by centralizing procedures for the payment of graft. (President's Commission, *The Challenge of Crime in a Free Society* 1967, 189)

Since this was written, computerization of the operations of these syndicates has made it even more difficult for law enforcement to be effective in controlling them.

Loan sharking (also called usury), which is defined as the loaning of money at an exorbitantly high—usually unlawful—interest rate, nets very large sums of money for organized crime. With the exception of dealing in controlled substances, loan sharking and gambling are the most lucrative practices for organized crime groups. Much of the lending money is derived from gambling and drug operations. Loans are made to small businesspersons whose channels of credit are closed, and to gamblers, narcotic users, politicians and others who need money quickly to cover their expenses or debts.

Dealing in controlled substances is the largest source of income for organized crime today. Drug traffic brings in enormous sums of money to those organizations involved in it. Narcotic and drug sales are organized like a legitimate production-import-retail business involving the distribution of drugs through a series of levels, down to the street corner seller. During the 1980s and continuing to this day, known members of organized crime groups—the Mafia, for instance—have increasingly been identified, tried and imprisoned as high-level drug dealers (President's Commission on Organized Crime 1986). The increasing participation of Asian groups in drug smuggling and distributing has recently alarmed law enforcement officials. For example, in New York City's Chinatown an organized syndicate known as the Flying Dragons was implicated in smuggling hundreds of pounds of pure heroin into the city; one of its pivotal leaders was convicted on 14 felony counts (*New York Times,* December 1, 1992, "Ex-head of Chinatown Gang Is Guilty of Leading Drug Ring").

Organized crime plays a part in shakedowns in prostitution, in the ownership of topless and nude bars and massage parlors and in the distribution of pornographic literature and films depicting sex acts of adults as well as children. Concern over an increase in the production and dissemination of pornographic films and other materials has opened the question of the extent to which the production and distribution of these materials is controlled by criminal syndicates (Reuter 1983). As an additional source of revenue, organized syndicates have engaged in the sale of valuable goods. Many of these commodities are stolen from airports and similar loading and warehouse facilities. More recently, the syndicates have moved into the sale of stolen and counterfeit credit cards (Tyler 1981).

Control of Legitimate Business

In addition to the control of illegal activities, organized crime has infiltrated legitimate businesses. This has been accomplished by employing illegal means and by investing large financial resources. Organized crime has at times, of course, used legitimate business as a front for other criminal activities. More recently, however, organized crime has used legitimate business as a major source of income. Organized crime has a vested monopoly in some legitimate enterprises, such as vending machines and electronic games. They are owners of a wide variety of enterprises, such as real estate, retail firms, restaurants and bars, hotels, automobile agencies, trash collection routes, laundering services and other services. In the past, various federal investigations have disclosed that one such organization, the *Cosa Nostra* (or Mafia), controlled one of the nation's largest hotel chains and a bank with assets of more than $70 million. Special investigating committees found that organized crime had infiltrated approximately 50 areas of legitimate business, including advertising, the entertainment industry, the automobile industry, banking, insurance, the liquor industry, loan businesses, the oil industry, radio and TV stations, real estate and scrap surplus sales.

Organized crime often invests the profits it derives from illegal services in legitimate businesses, and these funds serve to establish a legitimate source of profits for income taxes and help to avoid prosecution. The business organizational arrangement involves business consultants, accountants and attorneys who work full-time for the organization. The control of business concerns is secured through (1) investing concealed profits acquired from gambling, drugs and other illegal activities, (2) accepting business interests in payment of the owner's gambling debts, (3) foreclosing on usurious loans, and (4) using various forms of extortion. A favorite operation is to place a concern it has acquired into fraudulent bankruptcy after milking its assets (Cressey 1969). (This latter practice, however, is not the monopoly of organized crime, for individuals and corporations also engage in this sort of conduct.)

Somewhat related to the control of legitimate business is the infiltration of organized crime into politics. Political graft and corruption are usually mentioned as forms of organized crime. Few groups of organized criminals, however, become involved in politics for the sole purpose of economic gain. Such infiltration is usually for the purpose of protection from legal interference in other criminal activities. The liaison with public officials is actually a method of achieving immunity from the law, and should be so considered rather than regarded as a separate type of organized crime.

> All available data indicate that organized crime flourishes only where it has corrupted local officials. As the scope and variety of organized crime's activities have expanded, its need to involve public officials at every level of local government has grown. And as government regulation expands into more and more areas of private and business activity, the power to corrupt likewise affords the citizen. Contrast, for example, the way governmental action in contract procurement or zoning functions today with the way it functioned only a few years ago. The potential harm of corruption is greater today if only because the scope of governmental activity is greater. In different places at different times, organized crime has corrupted police officials, prosecutors, legislators, judges, regulatory agency officials, mayors, councilmen, and other public officials, whose legitimate exercise of duties would block organized crime and whose illegal exercise of duties helps it. (President's Commission, *The Challenge of Crime in a Free Society* 1967, 191)

In Japan the involvement of organized crime, called the *yakuza,* in the political system is endemic, systemic and traditional. There are approximately 10 major *yakuza* syndicates, with 990 affiliated groups and tens of thousands of members. They are politically powerful and extend their influence to the highest levels of Japanese government. In contrast to organized crime in the United States, the *yakuza* are extremely politicized. Their modern history is intertwined with that of Japan's extreme right wing, a group of pro-Emperor activists who were the most virulent force behind Japan's rise to fascism and military expansion before World War II. Organized crime groups constitute a violent coalition of rightists and gangsters, and have served as a sort of paramilitary force for Japan's ruling Liberal Democratic Party, which has held continuous power in that nation's postwar politics (Tasker 1987). In the early 1990s, Japan's leading politician resigned his post as parliamentary leader over mob-related scandals. He played a central role in a corruption scandal and there were links between the Liberal Democratic Party and organized crime. A short time later, a former Prime Minister who came to power in 1987 with the assistance of Japanese *yakuza* was found to be at the center of an influence-peddling scandal linked to organized crime (*New York Times,* October 15, 1992).

Racketeering

The third and final type of organized crime is racketeering, the systematic extortion of money from persons or organizations. For the most part, racketeering in the United States has been concentrated in organizations engaged in the distribution of services and commodities.

Powerful organized criminal groups may extend their operations to the control of many kinds of products and services. The wholesaling of perishable products, such as fruit, vegetables and fish, is another field of racketeering operations. Racketeering is prevalent in laundry businesses; cleaning establishments; truck, rail and shiploading businesses; and among such workers as motion picture operators, bartenders, food service personnel, truck drivers and retail clerks. These organizations are especially vulnerable to the operation of rackets. One of the simplest forms of this type of racketeering is the protection racket, in which persons or organizations are "protected," by payment of regular fees, for the privilege of operating without being injured, damaged or destroyed by the organized criminals. This kind of operation may be used as a means of maintaining control over various services and commodities.

Racketeering has operated successfully for a number of years in controlling some groups of organized labor. In the past, the International Brotherhood of Teamsters was particularly vulnerable. Various schemes are employed, such as the infiltration of certain labor unions, extortion of money from employees for union cooperation, and the cheating of members of the union through nonpayment of union wages or misuse of union welfare and pension funds. Workers may be forced to pay high fees and dues in order to find and hold jobs. Union leadership may be taken over by organized criminals. A considerable portion of the operating funds of unions may go to organized crime. Furthermore, money may be extorted from employers. Strikes are often threatened as a means of controlling employers. The building trades are particularly vulnerable to racketeering because of the importance of purchasing materials at crucial times and the need to complete projects by a certain date.

When organized crime (the *Cosa Nostra*) first became involved in labor racketeering, there were four fundamental operations (Cressey 1969, 95-99).

1. Real unionization is often prevented by pretending, after the organization is paid, that the shops are really "unionized." A larger business concern, for example, may think it is cheap to pay $6,000 for a nonunionized union shop. Such a company may be "unionized," but the employees do not get union wages and there is no "union trouble" for the employer.

2. Employees are made members of fictitious "paper locals," which are established partly to help the employer reduce his labor costs. Cosa Nostra members may even "sell" unions to one another.

3. Employers may be threatened with strikes or violence if they do not pay bribes to Cosa Nostra members leading the controlled unions.

4. Union funds are stolen or diverted illegally from pension or welfare funds.

Criminal Career of the Offender

As with any large-scale enterprise, organized crime requires a structure of positions with an accompanying hierarchy of command. It has been noted often that the hierarchical structure of organized crime represents a feudal system (Serio 1992). At the top of the clan-like pyramid are powerful leaders, the "lords," who make the important decisions and run the organization. These leaders maintain a master-serf relationship over other persons in the feudal structure. A middle echelon of gangsters, lieutenants and flunkies carry out the demands of the leaders. At the bottom of the structure are persons marginally associated with organized crime—drug peddlers, prostitutes, bookies, runners—who deal directly with the public. The structure is held together by a chain of command, personal loyalties, a code of behavior, alliances with rival groups and hostility toward conventional society.

The hierarchical structure of organized crime makes generalization about the careers of its members difficult. Some have specialized training and are directly recruited from the law and accounting professions, while others, as young men, are given university training with the understanding that they will join the syndicate. "Cosa Nostra members occupying the higher echelons of organized crime are orienting their sons to the value of education, if only as a part of the general move toward respectability. . . . [T]hey are sending their sons to college to learn business skills, on the assumption that these sons will soon be eligible for 'family' membership" (Cressey 1969, 241-242). There are rarely, if ever, female members of organized criminal gangs, whether in Asia, Russia, Europe or the United States. Women and girls may be used for specific purposes on specific occasions, such as the transporation of illegal commodities or money, but they are not normally considered members of the syndicate proper.

Many organized criminals, especially those lower in the hierarchy, have careers similar to the conventional offender, in which there is association with young gang members and a long series of delinquencies and crimes. Instead of ending their careers in their early twenties, however, they continue their criminal activities in association with organized criminals. Nearly all Mafia leaders in Sicily have this type of background. For example,

> Salvatore (Toto) Riina, a native son of the town of Corleone, is a man of many distinctions. Corleone is the Sicilian town that gave the Mafia its most brutal leaders, and Riina is reputed to be the first among them. He is said by informers and investigators to the *"capo di tuti capi,"* the boss of all bosses of the Sicilian mob, a status that places him high in the rankings of international crime. He is the mobster whose ruthlessness finally killed the vestigial myth of the Mafia as "men of honor" and godfathers to this island off the toe of the Italian boot. (*CJ Europe* 1992, 6)

Some who grow up in certain slum areas in this country tend to emulate the older members of organized crime and aspire to a career in organized crime. One study found that eight out of the 10 delinquents in an inner-city area selected an association with organized crime as the occupation they would most like to have in 10 years (Spergel 1964). Such youths stressed the need for connections, such as belonging to the right club or having certain criminals as sponsors. This phenomenon is probably largely true today. In such areas the relationships between organized criminals and conventional businesses tend to be mutually supportive. Organized crime uses a legitimate business as a front for various operations to the latter's profit. Organized criminals involved in such practices, operating in gambling, among unions and in usury, have considerable power and influence on the conventional social structure.

> Frankie, a young adult who still considered himself a member of a delinquent group, when speaking about the influence of the racketeers, said that they were known to everybody in the neighborhood. If you wanted to open up a legitimate business and needed additional capital, you could sometimes borrow money from the racketeers. If you were losing out in business, they might be helpful. If somebody got "busted," or arrested, a racketeer would put up bail money and, in an emergency, the racketeer could be called upon for a payoff, since he had the right contacts in the police department. Of course this was strictly business, and you had to repay the loans or favors. (Spergel 1964, 18)

Delinquents are selected by organized criminals not on the basis of the technical knowledge they display but based on attitudes such as being loyal, willing and trustworthy. In neighborhoods where organized crime is important, a boy might drive his uncle's car to pick up gambling receipts or he might be given other roles to prepare for an organized criminal career. For example, the youth may be used to transport incriminating and highly secret information among mob members: "In May, investigators questioning a teen-age hoodlum discovered in his possession a so-called 'master book' listing businesses targeted for extortion and the names of those who would profit from it" (*New York Times,* November 12, 1992).

Usually it is the delinquent gang that produces the adult gangster who uses strong-arm methods and is employed for this purpose by organized criminal groups. Gangsters usually come from the slums of large cities, frequently have long criminal records of armed robberies and generally have a conception of themselves as "tough" or "bad." Those who are successful in organized crime sometimes later become its leaders.

> In many instances organized criminal machines have called upon the services of gangsters for protective or offensive operations only to have the gangsters take over the operations themselves. In other instances gangsters have been content to be on the payroll of a prosperous organization and to get a considerable cut of the profits without assuming full control. Gangsters are usually recruited from the slums of American cities. They have come up through the sand lots of crime and have made crime their career. Most of them have been members of small boys' gangs and have graduated to larger boys' gangs and later to affiliation with organized crime and political machines. They have made themselves useful to both political machines and organized crime. (Reckless 1961, 203)

Organized crime may thus provide a person with the opportunity for a lifetime career in crime. Selection of a career in organized crime, rather than one of the other criminal careers, is apparently dependent upon the existing social conditions, or subcultures, of the area in which the person lives. Little is known, however, of the specific mobility of the criminal from one position to another, once a part of the hierarchy of organized crime. The career histories of organized criminals are not usually available because of the secrecy and nature of their work. Nevertheless, there are indications that as organized crime has moved from the bootlegging and prostitution rackets of the 1920s and 1930s into gambling, usury, drug trafficking and the control of legitimate businesses, there is more need for expertise in management operations and less need for security and secrecy, because the new operations are more open and more closely resemble legitimate corporate activity. Organized crime syndicates, therefore, are becoming more flexible and creative and, rather than only punishing wrongdoers, they are rewarding those in the organization who display the ability to make profits. This is the pattern of legitimate business enterprises. This contemporary skill acquired by criminal organizations is difficult to defeat.

It is important to bear in mind, however, that the speed and efficiency of criminal organizations is not necessarily due to their organizational structure alone. Such feats of organized crime are made possible in part as a result of circumventing official permits and other requirements of regulatory agencies, all of which consume a great deal of time. If a legitimate corporation could evade all federal, state and local business regulations and controls, it too would be more efficient.

Except for some movement up the scale in the organization, there are indications that mobility varies with the type of position in the hierarchy, for example, making money or enforcing discipline.

> One young man with the right connections and the right attitudes might be rewarded with a job as a collector of street-level bets, as a courier who picks up and delivers usury monies, or as a truck driver in a cigarette smuggling operation. If he is ambitious and talented, he may do all three. Another young man may be rewarded with an executioner position, such as "wheel man," "finger man," or "hit man." Both men are either salaried employees or behave as if they were, even if unpaid or paid on a piecework basis. Neither has high status, and neither has necessarily been admitted to membership in Cosa Nostra. But the career-development pattern for the first man is much clearer than the pattern for the second. If either man is admitted to membership, his initial position is likely to involve moneymaking, perhaps at a supervisory level such as bookmaker, rather than discipline. On occasion, an executioner may be given a salaried position as bodyguard to his boss, but bodyguards do not ordinarily move up to supervisory positions oriented principally to discipline, such as enforcer and buffer. Either of the two men may, after years of work as a soldier-bookmaker who shares his profits with his superiors, move up to lieutenant-enforcer, lieutenant-buffer, lieutenant-corrupter, or lieutenant-money mover. The four positions are listed in ascending order of status. The person occupying a high-status money-mover position is self-employed to a greater degree than is the corrupter and, in descending order, the buffer and enforcer. His frontiers of action are wider, and his income is greater. (Cressey 1969, 243-244)

Progression into organized crime usually represents for the offender an increasing isolation from conventional society. While there are undoubtedly variations according to the location of the person within the hierarchy of organized crime and according to the ethnic group involved, most organized criminals are committed to the world of crime. Their sole commitment to the larger society is concentrated on the goal of pecuniary success, and they use illegal means to achieve it. Although they generally are interested in the welfare of the local community from which they come, organized criminals tend to have little or no interest in the welfare of the larger society (which explains their disregard for the negative effects of distributing heroin or corrupting public officials). A number of social conditions and forces in American society are conducive to the separation of the organized criminal from the larger society. In coming up through the ranks of street gangs, organized criminals have been nominally separated from the dominant culture (Tyler 1962).

The leaders of organized crime are involved in activities that are in continuous conflict with the law, though in many cases they manage to persuade corrupt law enforcement officials to work for them. Normally, however, a philosophy of justification allows the leaders to carry out their illegal activities. They hold the government in contempt, as well as its officials and the general public. The leaders of organized crime do, however, often choose to live segmented lives, donning the role of respectability in their community, as did John Gotti, New York's much publicized organized crime leader of the 1980s and early 1990s, before his convictions and imprisonment. (Gotti was much loved and respected in his home community, every year throwing lavish street parties for the community.) Their commitment, nevertheless, remains with the world of crime, where in detachment from the values of the larger society they receive their prestige, power and a lifestyle of opulence and luxury.

Group Support of Criminal Behavior

The very nature of the activities of organized crime requires that persons involved in most levels associate regularly with other criminals and receive intensive group support for their criminal activities. Since many persons in organized crime associate with a particular group of criminals (usually having a common ethnicity), support and prescription of behavior come from a specific group of criminals. These groups are organized for the sole purpose of gaining monopolistic control over a sphere (or spheres) of activity. During Prohibition in the United States, for example, specific organized criminal groups competed in an attempt to control the manufacture and distribution of liquor. More recently, organized criminal groups have attempted to gain monopolistic control of drug trafficking, gambling and various other rackets that often lead to violence and death.

Monopolistic control of a criminal activity by criminal groups often entails an interlocking control over other illegal activities. Such interlocking interests are found in organized crime patterns similar to those in corporate business. In connection with their illegal activites, most organized crime groups eventually need to launder money (an activity requiring a very elaborate structure of group support). Money laundering is the process of converting illegally earned assets to one or more alternate forms to conceal their illegalities and true ownership. Furthermore, in achieving monopolies, organized crime is not restricted by traditional political and geographical boundaries. For example, money laundering strategies involving foreign exchange activities are often required.

Organizational Structure

From an organizational standpoint, all of organized crime operates on a syndicated basis. That is, skilled persons with considerable capital resources are organized to establish and maintain a large-scale business enterprise devoted to the coordination and control of products or services. The nature of the coordination and control may be illegal, and/or the products and services may be illegal. Given the syndicated pattern of organized crime, there are questions regarding the pervasiveness and geographical extensiveness of the organization of illegal activity. For example: In the United States are there a great number of criminal groups organized on a syndicated basis? Are some groups interlocked according to a plan? Or is there a single crime syndicate in the United States that coordinates all the activities of organized crime? There are a variety of different views on these questions.

Most criminologists and crime control officials traditionally have held that there are about 24 "families" of Cosa Nostra alone, which operate in large cities and are directed by a council that governs the activities of these families. When all is working well, this council divides operational territories and settles jurisdictional disputes among the families without employing violence. Most cities have only one such family, if any, which may contain as many as 700 members. Until relatively recently, New York City was reported to have five such families. When things go astray, however, and a "mob war" breaks out—usually over jurisdictional disputes—there is a rash of inter-family murders. Many observers believe that the most influential families reside in New York, New Jersey, Illinois, Florida, Louisiana, Nevada, Michigan and Rhode Island, and that there are syndicates in other places as well (Rowan 1986). Most criminologists accept the idea of a *Cosa Nostra,* but some argue that the claims for the existence of such organizations are simply the result of a combination of ulterior motives, sensationalized reporting and the "media effect" (Smith 1975). Yet others have argued that the very existence of a national organization of criminal synidcates has never been empirically shown (Reuter 1983).

Perhaps the most complete description of the structure of organized crime in the United States was reported by the President's Commission on Law Enforcement and Administration of Justice (1967). According to that report, the core of organized crime consists of 24 groups, which operate as criminal cartels in large cities. Each family is headed by one man, the *"capo di tuti capi"* or "boss," who maintains order and maximizes profits. Beneath each boss is an "underboss," who collects information for the boss, relays messages to him and passes instructions down the line to underlings. On the same level as the underboss is the *consigliere,* who is a counselor or adviser to the boss. Below the level of the underboss are the *caporegime,* some of whom serve as buffers between upper-level and lower-level personnel, while others serve as chiefs of operating units.

The lowest-level members are the *soldati,* the soldiers or "buttonmen" who report to the caporegime. Outside the structure of the family are a large number of employees and agents who do most of the routine work in the various criminal enterprises. Finally, the 24 families or criminal cartels are ruled by a "commission." This body is a combination of legislature, supreme court, board of directors and arbitration board, but functions primarily as a judicial body mediating disputes. The commission is composed of the bosses of the most powerful families and varies from nine to 12 men.

The balance of power of this nationwide council was traditionally centered in New York City. However, since the enactment of the 1970 Racketeer Influenced and Corrupt Organization (RICO) Act, which was Title IX of the Organized Crime Control Act of that year, and the consequent modest successes of federal law enforcement agencies, much of the traditional structure of this model of organized crime has been disrupted and thrown into disarray (RICO Task Force 1985). For example, as a result of the RICO legislation and the law enforcement efforts stemming from it, in 1985 a New York-based task force succeeded in obtaining indictments for members of the Bonnano, Lucchese and Genovese crime families. Similar successes were achieved in Boston, Miami and Chicago during the latter part of the 1980s. While many view these developments as favorable, the dark side is that, with many of the traditional bosses either dead or in prison, much inter- and intra-mob violence has erupted. Furthermore, other groups have taken over activities such as drug trafficking, and the once powerful and relatively united structure of organized crime has begun to splinter. Some law enforcement authorities are saying, in effect, "give us back our old organized crime." It is easier to go after one tightly organized structure than it is to bring to prosecution a series of undisciplined multiple warring gangs.

In other settings organized crime has taken on different forms. For example, in the countries that emerged out of the former Soviet Union, a number of ethnically organized groups have been formed that shun the traditional structures of organized crime under communist rule.

> The ethnic groups are generally homogeneous bodies governed by interpersonal feudal-like clan and tribal relations rather than the simple protector-protected relationship. Because the very nature of these groups is predicated on a notion of "family," the Russian understanding of "boss" as a single, powerful decision-maker attempting to maintain relationships among unrelated individuals for mostly economic reasons becomes superfluous. . . . One prime example of such a group with a rapidly expanding power base is the Chechen organization. . . . Most important for the Chechen is the organization, recruiting only from among their own people. Chechens actively recruit juveniles from the Chechen regions where unemployment is high. This also ensures a degree of "purity" in the membership, making it difficult for law enforcement agencies lacking personnel that speak Chechen to infiltrate the group. (Serio, *CJ International* 1992)

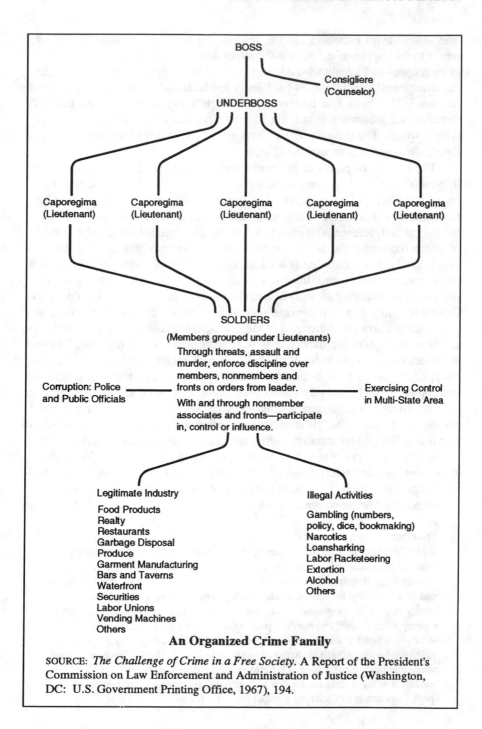

An Organized Crime Family

SOURCE: *The Challenge of Crime in a Free Society*. A Report of the President's Commission on Law Enforcement and Administration of Justice (Washington, DC: U.S. Government Printing Office, 1967), 194.

The homeland of the Chechen nationality is located on the western shore of the Caspian Sea, north of the Georgian republic.

Finally, the extent and complexity of group support is seen in the money laundering activities of virtually all organized crime groups.

> Money laundering thus provides the essential linkage between the drug and racketeering underworld and virtually limitless commercial and financial operations in the legitimate sector. . . . From the perspective of drug traffickers and other organized criminals and the money launderers who serve them, preferred negotiable instruments meet two basic criteria: (1) they are bearer instruments, or are made out to fictitious payees, entitling the holder to use them in commerce without inviting questions of true ownership; and (2) they are "liquid" assets, enabling owners to use them immediately, if desired, avoiding unacceptable personal inconvenience. (Karchmer and Ruch 1992, 2)

Here the division of labor becomes highly specialized. Laundering specialists include: (1) *couriers*, who arrange for the transport of monies to a laundering site where it is easily converted to another method of payment, such as money orders. Most frequently the couriers carry the money to a "safe" foreign jurisdiction; (2) *currency exchange specialists*, who operate either formal or informal businesses that can be legal to all appearances or that solely serve an illegal clientele. This provides organized crime with a quasi-banking service; (3) *white-collar professionals, attorneys and accountants*, who provide investment counseling, create nominee trust accounts, handle international funds transfers and use various tax avoidance schemes in foreign countries. These specialists, nonmembers of the organized crime group, are loose coalitions united by consensus related to the common goal of gaining a steady, lucrative income.

Code of Conduct

To a certain extent all career criminals observe a code of behavior in that they never inform the police on another's activities. With organized crime the code of conduct is highly developed and extends into areas such as the maintenance of internal discipline and the power of leadership. It is very similar to the Sicilian Mafia's code of silence, known as *omerta,* and it is effectively enforced. It involves "(1) *intense loyalty* to the organization and its governing elite, (2) *honesty* in relationships with members, (3) *secrecy* regarding the organization's structure and activities, and (4) *honorable behavior,* which sets members off as morally superior to those outsiders who would govern them" (Cressey 1969, 171). Loyalty, respect, honor and absolute obedience are expected of all members. Compliance is induced by custom, material rewards and violence (either through beatings or executions). Subordinates should not interfere with the leader's interests, they should not inform the police, and if necessary, they should (and often do) go to prison to protect those in power in the organization.

Largely as a result of the RICO prosecutions, however, this code of honor has begun to collapse in some sectors of the Mafia:

> Salvatore (Sammy Bull) Gravano, the Mafia turncoat who helped prosecutors win conviction of John Gotti earlier this year, testified yesterday that Mr. Gotti had supported efforts by Victor Orena to become the official boss of the Colombo crime family. . . . Mr. Gravano identified Mr. Orena, the defendant in a racketeering-murder trial. The trial focuses on a power struggle that turned into a murderous conflict between two rival Colombo factions. (*New York Times,* December 1, 1992)

Gravano also broke with tradition in identifying the structure, rules and recruiting processes of the Mafia. Other former gang members have recently begun to follow his lead in breaking the code of silence. Such departures from the *omerta* tradition are highly threatening and dangerous to the leadership of organized crime groups, and in the long run they threaten all the members.

> Although the code of organized criminals is purportedly for the protection of "the people," it is administered and enforced for the protection of each boss. Since the boss of a "family" has the most to lose if the organization is weakened through an attack by outsiders, he enthusiastically promotes the notion that an offense against one is an offense against all. Moreover, this same principle protects the boss from his own underlings. The principle gets transformed so that it deals with matters of safety rather than matters of offense—the safety of all depends upon the safety of each. Since each conforming member is guaranteed a livelihood without fear of encroachment by other members or by nonmembers, each member must be "protected." (Cressey 1969, 186)

Force and Violence

Organized crime is distinguished by its dependency on the use or threat of force and violence, plus intimidation and bribery, as methods of operation to ensure large economic gains, control illegal activities and survive in competition with other criminal groups. The "gangster," who is usually associated with organized criminal enterprises, actually performs the violent acts. There is continued slaying of rival gang members which is widely celebrated in film and television. Because of underground tactics, these killings are not usually cleared by arrest.

The infamous St. Valentine's Day Massacre of 1929 is still cited as the archetype of gangland warfare. Al Capone and his gang had acquired control of the illegal liquor field in the Chicago area during the Prohibition era. Eventually, rivals attempted to "muscle in" and compete for the large profits in much the same way that contemporary gangs compete for drug profits. Capone eventually exhibited superiority over his principal rival gang with summary dispatch. On February 14, St. Valentine's Day, Capone's gangsters, disguised as police officers, lined seven members of the Bugs Moran gang against the wall of a garage and mowed them down with submachine guns (Kobler 1971). Although such a mass killing in organized crime has never been equaled, hundreds of slayings have occurred over the years in the course of economic competition between organized crime groups.

Violence is also used in organized crime to "protect" businesspersons from possible harm. Through intimidation, organized criminals have been able to extort large sums of money from legitimate businesses. The laundry business is a classic illustration. Laundry proprietors in some cities have been visited by gang representatives who inform the proprietors that the laundry business is in "danger" and that they will provide protection. Failure on the part of owners to subscribe to the protection plan then results in destruction of laundry equipment or personal violence. Such demonstrations of force, provided by those who would otherwise "protect" them, usually convinces the laundry proprietors and other businesspersons that protection is worth the money demanded for it.

In addition, there is the well-known extreme violence associated with the drug trade. As the old organized crime families gradually begin to break apart and newer, smaller and less disciplined gangs take their place, the old codes are abandoned. In traditional organized crime groups a rule was *never* to attack police officers because it would "turn on the heat" for the group. There are some indications that this may not be rigidly followed with those government officials who interfere with organized drug trade.

Permanent Immunity

The existence of organized crime traditionally has been largely dependent on the maintenance of permanent immunity from interference of law enforcement agencies. Permanent immunity is achieved in a number of ways. First, because the leaders of organized crime stay behind the scenes of operation, they are not usually arrested and prosecuted. Gangland activity cannot be readily traced to its leaders.

Second, persons lower in the hierarchy of organized crime who are arrested are likely to be released as a result of actions by their superiors. Such release and avoidance of prosecution and punishment are assured through what is popularly known as the "fix." For various reasons, persons not directly involved in criminal activity contribute to the protection of organized criminals. Law enforcement officials, judges, businesspersons and others provide needed services for the protection of organized criminals.

A third way in which organized crime may acquire immunity is by gaining political clout through contributions to political organizations and parties. Elected officials may owe their election to organized criminals. Furthermore, regular "payoffs" to officials provide protection for organized crime. Thus, on a permanent basis, organized crime may be immune to law enforcement through political graft and corruption.

Fourth, because organized crime provides the public with illicit and desired goods and services (such as gambling and drugs), a certain amount of immunity from arrest and prosecution results from public toleration of organized crime.

A fifth means of immunity can be found in the functioning of the law itself. Existing laws and enforcement procedures have not been especially successful in coping with organized crime. The survival and continuance of organized crime is possible because legal action is kept at a minimum. Lack of effective legislation (prior to the RICO laws) and weak law enforcement are a reflection of public toleration of organized crime in this country.

Finally, through the infiltration of legitimate business, organized crime is able to evade the law. Organized crime often operates behind the facade of legitimate business, obscuring its operation and making its detection difficult. Also, in the case of racketeering, organized crime escapes the law because intimidated businesspersons must contend with reprisal if a report is made. In addition, organized crime and legitimate business may assist one another, as in the regulation of prices of given commodities and services or through the enforcement of labor contracts. Such mutual assistance, accompanied by public espousal of the profit motive under almost any arrangement, provides considerable assurance of immunity for organized crime.

Correspondence between Criminal and Legitimate Behavior

While many citizens strongly condemn the stereotyped picture of organized crime, they are often in favor of the economic enterprise that makes it possible and the services that it provides. As already indicated, a number of characteristics of American society and culture give support to organized crime. In fact, it may be argued that organized crime is a result of the particular structure of our society. To begin with, the motives for organized crime are largely the same as those valued so highly in the free enterprise system (Taft and England 1964). In fact, one criminologist claimed that the smuggling of drugs alone generates a gross volume of business of over $100 billion per year. "The largest corporation in the world has a gross volume of business less than that of illegal drug smuggling" (Chambliss 1988, 88). Organized crime, like legitimate business, attempts to achieve maximum returns with a minimum of expenditure, through efficient organization, skilled management and evasion of governmental regulations and taxes. Consequently, the only difference is that legitimate business operates within the law for the most part, while organized crime operates outside of it. From the standpoint of control, organized crime appears to be more significantly affected by economic facts of supply and demand and consumer habits than by legislation and sporadic attempts at formal control. This explains the public demand for stressing antidrug education programs over increased law enforcement to contain the problem.

A great deal of organized crime in the United States is tolerated by the public because of its close relation to legitimate business. In fact, it is often referred to as the flip side of legitimate business. As Vold concluded:

> One basic fact stands out from the details of this discussion, namely, that organized crime must be thought of as a natural growth, or as a developmental adjunct to our general system of private profit economy. Business, industry, and finance all are competitive enterprises within the area of legal operations. But there is also an area of genuine economic demand for things and services not permitted under our legal and social codes. Organized crime is the system of business functioning in the area. It, too, is competitive, and hence must organize for its self-protection and for control of the market. (Vold 1958, 240)

Organized crime engages in the activities of smuggling and distributing drugs. On the other hand, millions of Americans are occasional or regular users of illegal drugs such as marijuana, cocaine and heroin. Organized crime simply supplies a steady flow of a needed commodity, much as legitimate business deals in supplying the public with legal commodities. Without the demand, organized crime could not operate in the illegal drug trade. The "war on drugs" has failed to take into account two factors that help us understand the overall context of drug use. First, public concern over drugs is unstable and faddish. Some drugs are "in" during certain periods and "out" during others. Concern about drugs focuses for a relatively brief time on a particular drug and then moves on to another, independent of any characteristic of the drug or the result of the public attention. Second, the use of drugs is so much a part of the behavior pattern of Americans that it is inconceivable that all segments of the general public will abstain from all drug use. Consequently, drug-taking in one form or another will continue to be a widespread practice throughout the population. What varies is the kind of drugs that are used at any point in time.

Gambling, as a major area of operation for organized crime, is a deeply ingrained aspect of American culture. As Block pointed out decades ago, gambling is a natural consequence of a culture that encourages success, skill, competition and diversion (Block 1951).The element of chance and the tendency to speculate in certain risks not only are found in illegal gambling but are a major part of investment and finance in the legitimate business world. After all, the stock market itself is little more than an investment in chance occurrences based more on hunches than on empirical data. It is little wonder that a large-scale business (legal and illegal) has developed in America to satisfy the demand for gambling. Moreover, living on credit with interest has become an indispensable feature of American life and the American economy.

In an early writing on organized crime, Lindesmith stressed the social context of organized crime by noting that it is an integral part of our total culture (Lindesmith 1941). He observed that such factors as the profit motive, indifference to public affairs, general disregard for law, laissez-faire economics and questionable political practices have produced a fertile place for organized crime in our large cities. Criminologists have repeatedly noted the links between major crime syndicates and leading political and legal figures in many American cities (Block and Chambliss 1981). Finally, because America is a "melting pot" (some feel the pressure cooker analogy is more appropriate), its ethnic and immigration patterns show organized crime evolving among Chinese, Jamaicans, Mexicans, Vietnamese, Japanese, Cubans, Colombians, Irish, Russians, Canadians and other ethnic groups (Nelli 1987).

Organized crime continues to exist without a great deal of public action against it because of a hypocrisy in which citizens try to prohibit illegal practices in which they themselves often indulge. In this clash of values and interests, organized crime provides the illegal services that the public desires and needs. This observation leads us into the last section of this chapter: the social and legal reaction to organized crime.

Societal Reaction and Legal Processing

Although societal reaction against organized crime is strong, in actuality the public feels ambivalent about it (Morash 1984). While more effective laws and better law enforcement may assist in the control of organized crime, the structured paradox of public indignation at illegal behavior on the one hand, and toleration and approval of such illegal behavior on the other, provides American society with its most serious handicap in the control and prevention of organized crime. For example, most Americans are fascinated by organized crime. This is indicated by the fact that *The Godfather* films netted huge sums at the box office. In *The Challenge of Crime in a Free Society,* the President's Commission pointed out that "Usually, when a crime is committed, the public calls the police, but the police have to ferret out even the existence of organized crime. The many Americans who are compliant 'victims' have no incentive to report the illicit operations. The millions of people who gamble illegally are willing customers who do not wish to see their supplier destroyed." (President's Commission, *The Challenge of Crime in a Free Society* 1967) Likewise, citizens buying small bags of marijuana or vials of cocaine know full well that it is made available thanks to organized crime, and while they may decry organized crime per se, they do not wish to have their supply cut off.

Most students of organized crime argue that in spite of all the legal measures, it has not been controlled to any great extent. There are several reasons for this failure of control efforts: (1) The very nature of organized crime is itself a major dilemma. That is, as an "illegitimate" business, it consists of different kinds of individual crimes. The "organized" element is not a crime in and of itself. (2) As already noted, the general public demands many of the illegal goods and services of organized crime. (3) Proof of criminal activities is virtually impossible to obtain in many cases, especially as a result of the intimidation of witnesses. (4) Effective resources to launch a coordinated nationwide assault on organized crime are not available, and such an attempt may involve acts of questionable constitutionality in any case. (5) The corruption of government officials often blocks effective enforcement and prosecution. (6) There is no single, unified governmental agency to root out organized crime. Enforcement and prosecution are patchwork affairs on the federal, state and local levels. (7) The huge financial gains from organized criminal activities far outweigh the risk of being caught and serving time. Moreover, the sentences that are handed out are generally lenient (although there have been exceptions to this). (8) Organized crime figures are often idolized by their local communities, both inner-city and suburban, thus eliminating community support for law enforcement efforts.

In addition to these many factors, the profits made from illegitimate businesses are subsequently invested in legitimate businesses, which creates respectability and makes detection of illegal profits difficult. All of these activities are interrelated and consequently are confusing to the public (and sometimes difficult for prosecutors themselves). With no other criminal behavior pattern, except perhaps certain types of white-collar and corporate crime, is there such a complexity and confusion in public attitudes.

Nonetheless, law enforcement efforts have not been entirely fruitless. There have been indications recently that efforts have seriously damaged the power, influence and reach of certain criminal organizations in many cities (Raab 1990). Furthermore, criminologists have noted that organized crime leaders and bosses have aged and that the newer, younger leaders may lack the necessary leadership and managerial skills to carry on. In the past decade, RICO legislation has been effective, leaders have been imprisoned and as the demography of the American people changes, traditional groups have lost some of their power bases. The code of silence, the *omerta,* has been cracked. One leading criminological authority on organized crime has predicted that law enforcement pressures will steer organized crime toward "safer" activities such as credit card and airline ticket counterfeiting, illicit waste disposal, computer crimes and the infiltration of legitimate business enterprises (Albanese 1989).

It has become evident that it is more productive to deal with organized syndicates than with individual criminals. Prosecution of individual offenders does not go very far in changing the fundamental structure of public demands for goods and services that are currently illegal. A number of estimates have placed the potential income from what is referred to as the "hidden economy" as being over $100 billion, a figure that is constantly adjusted upward as a result of both inflation and increased business (Simon and Witte 1982).

If a leading member of a crime syndicate is sent to prison, the organizational structure is such that someone else is available to move into the vacated place. Moreover, vigorous enforcement is likely to result in more clever evasive devices to circumvent the law. Only if something can be done about organized crime as an entity might prosecution be successful, but this would involve serious constitutional questions regarding due process under the law. Organized crime can be looked upon as a behavior system; it is as yet not a legal entity.

> The fact is that "organized crime," as such, is not now against the law. It is not against the criminal law for an individual or group of individuals rationally to plan, establish, develop, and administer an organization designed for the perpetration of crime. Neither is it against the law for a person to participate in such an organization. What is against the law is (unlicensed) bet-taking, usury, smuggling and selling narcotics and untaxed liquor, extortion, murder, and conspiracy to commit these and other specific crimes. (Cressey, 299)

In the end, when all is said and done, the struggle against organized crime and its activities will only be ended when the very fabric of American society and culture is changed.

References

*Albanese, Jay (1989). *Organized Crime in America.* 2nd ed. Cincinnati: Anderson.

Beirne, Piers, and James Messerschmidt (1991). *Criminology.* New York: Harcourt Brace Jovanovich.

Block, Alan, and William J. Chambliss (1981). *Organizing Crime.*

Block, Herbert A. (1951). "The Sociology of Gambling." *American Journal of Sociology* 57:215-221.

Chambliss, William J. (1988). *Exploring Criminology.* New York: Macmillan.

CJ International (1993). "Enter the Mafia—Blood, Fire and a Code of 'Honor'." *CJ International* 9 (1): 6.

*Clinard, Marshall B., and Robert F. Meier (1992). *Sociology of Deviant Behavior.* 8th ed. New York: Harcourt Brace Jovanovich.

*Cressey, Donald R. (1969). *Theft of the Nation: The Structure and Operations of Organized Crime in America.* New York: Harper and Row.

Haller, Mark H. (1990). "Illegal Enterprise: A Theoretical and Historical Interpretation." *Criminology* 28:207-235.

Karchmer, Clifford, and Douglas Ruch (1992). "State and Local Money Laundering Control Strategies." *National Institute of Justice: Research in Brief* (October). Washington, DC: U.S. Department of Justice.

Kobler, John (1971). *Capone: The Life and World of Al Capone.* New York: Putnam.

Kobrin, Solomon (1951). "The Conflict of Values in Delinquency Areas." *American Sociological Review* 16:653-661.

Kopkind, Andrew (1993). "From Russia With Love and Squalor." *The Nation* 256(2): 45-46.

Light, Ivan (1977). "Numbers Gambling among Blacks: A Financial Institution." *American Sociological Review* 42:892-904.

Lindesmith, Alfred (1941). "Organized Crime." *The Annals* 217:76-83.

Morash, Merry (1984). "Organized Crime." In *Major Forms of Crime,* edited by Robert F. Meier. Beverly Hills, CA: Sage.

*Nelli, Humbert S. (1987). "A Brief History of American Syndicate Crime." In *Organized Crime in America: Concepts and Controversies,* edited by Timothy S. Bynum. New York: Willow Tree Press.

New York Times (1992). "Japan's Scandal: The More Things Change." October 2, A10.

New York Times (1992). "Japan's Top Politician Quits Post Over Mob Scandal." October 15, A10.

New York Times (1992). "Italians Defying Shakedowns Pay With Lives." November 12, A13.

New York Times (1992). "Ex-Head of Chinatown Gang Is Guilty of Leading Drug Ring." December 1, B4.

New York Times (1992). "Mafia Turncoat Testifies on Gotti Role in Crime Family Power Struggle." December 1, B1.

New York Times (1992). "A Look Into the Violent World of a Young Neo-Nazi." December 12, A12.

New York Times News Service (1992). "Sicilian Capo Symbolizes Mafia's Durability." *CJ Europe* 2 (6): 6-7.

*Pace, Denny F. (1991). *Concepts of Vice, Narcotics, and Organized Crime.* 3rd ed. Englewood Cliffs, NJ: Prentice-Hall.

Plate, Thomas (1975). *Crime Pays!* New York: Ballantine.

President's Commission on Law Enforcement and Administration of Justice (1967). *The Challenge of Crime in a Free Society.* Washington, DC: U.S. Government Printing Office.

President's Commission on Organized Crime (1967). *Task Force Report: Organized Crime.* Washington, DC: U.S. Government Printing Office.

President's Commission on Organized Crime (1986). *American Habit: Drug Abuse, Drug Trafficking and Organized Crime.* Washington, DC: U.S. Government Printing Office.

Raab, Selwyn (1990). "A Battered and Ailing Mafia Is Losing Its Grip on America." *New York Times* October 22, 1.

Reckless, Walter C. (1961). *The Crime Problem.* 3rd ed. New York: Appleton-Century-Crofts.

*Reuter, Peter (1983). *Disorganized Crime: Illegal Markets and the Mafia.* Cambridge, MA: MIT Press.

*Rhodes, Robert P. (1984). *Organized Crime: Crime Control vs. Civil Liberties.* New York: Random House.

*RICO Task Force (1985). *Report of the Ad Hoc Civil RICO Task Force of the ABA Section of Corporation, Banking and Business Law.* Chicago: American Bar Association.

Rowan, Roy (1986). "The Biggest Mafia Bosses." *Fortune,* November 10, 24-38.

Rush, George E. (1991). *The Dictionary of Criminal Justice.* 3rd ed. New York: Dushkin Publishing Group.

Sellin, Thorsten (1963). "Organized Crime: A Business Enterprise." *The Annals* 347:12-19.

Serio, Joseph (1992). "Shunning Tradition: Ethnic Organized Crime in the Former Soviet Union," *CJ International* 8(6), 5-6.

Simon, Carl P., and Ann D. Witte (1982). *Beating the System: The Underground Economy.* Boston: Auburn House.

Sinclair, Andrew (1964). *Era of Excess: A Social History of the Prohibition Movement.* New York: Harper and Row.

Smith, Dwight C. (1975). *The Mafia Mystique.* New York: Basic Books.

Spergel, Irving (1964). *Racketville, Slumtown, Haulburg: An Exploratory Study of Delinquent Subcultures.* Chicago: University of Chicago Press.

Taft, Donald R., and Ralph W. England, Jr. (1964). *Criminology.* 4th ed. New York: Crowell-Collier and Macmillan.

Tasker, Peter (1987). *The Japanese: A Major Exploration of Modern Japan.* New York: E.P. Dutton.

Tyler, Gus (1962). "The Roots of Organized Crime." *Crime and Delinquency* 8:338.

Tyler, Gus (1981). "Sociology and Professional Crime." In *Current Perspectives in Criminal Behavior,* edited by Abraham Blumberg, 153-178. New York: Knopf.

Vold, George B. (1958). *Theoretical Criminology.* New York: Oxford University Press.

Chapter 10

Professional Criminal Behavior

Among the almost infinite variety of law breakers, the "professionals" have the most highly developed criminal carrers, social status (among other law violators) and skills (Roebuck 1983). Sociological concepts can probably help us understand this pattern of criminal behavior more than any other form of crime. Professional criminals have most likely never been very numerous at any time, and there is every indication that their numbers have declined to such an extent that some criminologists have referred to them as "old fashioned criminals" (Cressey 1972, 45). For example, a variety of preventive devices have made professional forgery more difficult, and there is a possibility that it is declining, as are other other types of professional crimes. While it is not true that they have "gone the way of the dinosaurs," they are nevertheless a fading breed of offenders.

Professional crime differs from conventional crime in several significant ways.

1. The professional criminal engages in illegal behavior for the purpose of economic gain, or even (what is more probable) economic livelihood.

2. The criminal career of the professional criminal is highly developed.

3. Considerable skill is usually involved in the crimes of the professional criminal.

4. The professional criminal enjoys high status among criminals.

5. The professional criminal is usually able to avoid detection and is fairly successful in keeping out of prison.

6. The professional criminal is involved in a more complex social network than is the conventional criminal.

Professional crime also differs from organized crime in a number of important ways. First, professional crime is not as highly organized in size and complexity as is organized crime. Second, the degree of economic gain in professional crime comes nowhere near that of organized crime. Third, with the exception of robbery, the element of violence is virtually absent in professional crime. Finally, the nature and extent of social harm and social injury wrought by professional crime does not approach that which results from organized crime.

Most illegal conventional activities, such as robbery and burglary, can be performed by professional criminals. Over 40 years ago, one observer of armed robbery noted that a professionalized form of armed robbery ("the heist") was emerging in the United States (DeBaum 1950). It consists of finding a mark (the location for the holdup), getting together a team of specialists, planning the holdup and executing the job.

Traditionally, however, professional crime has been limited to nonviolent forms of behavior and activities that do not require the use of strong-arm tactics. In this sense, criminal activities that involve the *theft* of sums of money through the use of skillful, often sophisticated, nonviolent methods best represent professional crime. As such, over half a century ago in Sutherland's classic research, *The Professional Thief* (1937), the varieties of professional theft were divided into the following traditional categories, as stated by professional criminals in their own argot:

1. Picking pockets (cannon)
2. Sneak thieving from stores, banks and offices (the heel)
3. Shoplifting (the boost)
4. Stealing from jewelry stores by substituting inferior jewelry for valuable jewelry (pennyweighting)
5. Stealing from hotel rooms (hotel prowling)
6. Confidence games (the con)
7. Miscellaneous rackets such as passing illegal checks, money orders and other papers (hanging paper)
8. Extorting money from others engaged in or about to engage in illegal acts (the shake). (Sutherland 1937)

Sutherland's model of professional theft long dominated criminologists' thinking about professional crime. With more recent studies of professional criminal activities, the concept has expanded greatly (Roebuck 1983). Professional crime as a behavior system is in the process of change, as it meets the demands of ever-changing social structures and technologies. Society changes and crime patterns change with it. Therefore, for our purposes, professional crime can now be divided into six subtypes:

1. Larceny (including shoplifting, pickpocketing, sneak thieving)
2. Confidence games

3. Robbery
4. Burglary
5. Forgery (including counterfeiting)
6. Extortion

In all cases, the crimes differ from conventional crimes in terms of the distinct behavior system of the professional criminal.

Legal Aspects of Selected Offenses

Generally, the character of professional crime is determined apart from the criminal law. That is, it is not the legal definition of the behavior that distinguishes professional crime from other crimes, but rather the way in which the crime is performed that determines the professional character of the behavior. For example, the criminal law is not of much help in defining the "confidence game." Most jurisdictions do not even reserve a special statute for confidence game crimes. Instead, confidence game crimes are included under such general practices as fraud, embezzlement, forgery, gambling and swindling.

In the confidence game, the important factor is the way in which the victim is involved. The victim is never innocent, but is led into a scheme where he or she may benefit through his or her own dishonesty and complicity.

> The practices of swindling and forgery and the perpetration of various fraudulent schemes which prey upon the victim's innocence, ignorance, or gullibility are not classified as confidence. Such schemes merely seek to cheat someone because of his ignorance or naivete. Therefore, cheating little old ladies or amorous widows cannot be considered as confidence unless these ladies are led into some scheme they know to be dishonest—a scheme which they believe will help them achieve some gain. They, however, are "taken" themselves. The practice of confidence, then, is the manipulation of the victim through nonviolent methods into a situation of dishonesty in order to take advantage of the victim's dishonesty. (Gasser 1963, 27)

Such a definition of the confidence game is not usually found in the criminal law. Professional crimes, for the most part, are sociological constructs that denote a particular pattern of criminal behavior rather than a legal category. Perhaps the most entertaining portrayal of such a pattern of behavior called the "con game" was depicted in the popular film *The Sting*.

What distinguishes professional crimes such as the confidence game from legal categories such as fraud are the concrete facts and situations that are associated with the commission of the act.

> Professional crime of any sort is necessarily embedded in a complex set of conditions, which include the normal structure of business transactions, public attitudes toward the criminal and his victims, prevailing police and court practices, and the market for stolen or contraband goods. Taken together these factors (and many more) constitute a system, and a change in one element will produce changes in others, including the type and volume of professional crime. (Walker 1981, 174)

Most of the laws violated in the course of pursuing professional crime have been created to regulate conventional behaviors. This is nowhere better illustrated than in the case of the law of theft. It was with expanding production and trade that the law was established, primarily to protect the property of the classes that owned it. Whether or not that property was taken by amateur, conventional or professional criminals was not the issue. Protecting the property of the merchant from theft was the overriding issue.

The law of theft emerged out of the Carrier's Case in fifteenth-century England (Hall 1952). The legal problem in the case was that of precedent. Prior to that, the common law held that anyone in possession of property could not technically steal that property, but in the Carrier's Case, property (probably wool or cloth) was taken by the person transporting the property, who did not own it (the bailee). The judges, in order to meet the changing social and economic demands of the newly emerging merchant class, departed from precedent—opening the door for the modern law of theft.

The social and economic conditions of the period were crucial forces behind the decision of the judges in the Carrier's Case. A new order, based on industry and trade, was developing. Even the Crown was heavily involved and, like all merchants, needed the protection of laws to successfully carry out trade. To assure the safe transport of their products, the broader law of theft was created. Eventually, with the growth of banking and the use of paper money, the law was expanded to include embezzlement by clerks, officers and the like. Thus, the legal protection of property has always been to the interest of the propertied classes of society. How that property was taken, and by whom, was of less importance than the loss of the property.

Only in recent years have laws considered the nature of professionally executed offenses. The federal government, for example, now has the power to prosecute the confidence artist if the victim has been induced to cross a state line in obtaining money, provided the amount is above a fixed sum. In addition, the United States Postal Service can have confidence artists prosecuted when such offenses infringe upon using-the-mail-to-defraud laws. Tax laws also regulate some of the activities in the confidence rackets, and increased regulations of the stock market serve to control the professional trade in fraudulent stocks to some extent.

Professional criminals, however, are still quite able to operate around these laws. Such is the very nature of professional crime. Maurer, in his frequently cited study, *The Big Con,* thus concluded:

Confidence men trade upon certain weaknesses in human nature. Hence, until human nature changes perceptibly there is little possibility that there will be a shortage of marks for con games. And so long as there are marks with that fatal combination of larceny and money, the law will find great difficulty in suppressing confidence games, even assuming a sincere interest on the part of local officials. Increased legal obstacles have, in the past, had little ultimate effect upon confidence men except, perhaps, to make them more wary and to force them to perfect their work to a still finer point. As long as the political boss— whether he be local, state, or national, foreign or of the home-grown variety— fosters a machine wherein graft and bribery are looked upon as a normal phase of government, and as long as juries, judges, and key enforcement officers can be had for a price, the confidence man will continue to live and thrive. (Maurer 1940, 256)

Criminal Career of the Offender

Of all the criminal offenders, the professional criminal has the most highly developed criminal career; and, as the word *professional* implies, they are accorded great prestige by other criminals. They engage in a variety of highly specialized crimes, all of which are directed toward economic gain. By means of skill and sometimes elaborate techniques, professional criminals are often able to acquire considerable sums of money without being arrested or prosecuted.

Professional criminals also tend to come from higher socioeconomic backgrounds than do conventional and organized criminals. Many start out their careers in legitimate employment and gradually move into professional crime. Persons entering professional crime may continue to engage in legitimate employment until they are successful in crime and have mastered the required skills, which are often quite formidable. Professionals acquire substantial skills in committing one particular crime, such as pick-pocketing, shoplifting, confidence games, stealing fom hotel rooms, passing forged checks and securities, counterfeiting, and forms of sneak-thievery from offices, stores, and banks.

The professional criminal is also likely to begin his or her career at a relatively late age. Furthermore, once in professional crime, he or she tends to continue in it for the remainder of his or her life. Two quotations illustrate this. The first is from a criminologist:

The con man begins his special career at a much older age than other criminals, or perhaps it is better said that he continues his criminal career at a time when others may be relinquishing theirs. Unemployment occasioned by old age does not seem to be a problem of con men; age ripens their skills, insight, and wit, and it also increases the confidence they inspire in their victims. With age the con man may give up the position of the roper and shift to being an inside man, but even this may not be absolutely necessary. It is possible that cultural changes outmode the particular con games older men have been accustomed to playing and thereby decrease their earnings somewhat, but this seems unlikely. We know of one con man who is seventy years of age and has a bad heart, but he is still as effective as he ever was. (Lemert 1951, 323-324)

A professional "fence" (disposer of stolen property), makes a similar point:

Your younger person isn't worldwise, is too half-assed to be a fence. He thinks he knows but he doesn't have the knowledge. Same as any business, you need the experience and the money to make money. The other thing is, people are less leery of an older person. In any business, the people have to have confidence in you and it's hard for your younger person to get that. Most of your fences are like your legit businesspersons, are older, and most people feel more at ease doing business with an older person. Even your thieves which are mostly young would rather deal with an older person. You don't have kids running a fencing business, same as they don't run a legitimate one. (Steffensmeier 1986, 21)

In another case study of the genesis of a professional fence, Klockars traced the man's career from hustling as a 14-year-old through to late middle age and a $1 million a year business. Commenting on the process of becoming a successful fence, Klockars comments:

Although one could continue to pick passages from the romantic correctional literature on the fence that would buttress notions of "ingenuity, cunning, resource, energy, and that mysterious power we sometimes call personal magnetism," the theoretical point intended here is quite modest and would not be advanced by doing so. Simply stated the point is this: unlike many forms of deviance that have been studied by criminologists, becoming a professional fence cannot be managed by just anybody. Ability, energy, ingenuity, and certain persuasive skills are absolute prerequisites. Even though there is a discernible institutional path to becoming a professional fence, the sociological forces alone are simply not strong enough to carry someone without such talents into the role. To be sure, talents are plastic attributes subject to growth and development in the course of a career, but the distinctive feature of becoming a professional fence that makes certain talents prerequisite is that errors of judgment, lack of effort, or failed persuasion, especially early on in one's career, can end it. (Klockars 1974, 177)

Also, longevity and success in professional crime are attributable in part to the fact that very few professional criminals are arrested, brought to trial, convicted or incarcerated. In another vein, since it is not a career that requires high-risk and large financial investment, it is relatively free of stress. Nor does it normally make great physical demands.

A significant characteristic of professional criminals is the philosophy of life they develop to justify their criminal careers. As one criminologist observed in the 1930s, when interest in professional crime was relatively new, "the philosophy of criminals does not differ from that of any other group. So far as other men believe in a set of assumptions and use them to explain their conduct, they do no more and no less than the criminal does. Each uses his philosophy of life as a means of making his activities seem reasonable" (Tannenbaum 1938, 177). In their relations with others of similar interest, professional criminals acquire a philosophy that gives answers to questions related to the worth of the activity and to the person's own self-image.

Basic to the professional criminal's philosophy of life is the conviction that nearly all people are basically dishonest, given the opportunity, and that professional criminal activity is similar to the activity of other businesspersons. The professional criminal also justifies his or her behavior by the belief that all non-criminals would commit crime if they could. One successful long-time confidence man, Joseph "Yellow Kid" Weil, said:

> The men I fleeced were basically no more honest than I was. One of the motivating factors in my action was, of course, the desire to acquire money. The other motive was a lust for adventure. The men I swindled were also motivated by a desire to acquire money, and they didn't care at whose expense they got it. I was particular. I took money only from those who could afford it and were willing to go in with me in schemes they fancied would fleece others. (Weil and Brannon 1948, 293)

The victim of the con game, after all, has been willing to participate in a crime in order to make money. The professional criminal can justify his or her own crime in terms of the behavior of the victim. Such justifications are, of course, shared and supported by professional criminals in their associations with one another.

There are distinct variations in the careers of the different types of professional criminals. Among confidence artists alone, for example, there is a "continuum ranging from the unsuccessful bungling, frequently arrested short-con man ("flimflammer"), whose modus operandi is dated and pitched at a low level, to the highly successful, accomplished big-con man who is infrequently arrested and whose modus operandi is original and pitched at a high level" (Roebuck and Johnson 1964, 237). Although the former learn their "trade" from the latter, they lack the finesse, skill, patience, planning abilities and industry necessary to become successful in the big con games. They are able, nevertheless, to maintain a rationalization for their behavior, comparing it to other criminal behavior as well as to other occupations:

You know how it goes in this dog-eat-dog world. You got to take the other guy before he takes you. You know, the real sharpie outwits the marks. Of course, it all depends on how you get ahead. My way was no different from, say, a lawyer or businessman. You know, a lawyer has a license to steal. The cops should lay off con men. We don't hurt nobody. You can't con an honest man. The mark has more larceny in his heart than we do. The cops should do their job and clear the streets of the muggers, heist men, hop heads, and the rest. Why, it's dangerous for a decent man like me to walk down the street at night."
(Roebuck and Johnson 1964, 243)

Most professional criminals are extremely careful in selecting their victims. They believe that some people and businesses are more worthy of being victimized than others and that some people and businesses are easier to victimize than others. The professional robber, for example, makes a conscious effort to choose victims that can well afford the loss, and sites where considerable sums of cash are likely to be found (primarily large organizations such as banks, supermarkets, fast food restaurants or chain convenience stores). Employees or customers are not seen by the professional robber as victims who will suffer personal loss; rather they are viewed as agents or patrons of the impersonal organization being victimized. The offenses are usually well-planned, and executed in such a way as generally to escape detection.

Bob is a twenty-five year old white man. His arrest record indicates no recent arrests. According to him, he and his accomplices had committed a series of seven or eight robberies of public utility offices in the months before they were arrested. He is now serving a ten-to-twenty year term for robbery in a state prison.

He became involved in this series of robberies at his brother's suggestion. The latter was out of jail on bail pending trial for another robbery and needed money to hire a lawyer. In the past, his brother had found that public utility offices were lucrative targets to rob, providing large sums of money and minimum resistance. Because Bob's brother was "hot," he stayed in the car during the robbery while Bob and another accomplice entered the office to get the money.

One of the rules observed during the series of holdups was that no customer who happened to be in the office was to be robbed. One reason for this was that such an act would be another charge of robbery if they were caught. More important was the feeling that since the customer would be parting with his own money, resistance was more likely. Such resistance might lead to injury to the victim or create a disturbance which would bring the police to the scene. Another reason for not robbing the customer was that the amount of money he was carrying was apt to be small when compared to the sum that would be taken from the public utility.

These robberies were spaced every two or three weeks over a six-month period. Experience with this crime meant that the gang knew they could get about

$5,000 to $10,000 each time they robbed, and that less planning was needed each time they robbed. They knew how roles would be allocated, how the money would be divided (equally among the partners), and what obstacles they might encounter inside the office. Mapping the escape route was the only thing that had to be done differently each time. (Conklin 1972, 63-68)

The professional thief has similar rationalizations for his or her acts. One case history of a professional thief who specialized in safe-cracking, a "box man," highlights the professional's disdain for "straight" society (Chambliss 1972). He or she can easily hold that stealing is as honest a way to make a living as any other way. Talking about his lifestyle, another professional thief in California's San Quentin prison makes the following observations:

The way I see it a guy has several ways to go in this world. If he's not rich in front, he can stay honest and be a donkey. Only this way he works for someone else and gets fucked the rest of his life. They cheat him and break his back. But this way is honest.

Now another way is he can start cheating and lying to people and maybe he can make himself a lot of money in business, legally I mean. But this guy isn't honest. If he's honest and tries to make it this way he won't get nowhere.

Another way he can make it and live a halfway decent life and still be honest is to steal. Now I don't mean sneaking around and taking money or personal property from assholes who don't have nothing. I mean going after big companies. To me this is perfectly honest, because these companies are cheating people anyway. When you go and just take it from them, you are actually more honest than they are. Most of the time, anyway, they are insured and make more money from the caper than you do.

Really, I think it is too bad it is this way. I mean it. I wish a guy could make a decent living working, which he can't do because those people who have it made got that way fucking the worker. And they are going to keep it that way. And all the crap about having to have laws protecting property. These are just laws set up by those people who got all the property and are going to make sure they keep it. (Irwin 1970, 11)

Such comments on the nature of law and society might enlighten the work of most criminologists and sociologists of law.

Group Support of Criminal Behavior

Sutherland observed the group nature of professional crime and found it characterized by:

1. *skill*—a complex of techniques exists for committing crime;

2. *status*—professional criminals have a position of high prestige in
    the world of crime;

3. *consensus*—professional criminals share common values, beliefs
    and attitudes, with an *esprit de corps* among members;

4. *differential association*—association is with other professional
    criminals to the exclusion of law-abiding persons and other crimi-
    nal types; and

5. *organization*—activities are pursued in terms of common knowledge
    and through an informal information and mutual assistance system.

Related to these characteristics are several others that are also associated with the
group support that underlies professional crime.

The recruitment of persons into professional theft is fairly well established.
Recognition by other professional thieves is the definitive characteristic of the
professional thief. Without such recognition, no amount of knowledge and experience can provide the criminal with the requirements for a successful career in
professional crime.

Included in the process of acquiring such recognition are two necessary elements: (1) selection, and (2) tutelage. A person cannot acquire recognition until
he or she has had tutelage or the neccessary training, and such tutelage is granted
only to a few selected persons. Selection and tutelage are interrelated and continuous processes. A person is tentatively recognized and selected for limited training and, in the course of tutelage, advances to more certain stages of recognition.

Contact is a necessary requisite for selection and tutelage. Professional
criminals may come in contact with prospective professionals though their limited association with other criminals (amateur thieves, burglars), with persons on
the fringes of criminal activity (pimps, prostitutes, hustlers) or with persons
engaged in legitimate occupations. The contacts may first be made in places
where professional criminals are working, in places of leisure-time activities
such as pool halls, or (more likely) in jails and prisons. Selection is reciprocal in
that both professional thieves and prospective "students" must be in mutual
agreement regarding the arrangement.

Tutelage involves the learning of skills, techniques, attitudes and values
through informal means. Rather than receiving formal verbal instruction, the
neophyte learns in stages while engaging in increasingly sophisticated criminal
activity. During the probationary period the neophyte assimilates standards of
group morality (such as honesty among thieves and not informing on others),
learns methods of stealing and disposing of goods, and becomes acquainted with
other professional criminals. For example, it is essential that the new profession-

al thief be introduced to fences (outlets for goods). Gradually the person comes to be accepted as a professional thief. Perhaps the only ritual that differentiates becoming a professional criminal from becoming a member of a legitimate business group or profession is that there is no graduation ceremony or formal reception. As long as the recognition continues, whether the individual continues in criminal activity or not, he or she is regarded as a professional criminal by other professional criminals.

The social nature of other forms of professional crime is somewhat different from that of professional theft. Some professional criminals may work alone or with others only sporadically. Some professional criminals are self-taught, requiring little tutelage or recognition. Consider the example of two California professional bank robbers who decided to go into crime on their own after researching the possibilities:

> So we decided to go into crime, and, in order to decide which branch we wanted to go into, since we were both inexperienced criminals at the time, we decided to do as much research as we could and find out which made the most money the fastest and that percentage-wise was the safest. I think you'll find that every public library in a city has statistics of the number of crimes committed the previous year, how much money each crime was, and you could figure out, from the amount stolen, the number of crooks caught, and the number of convictions, what you wanted to know. We spend four days at the public library and we researched, and we came up with armed robbery as the most likely for us. (Jackson 1969, 20)

In the case of professional fraudulent check writing, little training is necessary. The skills required are elementary. The learning of check writing has been described as follows:

> He was first a check writer, which is a craft requiring little or no tutelage. It takes no great flash of wisdom to realize that people will give you money for a slice of paper or to realize that if you are going to depend on that for your livelihood, it might be more pleasant to use names other than your own. Highly skilled craft aspects, such as check raising, are now fairly rare. The problem in check passing is handling the person with the money you want, and that is dependent on personal style rather than technical skill. Check writing is a solitary profession, it is better done alone, it is one in which the worst thing that can happen is to become well-known. Check writers do not socialize very well; they may meet in jail, but they do not tend to hang around together outside. (Jackson 1969, 23)

Similarly, one criminologist found in a study of professional check forgers that these offenders work alone, carefully avoiding contacts and interaction with other criminals. "Moreover, their preference for solitude and their secretiveness give every appearance of a highly generalized reaction; they avoid not only cooperative crime but also any other kinds of association with criminals. They are equally selective and cautious in their contacts and associations with the noncriminal population, preferring not to become involved in any enduring personal relationships" (Lemert 1958, 142).

Thus, many professional criminals today, especially the professional "heavy" criminals, form into work groups only for specific purposes, to pull off specific crimes or heists, and disband when the need for one another's skills and assistance no longer exists. Some professional criminal groups are only loosely organized, and the degree of group activity varies according to the requirements of their situation and the particular "caper." In the case of professional armed robbery, when social organization does exist among career offenders, it is usually in the form of a partnership. Rather than the permanent association of offenders, group activity is on a smaller and more flexible basis.

> Hence there is little evidence in the social organization of robbers of group cohesion during periods of stress in the manner described by Sutherland. The robber's organization is a more fluid arrangement taking into account existing conditions; it is not conceived by those involved as a permanent group but more or less a loose confederation of individuals joined together for a specific purpose on a short-term basis. Among certain types of robbers specific role relationships do develop; however, these always are assumed to be temporary by the robbery participants even though the association is of some duration. When this type of social organization exists no provision need be made for incapacitated members; each member considers himself on his own. (Einstadter 1969, 67-68)

Another way of understanding the social nature of professional crime is through the language of offenders. Some types of professional criminals have an extensive and colorful argot. The hundreds of terms used by these professional offenders have developed over a considerable period of time; many were common in the seventeenth century. The language has evolved out of the specialized activity of the professional criminal; and the argot reflects the attitudes of the professional toward the law, himself or herself, the victim, other criminals and society in general (Maurer 1964). Maurer, in an extensive analysis of the argot of the professional pickpocket, quotes a professional pickpocket who gave the following account in a police court of what happened to him:

Judge: Now you just tell the Court in your own way what you were doing.

Me: Well, Judge, your honor, I was out gandering around for a soft mark and made a tip that was going to cop a short. I eased myself into the tip and just topped a leather in Mr. Bates' left prat when I blowed I was getting a jacket from these two honest bulls. So I kick the okus back in his kick and I'm clean. Just then this flatfoot nails me, so here I am on a bum rap. All I crave is justice, and I hope she ain't blind. (Maurer, 1964, 55)

Within professional crime, there are distinctive argots according to the various types of criminal activity and to the racial or ethnic composition and background of the offenders. Some argots are closely related, while others are widely divergent. Extensive knowledge of the argot associated with their particular crime is the mark of the professional, and many years are required to use it effectively.

Why do specific speech patterns, vocabularies and argots evolve? According to Maurer there are several reasons. First, because professional criminals work outside the law, there are strong pressures to consolidate the criminal subculture. A common argot serves to develop a degree of group solidarity and provides a sense of camaraderie among members of the subculture. Second, specialized work requires and fosters the creation of a special language. Anyone who has heard doctors or attorneys—even criminologists—speak *as* professionals can understand this. Professional criminals within a particular racket, as craftspersons, are faced with identical problems that must be solved with certain known techniques. Third, many concepts exist for professional criminals for which there are no terms in the vocabulary of the outsider. It is necessary that professionals create, borrow or adapt words to meet their unique needs. Most professionals speak argot only among themselves, not in the presence of outsiders. This is somewhat analogous to the way an ethnic group would speak its own particular dialect only among themselves. It appears that secrecy and deception are only very minor reasons for the formation and use of argots among professional criminals. The specialized language serves, instead, as a means of social support for the way of life of the professional criminal.

Correspondence between Criminal and Legitimate Behavior

A marked similarity can be found between the behavior of professional criminals and that of outsiders in a mostly law-abiding society. The professional criminal is engaged in earning a livelihood, as are we all. He or she is a self-employed earner. In addition, law-abiding citizens must serve as "accomplices" in order for some forms of professional crime to exist. The confidence game perhaps best illustrates the correspondence between professional criminal behavior and the behavior of mainstream, conventional citizens.

Of all the types of professional theft, the confidence game is the most elaborate, complex and sophisticated. It is also the most respected. Furthermore, the "big con" is the aristocrat of professional crime and is granted the greatest prestige in the world of crime. Con men and con women receive this deference not only as a result of their uncanny ability to gain large amounts of money through skill, without the use of force or the threat of force or violence, but also because of their often cultured backgrounds, their dress and manners, their "rap" or "line" and their general lifestyle. They are almost universally thought of as "smooth, cool dudes."

As a general rule, confidence games are divided roughly into big con games and short con games. Short con games require only a short period of time to execute and are limited to relatively small amounts of money. Big con games require a longer period of time and net much larger sums of money. Short con games take place between one or two cons and their victim. Big con games generally require the abilities and intricate planning of a number of persons. They proceed through a series of steps, all carefully planned to secure the trust of the victim and eventually to walk away with the victim's money. Thus, the first requirement for the operation of a con game is the willing participation of an accomplice. A prospective victim, the "mark," must first be found and must agree to enter into an illegal scheme. Such an alliance assures the con artist a degree of protection and makes the victim a partner in the proceedings. The legitimate behavior patterns of our society are suggestive of, or at least neutral toward, participation in the confidence scheme.

Maurer and other observers of con game operators have noted that the mark is usually a fairly wealthy, high-status person who has access to capital—his or her own or that of someone else. Marks may include bankers, professionals (doctors, lawyers, dentists, etc.), businesspersons and even religious leaders. People with access to money and who are willing to gamble to increase their personal gain through illegal methods are the people most easily conned. Thus, the confidence game can be best understood as a sociological phenomenon in relation to legitimate behavior patterns. It is truly a game, reflecting the playful, sporting, risk-taking and manipulative aspects of American culture (Schur 1957). Seen as such, con games appeal to the American value of successful sales ability. The con artist, as a successful businessperson, is able to outwit members of the legitimate world who are willing to take a chance and participate in illegal activity.

Maurer, who has extensive studied forms of the big con, such as the "wire" and the "pay-off" (racing swindles) and the "rag" (involving stock that is stolen or counterfeit), lists the following steps in a big con swindle:

1. locating and investigating a well-to-do victim (putting the mark up)

2. gaining the victim's confidence (playing the con for him)

3. steering him to meet the insideman (roping the mark)

4. permitting the insideman to show him how he can make a large sum of money dishonestly (telling him the tale)

5. allowing the victim to make a substantial profit (giving him the convincer)

6. determining how much he will invest (giving him the breakdown)

7. sending him home for this amount of money (putting him on the send)

8. playing him against a big store and fleecing him (taking off the touch)

9. getting him out of the way as quickly as possible (blowing him off)

10. forestalling action by the law (putting in the fix) (Maurer 1964 15-16)

Another indication of the relation between professional crime and legitimate behavior is found in the fence who assists in the successful operation of professional theft. In fact, the fence is as indispensable to the professional thief as a market outlet is to a legitimate producer of goods or services (Steffensmeier 1986). Since nearly all professional theft is undertaken for economic gain, the stolen merchandise must be marketed. The fence, often a clothing or appliance dealer, a jewelry merchant or an operator of a pawn shop, serves as the middle-person between the thief and the sale of the merchandise to customers. To steal a painting by a master, for example, is of no use unless there is an intermediary in touch with an art dealer who has access to buyers. In addition, the professional thief reduces the risk of being arrested with the goods in his or her possession and avoids the necessity of having to sell the goods personally on the open market. The fence is able to supplement a legitimate business. In effect, the fence breaks the bond betwen the theft, the thief and the ultimate sale of the stolen property.

Finally, professional crime mirrors legitimate activities oriented toward economic gain in the fact that, as times change and social and economic patterns change, patterns of professional crime must adapt. Professional crime, like legitimate activity, must alter its enterprises, diversify or reorganize in order to remain solvent. And in order to remain solvent and do business, professional criminals frequently find it beneficial to interconnect with various other kinds of criminals: gamblers, drug distributors and users, usurers, prostitutes and the like (Chambliss 1988).

Societal Reaction and Legal Processing

The relatively high status of professional criminals is indicated not only by their relation to other types of offenders, but also by the special treatment they are accorded by the police, court officials and others. Because of their favored position, professional criminals are able to make arrangements with public officials that allow them to avoid conviction and punishment. The professional criminal may even be able to avoid arrest by regular payments to certain officials.

This does not mean, however, that law enforcement does not make serious efforts to arrest professional criminals. One study evaluated the efforts of law enforcement officials to arrest professional criminals by setting up their own storefront sting operation to ensnare the professionals. The study found that the goal of decreasing automobile theft in Birmingham, Alabama, was not attained. Instead there was actually an increase of vehicular theft as a result of the sting operation by the police. The author concludes:

> This study began with the observation that police storefront stings have been a popular police tactic for a number of years. . . . On the basis of the results of this study and others, however, it appears that the transitive police organizational agenda (i.e., a decrease in vehicular theft) is not served by this tactic. This finding suggests that the socially noxious behavior engaged in by the police (receiving stolen property) must be justified, if it can be justified at all, only on the basis of its ability to improve police public relations. (Langworthy 1989, 44)

This study reinforces the relative impotence of law enforcement (and the criminal justice system at large) in successfully prosecuting professional thieves. The professional criminal has the overall ability to fix cases because of the cooperation of influential others. Long ago a professional criminal wrote for Sutherland a detailed account of professional theft. He described the involvement of others in the "fix" as follows:

> In order to send a thief to the penitentiary, it is necessary to have the cooperation of the victim, witnesses, police, bailiffs, clerks, grand jury, jury, prosecutor, judge, and perhaps others. A weak link in this chain can practically always be found, and any of the links can be broken if you have pressure enough. There is no one who cannot be influenced if you go at it right and have sufficient backing, financially and politically. It is difficult if the victim is rich or important; it is more difficult in some places than in others. But it can practically always be done. It is just a question, if you have the backing, of using your head until you find the right way. (Sutherland 1937, 82-83)

A major point in the fix is the police department. Even before the arrest, provisions for a fix can be made by the professional criminal. As Sam, the checkwriter, observed:

> But about paying off, what we were talking about before: only once in a while can you do it, and the time to pay off is before you ever get arrested. If you got a policeman in town and you're going there—say he's chief of detectives or he's chief investigator for the service department or something like that—then before the case is ever even negotiated, before you've ever even done the

crime, you have given him a new hat or bought him a steak once in a while or taken him fishing or something like that, then you have a better chance. Then you can *talk* to him. (Jackson 1969, 82-83)

The selection of a lawyer is also important to the professional criminal in providing the "fix."

When you want a lawyer, you don't want a trial lawyer, you want a fixer. You don't care how good he is in the courtroom, you want to fix it; you don't want to go to trial. You're hiring him not to go to trial. And if you have to go to trial, you're hiring him to get the least amount of time, you're hiring him so whenever you walk into the courtroom, you already know what you're going to get because he'd already dealt out what. (Jackson 1969, 123-124)

Public toleration of professional crime results from a combination of factors, including the correspondence between some forms of professional crime and some legitimate behavior patterns, the involvement of the public as victims in illegal arrangements, and public apathy toward crimes that do not affect each person directly and concretely. Further, the myth that surrounds the operation of the legal process no doubt serves as a device for the public toleration of much professional crime.

Perhaps the greatest barrier to any form of societal reaction is the lack of social visibility enjoyed by professional criminals. Because of the lack of social visibility, professional crime escapes strong reaction from the legal system, the victim and society at large. The professional criminal usually is able to carry out his or her offenses without being detected. The criminal is able to escape being reported by the victim because the victim is often involved in the offense. Furthermore, the acts of the professional criminal are usually attributed to conventional and amateur offenders. The result is the relative obscurity of the professional criminal, and the continuation of a low degree of social visibility, which is beneficial to the offender.

Finally, there is much indication that professional crime is changing as other changes take place in the carrier society. At the end of the last century, persons and organizations that were the victims of professional crime established a number of schemes that subsequently brought about a change in the organization and operation of professional crime. The establishment of banker's associations, the creation of merchants' protective agencies and improvements in police methods have made the risks for some forms of professional crime exceedingly great. In addition, because of the increasingly widespread use of business and payroll checks as well as credit cards, the systematic check forger no longer has as great an opportunity to employ the more complex procedures used in past decades. Thus, it can be seen that professional crime (as is true of other types of crime) is related to the structure of society. As society and the reaction to crime change, so do the organization and operation of the types of crime. No form of human behavior—legitimate or illegitimate—takes place in a social vacuum or escapes being affected by larger social forces.

Let us end this book with a reiteration of the theme that has guided our work. What is regarded as crime, and what has been sanctioned in the criminal law, covers a wide range of diverse behavior. Only an explanation at the highest level of abstraction could include all of the phenomena known as crime. By diving crime into types, each one analyzed by five dimensions, we can better comprehend the diversity of criminal behavior. We hope that our efforts will broaden an understanding of the world of which we are innate parts. We also hope that such an understanding becomes more practical and ever more real in how we define crime and those who have become defined as criminals.

References

Cameron, Mary Owen (1964). *The Booster and the Snitch: Department Store Shoplifting.* New York: Free Press.

*Chambliss, William J. (1972). *Box Man: A Professional Thief's Journey.* New York: Harper and Row.

*Chambliss, William J. (1988). *On the Take: From Petty Crooks to Presidents.* Bloomington, IN: Indiana University Press.

Clinard, Marshall B., and Robert F. Meier (1992). *Sociology of Deviant Behavior.* 8th ed. New York: Harcourt Brace Jovanovich.

Conklin, John E. (1972). *Robbery and the Criminal Justice System.* Philadelphia: J.P. Lippincott.

Cressey, Donald R. (1972). *Criminal Organization.* New York: Harper and Row.

DeBaum, Everett (1950). "The Heist: The Theory and Practice of Armed Robbery." *Harper's* (February), 200.

Einstadter, Werner J. (1969). "The Social Organization of Armed Robbery." *Social Problems* 17, 64-83.

Gasser, Robert Louis (1963). "The Confidence Game." *Federal Probation* 27, 27-54.

*Hall, Jerome (1952). *Theft, Law and Society.* Indianapolis: Bobbs-Merrill.

*Irwin, John (1970). *The Felon.* Englewood Cliffs, NJ: Prentice-Hall.

Jackson, Bruce (1969). *A Thief's Primer.* New York: Macmillan.

Klockars, Carl B. (1974). *The Professional Fence.* New York: Free Press.

Langworthy, Robert H. (1989). "Do Stings Control Crime? An Evaluation of A Police Fencing Operation." *Justice Quarterly* 6(1), 27-45.

Lemert, Edwin M. (1951). *Social Pathology.* New York: McGraw-Hill.

Lemert, Edwin M. (1958). "The Behavior of the Systematic Check Forger." *Social Problems* 6, 141-149.

Maurer, David W. (1940). *The Big Con.* New York: Bobbs-Merrill.

*Maurer, David W. (1964). *Whiz Mob.* New Haven, CT: College and University Press.

*Roebuck, Julian B. (1983). "Professional Criminal: Professional Thief." In *Encyclopedia of Crime and Justice,* Volume 3, edited by Sanford H. Kadish. New York: Free Press.

Roebuck, Julian B., and Ronald C. Johnson (1964). "The 'Short Con' Man." *Crime and Delinquency* 10:235-248.

Schur, Edwin H. (1957). "Sociological Analysis of Confidence Swindling." *Journal of Criminal Law, Criminology and Police Science* 48.

*Steffensmeier, Darrell J. (1986). *The Fence: In the Shadow of Two Worlds.* New York: Rowman & Littlefield.

*Sutherland, Edwin H. (1937). *The Professional Thief.* Chicago: University of Chicago Press.

Tannenbaum, Frank (1938). *Crime and the Community.* New York: Columbia University Press.

U.S. Department of Justice, Bureau of Justice Statistics (1988). *Profile of State Prison Inmates 1986.* Special Report NCJ-109926. Washington, DC: U.S. Department of Justice.

Walker, Andrew (1981). "Sociology and Professional Crime," In *Current Perspectives in Criminal Behavior,* edited by Abraham S. Blumberg. New York: Knopf.

*Weil, Joseph R., and W. T. Brannon (1948). *"Yellow Kid" Weil.* Chicago: Ziff-Davis.

Subject Index

Name Index

275